FIRE WALKERS

Memoir

Bethlehem Terrefe Gebreyohannes

MAWENZI
HOUSE

We acknowledge the support of the Canada Council for the Arts for our publishing program. We also acknowledge support from the Government of Ontario through the Ontario Arts Council.

Cover design by Sabrina Pignataro

Cover photo: Davor Lovincic / *Springs and hot* / Getty Images

Library and Archives Canada Cataloguing in Publication

Gebreyohannes, Bethlehem Terrefe, author
    Fire walkers / Bethlehem Terrefe Gebreyohannes.

ISBN 978-1-927494-79-0 (paperback)

    1. Gebreyohannes, Bethlehem Terrefe. 2. Ethiopian Canadians—Biography. 3. Refugees--Canada—Biography. 4. Immigrants--Canada—Biography. I. Title.

FC106.E74T47 2016   971'.0049280092   C2016-904668-0

Printed and bound in Canada by Coach House Printing

Mawenzi House Publishers Ltd.
39 Woburn Avenue (B)
Toronto, Ontario M5M 1K5
Canada

www.mawenzihouse.com

For my father,
Terrefe Asrat Gebreyohannes,
who stopped at nothing to protect his children's future.

Contents

June 1980 – Life in the Garden of Eden

RAPID-FIRE GUNSHOTS WOKE ME early in the morning. The sound always felt like a new experience, shredding my heart into ribbons. I jumped out of bed, gasping. I ran outside in my bare feet, racing for my life. Ta, ta, ta and then silence. I tried to pluck the terrible thoughts out of my mind, but my heart knew that somewhere, not far away, life had ceased and everything had turned upside down. That's how it had been since the revolution.

I joined my two brothers, who were trying to distract themselves with a game on the veranda. Our dog, Metew, was spread out on the grass, nervously wagging her tail. We never spoke of the gunshots. We had silently figured out what they meant a long time ago, and we were forbidden to talk about it. So the three of us sat on the steps of our house, pretending nothing had happened, inhaling deep lungfuls of the Addis Ababa morning air that was filled with the aroma of the tall eucalyptus trees dominating our landscape. Soft white light filtered through the trees. The birds were chirping, neighbourhood dogs barked excitedly as the morning sun covered us like a warm blanket.

As long as I was with my brothers, everything was all right.

"Let's play gebeta." Yared offered.

"Last night, I was having this strange dream," Asrat said, collecting four pebbles from one of the eight gebeta holes and dropping one stone in each of the holes that followed. "I was walking and running a long distance, through strange places I had never seen before, when I arrived at a raging river. I stood trying to figure out how to cross it. I saw the flat head of a hippopotamus jutting out of the water."

Asrat studied the gebeta holes for his next move, but Yared was already beaming with a winner's smile.

Asrat gathered the five pebbles from where he had dropped the last stone and told us the rest of his dream. "I had to cross the river, so I entered the water and the head of the hippo turned into a rock. I jumped onto the rock. I could see the rough river twisting like a cobra beneath me, carrying dead animals, logs, and garbage. Sweating and feeling sick, I searched for another rock to jump to, but the water rose up, and the rock I stood on was now covered with water. I regretted entering the river in the first place. Finally, I spotted another rock next to me and jumped on it and then there were about eight or nine flat rocks on which I stepped to reach the other side of the river. I sensed I had to move quickly. I jumped on each rock as quickly as I could. The river slapped my legs, throwing me off balance, but I kept running until I crossed it. I sprang off safely and landed in a puddle of mud."

"You should tell Tetye," I said. (We always called our mother "Tetye," which meant "sweet sister," because we grew up hearing her four sisters calling her that.) Tetye always told us to pay attention to our dreams. She believed that dreams predicted the future and revealed aspects of our lives that we failed to see.

"It felt so real! When I jolted out of bed, I was drenched in sweat. *Ishi*, ishi! Okay, I will tell Tetye."

"I can interpret your dream for you," Yared said, the wide smile on his face growing wider. He gathered up the pebbles from one of the holes, and took his turn. "It means you are going to lose this game very badly, ha, ha, ha!"

Yared was the champion at every game we played—cards, checkers, ping pong, and marbles. He was eighteen, Asrat was sixteen, and I was fourteen.

I liked comparing my brothers' twinlike appearances. Their hair, shaved around the ears leaving only a curly crown of hair on top; now both were the same height and at times it was difficult to tell them apart. They were taller than most of their classmates, and while Asrat maintained a clean-cut look, Yared had an Afro. When I stood between them for family pictures, because of the height difference we formed the letter M. One thing we all had in common was our slenderness. We were thin in a time and place where people preferred a chubby look in children and adults alike.

We could hear our baby sister, Kalkidan, crying inside, and my stepmother, Meskerem, soothing her. I used to be the youngest until nine months ago when Meskerem gave birth to Kalkidan. Meskerem, in her early twenties, had long thick black hair that was always oiled and kept in large curls on top of her head. It looked like a basket. When she met my father, she was the administrative assistant in his department at the Ministry of Agriculture.

The veranda was our favourite place. It was long and narrow, like a hallway, with a shiny hardwood floor. A few steps down from us the rose garden was in full bloom. Moist green grass covered the area up to the fence, and beyond that the rows of eucalyptus trees spread throughout the neighbourhood.

"Come on, Beth, it's your turn," Yared said. I got ready to play. A strong sun was now on my back.

I was distracted by the sound of a car horn.

"Is it Terrefe?" my stepmother Meskerem asked. Terrefe was my father. She rushed out to the veranda carrying Kalkidan.

The guard opened the gate and my father's green Land Rover pulled into the driveway. We hadn't seen Abba for two months. My brothers and I ran up to him, shouting "Papa, Papa!" Metew wagged her tail and leaped around as Abba stretched out his arms wide and we fell into his embrace. I knew he hated being away from us because he often took us with him. The new military government, the Derg, had dispatched him to the Afar district of Assayita, in the province of Wollo, to manage a settlement program. Assayita, he told us, was sweltering hot, without proper medical facilities or schools.

Abba's presence was like Christmas, Easter, and birthdays all combined. He had come laden with aromatic gifts from the distant province. Mine was a leather handbag, buttery smooth and fragrant. For Yared and Asrat, there was soft wool fabric to be made into suits. And for all of us, brand new Adidas shoes. Mine were blue and white.

A young man emerged from the back of the car, followed by a large, beige-coloured ram. I recognized him as the local butcher. He was wearing tattered brown shorts with patches on the back and black rubber sandals made from a car tire. He led the ram to the back of the yard to be slaughtered. I followed Yared and Asrat to the car to help unload. As we took the things into the house, I could hear the ram's bleat. It would not last long, the butcher would drop the animal to the ground, tie its four legs together, and then offer a prayer, *"Besme ab, beweld, bemenfes kidus"* (In the name of the Father, the Son, and the Holy Spirit) before slitting its throat.

To me, Papa was as tall as the pine tree in our garden. The desert sun had turned his skin a smooth dark bronze, just like the bronze bust of John F Kennedy on display in our living room. Abba's face and his short black wavy hair were beautiful. He dressed with casual elegance, his shirt sleeves rolled up and pants tailored to fit perfectly. He moved slowly and gracefully.

Our house was a wedding gift from my grandfather, Ato Asrat, after whom my brother was named. It had three bedrooms, a bathroom, a living-dining room, a guest room, and a kitchen. The living room was decorated with items Abba had brought from some of his trips. A couch had been replaced with chairs covered with light brown animal fur. The floor mat was a black and white cow skin. The bookshelf was filled with an A-to-Z encyclopaedia set he had bought in Israel when he was a student there. Above the shelf was a large white ostrich egg in a small, shallow, colourful hand-woven basket. One wall was decorated with dried starfish of all sizes, and on the other walls were pictures of my father's sister, Abby, who was living in New York, and his brother, Paulos, who lived in Paris. My parents divorced when I was six, when Tetye moved to her mother's house. We lived only with the servants and our dog, Metew.

We used the house as we pleased. We all slept in one room, including Metew. We played and often told stories late into the night. Yared was the storyteller of the family, regaling us with the plots of the Western movies he had seen. My aunt Kelem came to check on us once or twice a month, but said nothing about our unorthodox living arrangement to our father, although I sensed that he already knew her opinion on that.

Alganesh was our nanny. Mamma Truye was the cook. She was like a grandmother to us; soft wrinkly skin that I found comforting when she embraced me. Her eyes always looked sad. After school I would find her in the guest room seated on a pillow on the floor with her legs crossed. By her side lay a spindle and a pile of raw cotton. Spinning occupied most of her day.

Before Abba married Meskerem, our relatives pleaded with him to send us children to a boarding school, arguing that we needed supervision and discipline. But my father said, "My children don't need disciplining, they need to be free." I was happy in our family home. I could count the rules of the house on the fingers of one hand: come home straight from school, don't talk to strangers, and study hard. Abba repeated them each time he left. After solemnly promising to obey the rules, we were free to do whatever we pleased. Sometimes, though, we crossed the threshold into real danger.

When Abba married Meskerem, he told us we should treat her

like our mother. But though we respected her, we found it hard to obey her. After all, we had done well on our own. At times she seemed like a guest to us, at other times, a trespasser.

I stuck to the rules. Asrat, the middle child, was the controlling kind, adding more rules for us, but Yared rebelled and hung out with his friends and did whatever he pleased.

————◆•————

We were going to celebrate Abba's return with a feast. The cooks prepared *yebeg wot* (lamb stew), *doro wot* (chicken stew), and his favourite food, *kitfo*—fresh raw meat seasoned with *mitmita* (a mix of spices) and soaked in ghee. The fragrance reached every corner of our home. *Dabo* (Ethiopian bread) and cakes were baked. As news of Abba's arrival spread, friends and relatives converged on our house to celebrate.

I walked over to see my friend Seble. Her father, Ato Beza, greeted me at their door. He was heading over to our house dressed in a suit under his *netela* (a handmade cotton blanket) to give Abba the latest neighbourhood news. Ato Beza was even taller than my brothers, he was slender with cotton white hair and a beard and stood out like a light bulb on the streets of Kasanchis. He was a lawyer and a widower, raising six girls and a boy on his own. Because he walked everywhere, my brothers and I often bumped into him. Sometimes he remembered to supervise us. "It is past six o'clock; shouldn't you be doing your homework?" he would ask. Or, "This Sunday I am taking you to church." I would always obey him and accompany him and Seble to church.

Ato Beza walked with me back to my house. When we arrived, he embraced my father and they shook hands.

"We have so much to talk about," Ato Beza said.

"We do," my father agreed.

I could hear Meskerem's sandals flip-flopping around the house as she went from one room to another serving appetizers and offering soft drinks and *tej* (Ethiopian wine) and *tela* (Ethiopian beer) to the other visitors. The cook and nanny too were going back and forth bringing in the stews. Soon the green velvet-covered dining table was covered with food. Each guest was offered lemon water to wash their hands.

We heard a car horn. It was my aunt Kelem with her husband, Gashe Hailu, and their two boys, Merid and Bruck. Our nanny ran outside to the gate, peeked through and then opened the two doors wide enough to admit a white Peugeot 404. My brothers and I were excited; this meant an afternoon of soccer and gebeta.

Most of the guests stayed late into the night, conversing with Abba about his work and the political situation in Ethiopia.

———◆•◆———

A week later, Abba told us that he was taking us to Dire Dawa to Meskerem's home town and possibly to Assayita for our two-month vacation. I was thrilled. School was already out for the rainy season. We would miss the rains because in Dire Dawa it was hot and sunny.

No King and Many Killings

———◆———

If I do not remember thee, let my tongue cleave to the roof
of my mouth. —PSALM 137

ON ONE OF OUR VISITS to Tetye at her mother's house, Asrat
told her about his dream.

"Hmm, your dream is predicting the path of the revolution,"
Tetye interpreted. "We will be facing untold trials and hardship, and
it is not going to be an easy journey." A grim look took over her
face. "Pray, my children, that peace will return to Ethiopia."

According to my mother, a prayer was the only weapon that
turned a bad dream into something less catastrophic. "I will pray on
my knees like our ancestors, to the God of your great-great-grand-
fathers, to the Almighty who overpowered the Italian army, to the
God who never forgets Ethiopia," Tetye said, her eyes closed tight.

Then she looked sternly at all of us, who were sitting before her
in the bedroom. "Let's read from the Bible," she said, opening the
book. "Psalm 137 says, 'If I do not remember thee, let my tongue
cleave to the roof of my mouth; if I prefer not Jerusalem above my
chief joy.'" There was a long pause. "You must never forget your

Ethiopia," she finished.

Why would she tell us not to forget Ethiopia? Why *would* we? What could possibly make us forget who we were—*injera* and *wot*, *gebeta* and soccer games, the unmistakable Addis morning sun that blanketed us like velvet? Our *sefer*, our neighbourhood—Kasanchis?

There we were, in 1980, with no king and lots of killings by the Derg and opposing parties. It was said that all this was happening because poorly educated soldiers from the *bereha* (the desert) were running the country. From what I could gather, it all started in a small town, in the southernmost tip of Ethiopia, where an unhappy group of poorly treated soldiers decided to take matters into their own hands. When their numerous complaints about bad working conditions were ignored by their superiors, they mutinied. They jailed the senior officers and sent a message to Emperor Haile Selassie, informing him about their conditions. When the emperor did nothing about it, similar incidents happened elsewhere in support. And then workers, teachers, taxi drivers, and even students began protesting. It was the soldiers, however, who demanded greater power, eventually about approximately 120 of them overran the palace and seized control. Their organization was called the Derg, and their commanding officer was Colonel Mengistu Haile Mariam. Derg members could execute, imprison, or detain anyone at any time without being accountable.

The radio heralded a new Ethiopian socialism (*hibretesebawinet*), and newly posted signs urged *Ethiopia tikdem* (Ethiopia forward). There was one TV image that I will never forget—the emperor, *Abba ba jan hoy*, feeding his dogs from a tray, which had been brought to him by a servant, as he stood beside naked, lifeless, skeletal figures of famine victims. A film made by a foreign journalist, *The Hidden Famine*, was also broadcast. It seemed that the Derg would make everything right for all Ethiopians. There would be food for all, improved working conditions for the army, a better education system for the students, and cheaper gas prices for taxi drivers.

Now in 1980, five years later, nights and days in Addis Ababa continued to echo with the sounds of gunshots. This was *Key Shibir* (the Red Terror), with intense fighting among factions and indiscriminate executions and imprisonments. My neighbourhood was relatively safe for the most part, and I was spared the sight of dead bodies. But my friends at school had seen them.

————◆•◆————

Our house had been built over thirty years before in Kasanchis, a district about ten kilometres south of the city centre. I walked everywhere and explored every inch of my neighbourhood. The driveway out of our house was unpaved and went up a hill that joined an asphalt road; at the corner was the small Nocé Café, run by an old Italian, the only European in the area. Most of his customers were taxi drivers, and sometimes my mother met us there to treat us to the soft and fluffy Italian pastries Nocé was famous for. The café was on Marshal Tito Street, which was paved and ran for about one kilometre before joining the Asmara highway. Opposite the café, across the street, was a *medebir* (convenience store) where only the window was used for conducting business. Here I often bought two of my favourite sweets, cinnamon-flavoured gum and pure sugar rolled into coin-like disks. Further down Tito Street was the Department of Forestry, where my father worked. Then came a Shell gas station and the iconic Hilton Hotel. Down the hill from the Hilton was our favourite rooftop restaurant, the Kokeb (the Star), which gave an aerial view of the park and trees inside the Emperor's palace grounds.

I was fourteen when I first saw Cuban and Russian soldiers in military tanks on the streets, and life was never the same. The only foreigner I had known was Nocé but now the streets were flooded with Cubans and Russians, and they came not with soft pastries, but tanks and guns. The statues of Marx and Lenin, erected in the city centre, became a distracting landmark. I often stopped and stared at the heavy statues embedded in the soil in the heart of Addis. The army said they were to remind us of the changes that were to come to the good people of Ethiopia. And there were changes. The elders in my community, whom I once trusted, now carried rifles in broad daylight and patrolled the streets in order to sniff out anti-Derg activities. I never told anyone that the Cubans and Russians scared me, or that instead of the statues of Marx and Lenin I preferred the fields of the yellow *adey abeba* (daisies), or the fact that waking up to gunshots ripped my heart to pieces. All political discussions were forbidden by the military government. It was never clear to me when it was safe to walk to school, to my soccer game, or to the movies. It seemed unsafe to go anywhere.

"Vacation"

———◆———

The heaviest burden for a man to carry is his promise.
—AFAR PROVERB

A WEEK LATER, IN THE PALE light before dawn, we crammed our belongings into the Land Rover to begin our journey to Dire Dawa. My baby sister, Kalkidan, was crying a lot, having been woken up from her sleep, and Meskerem covered her with a blanket and held her over her shoulder in the front of the car. Yared, Asrat, and I got inside from the back door. There were two bench seats, covered in black plastic material, facing each other. Our two suitcases were placed in the centre.

As we pulled out of the driveway, my friend Seble, Ato Beza's daughter, came running over.

"Beth," she called out, "I came to say goodbye."

I jumped out and wrapped my arms around her. Her eyes were shining with tears. "It will be just two months. Remember, it is just like the last time when I went to Lake Abaya. We will be back before you know it."

"You won't be back for Buhe," she said.

"But I am always here for Enkutatash," I said.

"Well, then, let me come with you this time," she said, wiping her eyes.

"I wish you could," I replied and got back into the car.

I waved her goodbye and she ran after us waving back. She stopped, and she kept waving until we were out of sight.

And so began our journey east to Assayita, to the province of my father's field assignment.

Buhe was a religious celebration that took place in August, a few weeks before the Ethiopian New Year, Enkutatash. It lasted for the whole day, during which the boys went door to door singing a song called "Hoya Hoye." I liked Buhe because of the special bread known as *mulmul* that was made only at that time of the year and because of the bonfire celebrations.

The New Year celebration was my favourite. That was when the yellow daisies were in bloom all over Ethiopia and the girls made bouquets to give to their neighbours and relatives, singing, Abeba Ye Hoy. We were always home for the New Year.

As we left, the streets were empty, and they wouldn't come alive for another hour or two. We took Tito Street to Asmera Road, then we rolled on to the Addis Ababa-Dire Dawa highway. For the most part, the highway was two lanes and both lanes were busy with trucks covered in canvas carrying government-approved merchandise such as electronics, canned goods, and furniture. There were also herds of sheep on the highway.

We passed Akaki, the first town east of Addis, driving past the spiralling chains of the Error Mountains on both sides of the highway. Dust swirled all around us. The valley was covered with species of eucalyptus, baobab, bamboo, and acacia trees standing up like sentinels in multicoloured luxurious abundance. When these were gone, Abba, looking out the window, pointed, "Those short trees are pepper trees that we use to ward off mosquitoes." The landscape was quickly changing.

Farmers led longhorn humpbacked cattle, goats, sheep, and

camels in throngs, choking the road, but Abba's endless honking fell on deaf ears. We managed to thread our way through the sea of animals and continued. My father turned the radio on and we heard someone saying how the Derg's literacy policy was helping hundreds of people learn to read and write for the first time ever.

"This is good news, for a change," Abba commented.

Every now and then we passed Cuban and Russian armoured convoys. At times Meskerem put down Kalkidan in the space between Abba and herself to take a break. Soon we drove into Debre Zeyet, which was famous for its horse-and-carriage method of public transport. Most trips within the city cost less than one Ethiopian birr. Yared asked if we could try a ride on the carriages.

"We can't stay here long. The sun will get hotter. I will get some cookies and drinks, just wait in the car," Abba instructed. "We will take a longer break in Nazareth," he shouted back as he reached the *medebir*. I rolled down the window and stared outside. The air felt drier and dustier than in Addis, still the streets were filled with people. Coffee shops were open and people sat on the patios. Amharic music blasted from store windows. Business people hurried to their destinations. Abba returned and we resumed our journey, munching on our snacks and sipping soft drinks.

The ninety-nine-kilometre journey from Addis to Nazareth had taken three and a half hours. It was a pleasant ride because the roads were well paved. As in Debre Zeyet, the Oromiffia people were in the majority. According to Abba, at least forty percent of the Ethiopian population was composed of Oromiffia and they lived in every province in Ethiopia except Eritrea. The small children selling mangoes and bananas on the roadside spoke mostly in Oromiffia. My stepmother's fluency in the language helped speed up our purchase of the fruit.

Nazareth was a popular family vacation destination for Ethiopians because the climate was warm and comfortable. A few kilometres from the city were the popular resorts of Sodere. People who came to bathe in the hot springs reported being cured of a wide range of ailments, from arthritis to skin conditions.

Abba pulled up at a restaurant near the Awash Valley, on the Addis Ababa-Djibouti railway line. The train stopped here every day at lunch-time, and the valley was then inundated with travellers emerging to eat lunch near this scenic location.

"Kalkidan is awake. She must be hungry," Meskerem said.

"She will love a banana." Abba said, peeling one for her.

"Akam Jirta," a server with a dazzling smile greeted us in Oromiffia as we arrived.

"Feya," our parents both replied. Meskerem asked if we could sit outside. Abba said we could sit anywhere we liked. We sat under the shade of a flowering tree. The whiff of fried fish filled the air and my mouth began to water.

———◆◆———

From the Awash Valley we descended towards the northern tip of the magnificent African Rift Valley that stretches 6,000 kilometres from the Red Sea, south through Kenya and into Mozambique. The site was pure wonder. I couldn't believe that such a beautiful place could exist on the planet, let alone a few hours from Addis.

My brothers and I counted camels on the road while listening to Amharic music on the radio, totally absorbed during every minute of the journey. But sometimes Abba and my stepmother became frustrated. Meskerem tried to keep Kalkidan comfortable, holding her every which way. The car would bounce on the road and dust came blowing inside, or black fumes from a slow truck in front. On one of Abba's attempts to pass a bus, it seemed we would go over a cliff, and Meskerem became upset, saying, "I don't want to die today with my baby in my arms!"

After we crossed the Awash River, the landscape changed dramatically. The mountains were now broken hills. The air was as dry as the hot Sahara wind, and the area was almost devoid of vegetation. The little foliage that existed was in the form of tiny shrubs scorched by the sun. We were stunned.

"At one point I managed this whole area," Abba said enthusiastically.

After completing postgraduate study in regional development planning in Rehovot, Israel, Abba returned in June 1974, just in time to witness the military takeover of the country. He did not get involved in the new politics, and the Awash Valley Authority immediately dispatched him to the eastern district.

"But it's so dry!" I said.

"During the rainy season, the Awash River and Lake Afambo fill up. If we can find a way of saving the water for use during the dry season, we can farm all year long and harvest enough to feed the whole country," Abba replied.

"That's a good idea," Asrat said.

"But the problem is that the Afar nomads who live in the area constantly move with their cattle and won't settle long enough to see a harvest. Besides, the government won't help," my father added.

"Why not?" I blurted out.

"That's a good question," Abba smiled. "Sad, but the government believes the nomads' way of life is too backward and not worth spending money on."

He fell silent. I noticed the dark circles around his eyes. I wondered about his work, labouring from the forested end of the country to the desert and from the highlands to the lowlands with the hope of turning desolate lands into living greenery. *Could Abba, the only advisor who had volunteered to go to the region, make a difference?*

"Almost all of the inhabitants are Muslim Afar people and they move around the eastern provinces in search of water and markets," Abba continued. "In 1974, scientists were digging in this region, and you wouldn't believe what they found," he said, his eyes wide open. "The skeletons of Dinknesh! The scientists call her 'Lucy.'" Abba had a wide smile on his face now.

"They said the skeletons were of an ape, but it walked like humans and it lived millions of years ago."

Abba always told us strange stories whenever he came back from his travels and sometimes he brought back unusual things like ostrich eggs, starfish, and leather items, which we used to decorate our home.

"The skeletons are the oldest ever found anywhere on earth, and it will be so until even older ones are found elsewhere. They are saying this could mean human beings originated from this land. What I find so interesting is the idea that all human beings originated from Ethiopia, and on top of that the idea that all of us come from the same ancestors."

In the town of Metahara, it was so hot that even rolling down the car windows didn't cool us. The best thing about Metahara was its sugar cane, which my brothers and I chewed and chewed, sucking on the juice until the insides of our mouths were blistered. We bought about twenty canes, each the size of my arm, to take to Meskerem's relatives in Dire Dawa.

As we neared the city of Asebe Teferri, the road became more hazardous. We began our descent from the mountain plateau toward the Danakil lowlands on narrow, single-lane roads without any protective railings. The car moved quickly, spiralling downward and almost out of control, taking us very close to the edge of the cliff. Everywhere you looked there was a sheer drop, and we were, it seemed, a hair's breadth away from spinning into the earth's core. This insane manoeuvring went on for about half an hour until, near the town of Dengego, the road became somewhat flat and less crooked. We had finally left the highlands and arrived into the lowlands, and we had gone from the fierce heat of the Awash and Metahara districts to the moderate climate of Hararge province. Our destination was its commercial city, Dire Dawa.

Having driven some five hundred kilometres, we arrived just before sunset. My father let out a final cry, "If they just filled the ditches and added one more lane on each side, it would take under six hours to get here instead of the whole day. But, no, no, no, they need the money to buy fancy weapons and war planes." He sighed, and then announced, "We are in Dire Dawa, children."

I was excited. The air was dry, unlike the moist air of Addis. I took off my sweater and let the wind, rushing through the open window, blow onto my face. I loved it. The wind, the red soil, the relaxed manner of the people on the street—the freshness of the surroundings gave me a sense of freedom.

Suddenly I was full of energy. This was the first time I had travelled east of Addis Ababa.

Dire Dawa was unlike any place I had ever known. It was the end of June, the start of the rainy season. The evenings were cool and comfortable, and I found the air relaxing. Beautiful trees lined well-maintained single-lane roads, their trunks painted deep white and their tops umbrellas of red, orange, and pink flowers. A big brown building situated far behind the trees stood out in the evening scenery. "What's that?" I asked my father.

"That," Abba replied, "is the City Hall."

The men wore shirts and striped cotton *shirit* (sarongs) tied around their waists. Most walked barefoot, like our cook at home, Mamma Truye.

"Children!" Abba called out. "You see all these people on the street? They come from many different ethnic groups: Adre', Afar, Issa, Somali, and some are Amharas, and most of them speak more than two languages. It's said that in Dire Dawa you are sure to find someone from every Ethiopian ethnic group."

At least eighty different languages were spoken in Ethiopia. I spoke only the official language, Amharic. However, I didn't feel comfortable mentioning my ethnic background; I didn't believe there was one pure ethnic category, since so many people were in mixed marriages. I remember that when we lived in Kaffa, my grade one teacher, who was an Oromiffia, had asked Asrat and me what we were. We instantly replied, "We are Habesha." I believed that the Oromiffias, Tigrays, and the others were all Habesha, which I understood to be what most Ethiopians (if not all) referred to themselves when not mentioning their specific ethnic origins. The teacher laughed at our response, and then called the other teachers into the classroom and repeated the question so that they could hear our reply. It was only then that we realized that we were not saying something right. When we reported to our mother what had happened, she explained that the Italians called the Ethiopians "Habesha," which meant "burnt faces," when they invaded Ethiopia. "Next time proudly say you are Ethiopians."

"How can we tell who is from which ethnic group?" Asrat asked our father.

"By the way they walk, dress, and talk. But it is hard for you to tell because you are not from around here," Meskerem was quick to reply.

Abba was more specific: "If you see a man wearing a short skirt-like *shirit* with a shoulder-width long thin knife (*gile*) hanging across his belly button, then he is an Afar. Don't be afraid of them; however scary they may appear with their weapons, the Afars are not violent people. They need their knives for protection from animals or bandits and to cut meat when they move from place to place. They don't usually come to the city centre. They have a market on the outskirts of Dire Dawa. That is what I love about this city. The people, however different they may be from each other, whether in religion, customs, or languages, all can relate easily to one another and live side by side without any major clashes."

"The Issa people carry a sword similar to the Afar's, except that the one the Issa carry is thicker and longer," Meskerem added.

I wondered if I could distinguish the Afar and the Issa by just staring at their weapons.

We stopped at a gas station late in the evening to fill up, then continued on our way to Meskerem's family home. Past the gas station, the paved road gave way to a gravel one and suddenly the road split into two and went around a circular field. We drove around the circle and passed a furniture store, then a metal and woodwork shop, and finally several houses. Meskerem explained that sometimes the gas-station owner rented out the open space to truck drivers overnight. But during the day children played games there and learned how to ride their bikes.

We pulled up in front of Meskerem's family home, which was now owned by Ato Teshome, Meskerem's relative. We parked the car and unloaded our bags, but left Abba's behind; he would be lodging in a hotel near his workplace for a couple of days.

In the dimness of the evening, I could see a big veranda with a cement floor, upon which lounged a large cat, white as cotton. As Meskerem got out of the car holding Kalkidan in her arms, she called out, "Ayenachew. Come here. Here, here!" As soon as she saw our family approaching, laden with luggage, the cat slowly came towards us. "She must be missing Miriam. I think she was waiting for her," Meskerem said. Ayenachew rubbed her head against Yared's leg and he bent down to rub her.

"She is so friendly," he said.

"Let me try," I said, edging closer.

She lay down on the veranda with her belly up for me to keep stroking. Her fur was thick, soft, and shiny. She reminded me of our dog, Metew.

We walked into the living room and put down our bags without anyone greeting us. There were two couches, a coffee table, and a mirrored buffet which displayed a glittering china set. The living room ceiling was very high. It had a fan spinning from its centre at a slow pace, which kept the room pleasantly cool.

"Babye, Elaine, Hewan," Meskerem called out. "Where is everyone?"

Minutes later, a man in a pressed white shirt and grey trousers entered the room. He looked surprised to see us.

"Meskerem! Ato Terrefe! So good to see you," Ato Teshome smiled and glanced at me and my brothers. "Miriam is in Addis

Ababa with Rebecca. She said she was going to stop by your house and visit. She called this morning but she didn't tell me you were coming to Dire Dawa." He put his arms around my father. Then he kissed my brothers and me one by one. He took the baby out of Meskerem's hands and looked at my sister with glowing eyes. "There you are, my dear. I finally got to meet you, little girl."

"I saw a good opportunity to bring the children and show them this part of the country and we decided to do it now, before school starts," my father said before I heard him apologize for arriving so unexpectedly. Then he added, "If my family can stay with you for a couple of days, it would be a great help. I will stay at a hotel near my work station for the time being."

Ato Teshome was Miriam's husband. He had a medium build and a welcoming smile. I was wondering why my stepmother had not told her sister, Miriam, about our plan to come to Dire Dawa, but since people from Dire Dawa were considered very relaxed, with no serious rules about when you dropped in, we didn't think much of it. People here didn't even lock their doors at night. In fact, they slept in the afternoon from noon until about three, when they got up to go to work, just as they would in the mornings.

Ato Teshome called for help, and his three daughters came into the living room. They were wearing sandals and colourful cotton dresses of a thin, fine fabric. I recognized the eldest, Elaine, because I had met her in Addis Ababa before. Then Hewan and Rahel were introduced to us. They looked very much alike. They both had long black hair in a French braid and they were light skinned, like their sister Rebecca. They helped with our luggage. Since they were not expecting visitors, they had given their two helpers a week off. So for the three days we were to stay with them, the three young sisters would be responsible for the comfort of our family.

In less than an hour, Meskerem's family served *injera* and a nutritious meal with a variety of sauces, calling us to come and sit down at the dining-room table.

Afterwards, Abba and Ato Teshome excused themselves and

went into the living room to continue their conversation over peppermint tea.

As we finished our meal, Elaine asked us if we would like to take a tour of the city in the morning.

"Yes, if we are not troubling you," Yared replied.

"No trouble at all. You would like the contraband market. You can find watches, perfumes, and anything you want at a good price. But we need to leave the house before the sun gets too hot."

Meskerem had left the table with Kalkidan and I could hear Kalkidan's laughter from time to time from the back of the house.

⚊⚬⚊

A loud noise outside woke me up in the middle of the night. A man's clear voice reverberated in Arabic in the darkness. It sounded like a loudspeaker.

"It's four-thirty in the morning," Asrat sighed, also awakened by the sound.

"What's going on?" I asked, feeling irritated.

"It's the Muslim call to prayer," said Yared. He had recognized the words, *Allahu Akbar! God is Great!*

I heard my baby sister crying in the next room, and Meskerem singing a lullaby to put her back to sleep. By five o'clock, quiet returned, and we all fell back into our slumbers.

A short time later, a siren pierced the morning air, and frightened, I jumped out of bed. My brothers were up too. The noise went on for about another minute, while we sat on the edge of our beds.

"I don't know what this is," Yared said uncertainly.

Just then, Meskerem knocked on our door with the baby in her arms.

"Don't be scared," she told us. "I should have mentioned earlier that the siren will sound several times during the day. It's a wake-up call for the railway employees; it's six o'clock in the morning. You will hear it again at six-thirty, which means the workers have arrived at the railway yard." We all looked relieved.

After Meskerem left, I tried to sleep, but couldn't. Before I knew it, it was already time to get up.

It was seven o'clock when I headed to the living room with my brothers. There we found Ato Teshome seated on a couch drinking cold milk and eating bread. Elaine believed that her father was the exception in Dire Dawa, choosing not to have spicy tea or coffee with his breakfast. He refused to chew qat, and he did not allow it in his house either.

"Did *aya jibo* scare you this morning?" Elaine asked.

"*Aya jibo*? Hyenas? Well, we didn't hear any hyenas, but the Muslims' call to prayer and the railway siren woke us up," Asrat said.

"We call the siren *aya jibo* because it sounds just like a hyena's long howl," she said with a smile.

Meskerem with Kalkidan, my brothers, Elaine, and I gathered at the table to eat. Soon after, my brothers and I left the house with Elaine to begin our exploration of Dire Dawa. Meskerem had opted to stay behind with Kalkidan. The large trees in the compound had spread out their shadows. As we crossed the circle field on our way to the streets, I realized that the mornings in Dire Dawa were very different from those in Addis Ababa. Here the whole city was waking up noisily: neighbours greeted one another, big trucks clattered by, and chickens and dogs ran freely throughout the compound. Elaine stopped to greet the neighbours and introduced us as her cousins from Addis Ababa.

We reached the city centre within half an hour. People were eating their breakfasts on the go, not because they were in a hurry, but because it was their custom. In Addis Ababa, eating on the street was considered bad manners. Most people wore sandals, even those going to work. And since Dire Dawa had people of many ethnic backgrounds, every traditional colour was represented in the clothes they wore. Some men and women had wrapped their heads while others sported Afros. Some women looked like they were on their way to a wedding. Some men wore pants and others wore sarongs. Everyone shouted as they talked. The streets were flooded with blue-and-white Peugeot 404 taxis, the drivers seated sideways facing the passengers.

The scent of fried *melewa* and samosa filled the air. Clothing boutiques, small and large, were lined up on the streets among evenly spaced flowering trees. In the unshaded areas the sun was head-piercing, not as soft as in Addis. Schoolgirls in blue and white uniforms spoke French: they were from the French school run by nuns not too far from where we were. Although there were very few French people in Dire Dawa, the French still had a great deal of interest in neighbouring Djibouti where they controlled the shipping business in the Red Sea and maintained a large air force and an army base.

When we arrived in the market, there was such a rush of people that we had to hold hands to stay together.

"This market was once a slaughterhouse for sheep," Elaine explained. "Now it is called Taiwan Market, since most of their products are made in Taiwan." The market was in a huge space under an aluminum roof with a cement floor. It was packed with goods and overflowed into the street. People came from as far away as Addis Ababa to look for contraband goods at reasonable prices.

The train came into Dire Dawa from Djibouti three times a week, when taxis lined up at the station to pick up the goods for the market. Gold jewelry, shoes, watches, refrigerators, cassettes, olive oil, powdered milk, underwear, cookware, spices, and wall clocks could all be found here. There were mountains of coloured sandals on the sidewalks. The Taiwan Market had boomed after the military takeover.

Seeing how worn out we were from all the noise and pushing and shoving, Elaine guided us on to quieter streets and showed us Leul (Prince) Mekonen's palace. Like his father the emperor's palace in Addis, it was surrounded by a fence. The tall stone walls made it difficult to see what lay beyond the three-arched iron gate. As we circled around the perimeter, the loud railway siren blasted through the midday heat, and soon the muezzin's voice pierced the chaotic street with "Allahu Akbar." It was time to go back to the house for lunch and our very first siesta.

———◆———

Abba was at the house. He came to check how we were doing and was pleased to hear about our adventurous morning. At lunch, he told us we would stay in Dire Dawa for two more nights before heading out on a tour of his work site. After lunch, we played with Kalkidan for a while then went to our bedroom for a much needed rest. As I lay on my bed, it felt good not to be outside in the heat. The fan was running at a slow speed over my head, wafting a refreshing breeze upon me. The windows were closed, but bright sunlight still managed to seep through, keeping the room dimly lit. I breathed deeply and closed my eyes. I heard Abba's and Ato Teshome's voices in the living room. They were talking loudly enough for me to listen in to what they were saying.

"The revolution has ruined my children," said Ato Teshome. "Before, they would come home after school and study, and help their mother with chores. Now days go by before I even know where they are. They tell me they are called to teach the illiterate, to enforce the curfew, to ration food, to learn the teachings of Marx and Lenin. Two years ago, my daughters never went out without permission. But now they carry rifles and walk the streets of Dire Dawa at three in the morning, chewing qat! And I can't do anything about it!"

———◆———

Under the rule of Emperor Haile Selassie, I had felt a sense of peace. People—at least those around me—trusted one another. I had not heard the sound of gunshots; I had not known what a curfew was. But once the Derg came to power, anyone who spoke against it was jailed or executed. Ordinary citizens were suddenly split into factions. Family members no longer could trust one another. Everyone was suspected of being an informant either for the Derg or for some other political faction. I was always afraid to go to school in the morning. Almost daily there would be corpses on the streets, left there from routine executions. Whenever I saw a crowd gathered, I would instinctively walk on the opposite side of the road.

My brother Asrat had been recruited by the Derg to teach the illiterate elderly three nights a week for two hours a night. He had to join a marching band, chanting revolutionary songs, once a week. At first he was excited about his role of a teacher. He wore his best suit to go teach. He had about thirty students, most of them eager to learn. They loved my brother and would invite him for dinner or lunch, and if they saw him on the street, they proudly told everyone that he was their teacher.

But he barely had time to study for himself, let alone keep an eye on the house while our father was away. So he told the revolutionary leaders that he would not be teaching when the new session began. When asked why, he gave a straightforward answer: "I am bored." He could have said he was sick or a relative was sick, which was a common and more appropriate excuse, but he didn't. He was sentenced to three days in jail. Luckily, one of his students was assigned to be his jailer, and he was released the following day. He was never asked to teach again.

This was one of the biggest secrets we kept from our father.

————•◦•————

On our last day in Dire Dawa, all we did was shop. My father and Meskerem bought everything they could think of, as though we were going camping. Flashlights, first-aid kits, mats, powdered milk, medicine, malaria pills, mosquito repellent and other camping gear. We asked Abba why he was buying all these supplies. He said that he wanted to be fully prepared for any emergency because his beloved family was travelling with him. After we were done with the shopping, Meskerem and I got our hair done. Meskerem liked her hair set in rollers and that was what I did too.

On the fourth day, my father woke us up unusually early, and then he went outside while we were still having breakfast. Meskerem was in the bedroom packing, and Kalkidan was still asleep. Through the window we saw Abba talking to two tall men dressed in sarongs and T-shirts, with knives tied at their waists and Kalashnikov rifles slung over their shoulders. They had dazzling Afros, which looked as though they had never been combed.

I guessed that they were Afar or Issa. But why were they here? The younger man, who looked about eighteen, was standing next to a wheelbarrow. The other man, much older, was listening to my father attentively.

Abba came back inside. We pretended to be eating.

"I found some help. These two men will help us transport our luggage and bring it to where I am taking you so we don't have to worry about carrying it in and out of the car," he said. He was served his breakfast, but he took only his tea and said, "This is all I am having."

Meskerem joined us with a cup of tea already in her hand. "I forgot to tell them you don't like eggs. Should they cook something else?" she asked my father.

Abba declined and whispered, "They came on time."

Meskerem turned to look at us and, as my eyes briefly met hers, I felt as though she was going to tell us something. But she suddenly decided to go and check on Kalkidan. I squeezed the honey jar and poured out a generous portion onto my last quarter of *melewa*. Through the open bedroom door I could see Meskerem holding nine-month-old Kalkidan tight to her chest as if she were saying goodbye. Instinctively I moved my chair back and got up. I went to stand behind Meskerem and said, "Ayehush," to Kalkidan. I see you! She let out a big scream and kicked her legs in delight.

"We better get going," Meskerem said and put Kalkidan back on the bed, arranging pillows so that she wouldn't fall off. Kalkidan rolled over onto her tummy, lifted her head up and started crying.

"Rahel!" Meskerem called out to her cousin.

Rahel rushed in, and Meskerem said, "Will you please keep an eye on Kalkidan? Terrefe and I are going to take the kids to show them where he works."

"Sure," Rahel said, and went to pick up Kalkidan.

Meskerem and I joined my father and Ato Teshome in the living room. Abba was anxiously staring out the window with his cup of tea in his hand. He watched the two men pile our belongings onto the wheelbarrow and disappear behind a sycamore tree.

"I don't understand what the hurry is that you don't even eat your breakfast," Ato Teshome complained.

"I just want the kids to see the farm before the sun is hot. You know what the weather is like in Addis Ababa, and my children are not used to the Dire Dawa heat," my father replied.

"We will be back before lunch," Meskerem promised.

On the way to the car, I saw Meskerem wiping away tears. I wanted to ask her why she was crying but I was so excited about our trip that I hurried to the car instead. Other than a box of cigarettes, a large container of water, a radio, and something I couldn't identify that was covered in a white sheet, the car was empty.

After driving for about five minutes within the city of Dire Dawa, we stopped on a street to pick up two men that my father seemed to know. The skinnier of the two, wearing a T-shirt and a *shirit*, sat in the front with my father and stepmother. The other, dressed in a shirt and trousers, sat at the back with us. From his accent, I could tell that he was a Somali. His uncombed curly hair was dark, and his teeth were rusty brown. After the greetings, he seemed disinterested in my brothers and me, and paid full attention to what the adults in the front were saying.

After passing the Ras Hotel, the largest in the province, our car stopped again and we picked up a third man, who got into the back and sat next to Yared. The back seat of the Land Rover could comfortably seat four people, but now we were five and there was hardly any room to stretch. The new man wore a suit but without a tie, and from the way he spoke, I could tell that he was an Amhara.

He took a look at the Somali and it seemed that they had never met before. Since the strangers entered the vehicle, the air inside the car smelled of cigarettes, qat, and dust. I wondered why all these men were accompanying us on our vacation and why Abba never bothered to introduce them to us.

We drove for another twenty-five kilometres with very few words spoken. I couldn't wait to get out of the car; the smell, the limited space, the heat, and the twists and turns in the road made me nauseous. At the village of Melka Jebdu there was a checkpoint with soldiers. Two of them, carrying automatic weapons, approached us.

"Selam," my father greeted them in Amharic. "I brought my family on a vacation to show them where I work."

The soldiers recognized the government plate on our car and let us go.

We drove for another half hour on a winding dirt road that took us deeper into the rocky desert. Suddenly we made a sharp right turn to follow tire tracks in the dust. Then we stopped. The three men quickly got out of the car and instructed us to wait.

"Abba, why did we stop?" Yared complained.

My father hesitated before he replied, "We are here."

"What's there to see here?" whispered Asrat in my ear. "Do you see any farm?"

All I saw everywhere were rocks and dust baking under an intense sun. My back was drenched. Without a single cloud in the sky, the only shield from the oppressive sun was our car.

"Here, have some water," Meskerem tried to distract us.

But Yared was impatient. "What are we doing here?"

If any of us were to rebel, it would be Yared. Our family albums were full of pictures of Yared with crossed eyes, his hands on his waist, standing with his legs apart. Now I wondered why we had packed our albums. Abba was becoming irritated. "If you could just keep quiet for one minute, I will explain," he hissed.

He followed the men to the back of the car. They opened the

back door and hauled out the cigarettes, the radio, and the small item that was wrapped in white. We were told to get out of the car and follow them. Abba walked behind us like a military marshal, ordering us to hurry. We scampered along helplessly. There was a certain eeriness about the place and our situation. The urgency in my father's voice hinted that we were being watched. I looked around to see if I could spot someone hiding behind a rock or in a bush. Further up I saw some vegetation, and some anthills, but nothing was moving in the midday heat, even the air was surprisingly clear of dust. I looked up and stared at the cloudless sky, almost expecting soldiers to drop down like spiders. It all felt like a dream.

"Why did we leave our car?" I cried to Yared, who was walking alongside me.

"I don't know. Are you okay?" he asked.

Abba's voice thundered behind us: "Stop talking! Just follow the men and move quickly."

We followed his order. We ran behind the men, who led us to a desolate valley, and then proceeded towards a narrow passage between sand walls. Suddenly, there was a helicopter up in the sky and I could hear the sound of its tat, tat, tat, tat, tat following us.

My father's hand pushed me from behind. "Walk faster, just keep walking," he ordered. Frightened, I hurried but stumbled on something and fell face down in the dirt. In an instant my eyes began to burn, my mouth, nose, and ears filled with dust. I felt my breath ebb, and lifted my head in a panic, gasping for air. When I didn't hear anything, I began to spit out sand and rub my itchy eyes. "Get up, get up, you are okay," my father commanded. I slowly got up and the sand trickled off my clothes. The sky was still.

I was walking like a partially blind child as we continued, not quite sure where my next step would land. My eyes still burned, no matter how many times my brother Yared blew into them. My thin legs threatened to stick in the sand or snap like a branch. My brand new blue-and-white Adidas, my orange miniskirt, and yellow shirt had already turned brown. My hair felt like a pile of straw; perhaps I should have bought a watch like Yared did from the Taiwan Market in Dire Dawa instead of getting my hair done with Meskerem. A horrible stench blew into our faces, carried by the desert wind. As we walked further, the smell became more nauseating, until we stumbled across the carcass of a camel between two crumbling rocks. It was huge, and its stomach was bloated as if it had swallowed an ostrich, and its legs were pointing up to the desert sky. It must have been dead for a while. Its nose was missing, its face covered with maggots and insects. I ran past it holding my breath as the vultures hovered above us waiting to begin their feast.

Once we were past the dead camel, my father and the three strangers ordered us to stop in the middle of what looked like a wide crack in the ground. Then they sat down on the dirt to discuss their plan of action.

Looking at us, my father announced, "We are leaving Ethiopia and we will not come back, no matter what. We have no choice, and you must be strong. The Derg was planning to jail those people in my department who worked for the Emperor." He turned his head away to hide his tears. "You must believe me when I tell you . . . ," he swallowed hard and continued, "that this is the most . . . " He choked again, unable to control the tears now flowing down his face. He turned away. "This is the most difficult decision that I have made in my life," Abba said and took in a deep breath. "I thought about it a lot and I have a good plan which I am sure will work. I have hired the best guides and good transportation to take us to Djibouti."

Meskerem burst into tears. She said, "I have known about it for a long time, but we couldn't tell you. This is life and death. We wanted to tell you, but we were afraid that word might get out."

I was beyond speechless. I was hurt, panicked, confused, burning with rage, feeling betrayed and dizzy all at the same time. I wanted to scream at Abba and my stepmother for not telling us their plans in advance. I didn't know how to stop the pain. How could Abba tell Meskerem everything before he told us? I thought we were a team, that while Abba worked all over Ethiopia, we, his children, obeyed his rules even with no parent in the house. The teachers never once had to call a meeting to report an incident. The unfairness of it seemed immeasurable. Meskerem had had a chance to see her family. But my brothers and I never got a chance to say goodbye to our mother, and nothing they did was going to fix that.

The last time I had seen my mother, she took us to a Western movie that did not have Amharic subtitles. It didn't matter if we only understood half of what was said; we followed the actions and in the end arrived at our own conclusions. After the movie, my mother took us to our favorite Kokeb restaurant for dessert. A few days after that Asrat had gone to visit her at my grandmother's house, to lend her his watch because hers was at the repair shop. At least she had his watch and she would remember him whenever she looked at it. I couldn't think of anything of mine she might have had, and that made me even more sad. I felt like I was watching a movie or this was all just my wild imagination gone rampant.

Yared scrambled to his feet, wearing an angry look, and said, "I am not going anywhere."

"We have no choice, Yared. You are my first-born and I need you to be strong," Abba begged.

Yared started walking back in the direction we had come from and Abba was quick to follow him. I could see Yared kicking something invisible and wiping away the tears flowing down his face. Abba caught up with him and put his long arm around his shoulder and talked to him for a while. Much later, I was relieved to see them both approaching.

The strangers and my family sat quietly, each of us absorbed with our thoughts.

"What about Kalkidan?" Asrat gasped, looking horrified.

"Kalkidan has to stay in Dire Dawa, but once we reach Djibouti, we will find a way to bring her." Meskerem was crying. She looked at Abba. "We can't leave her for long, Terrefe. She needs me to nurse her. Three days is all we have, otherwise my milk will dry up."

Abba went to her. He said, "You and I have talked about this already. It won't be for long, I promise."

We sat there for what felt like a lifetime and cried.

The Edge of the Danakil Desert

---◀◆▶---

Those who don't know the desert will curse their journey through it. —AFAR PROVERB

IT WAS DECIDED QUICKLY that one of the guides, named Ali, would go back to the abandoned car and take it to a garage, supposedly for repair, while we waited for his return where we were, in the middle of the desert. The second guide, Hussein, was thin but muscular. He seemed to be in his forties and was wearing a torn T-shirt and a grey *shirit*. The third stranger, in a suit without a tie, was introduced to us more formally. "This is Mr Lema, the chairman of the Peasant Association of Dire Dawa," Abba said. "It was because of him that we didn't get caught," he stated matter-of-factly.

"I wish you a safe journey. May God be with you and guide you always. I suppose I'd better return before I change my mind and escape with you," Mr Lema said with a smile.

Abba shook his hand in gratitude. "I will never forget your help, Lema. You are a dear friend."

"You know there is nothing I wouldn't do for you, and this is the least I can do considering all that you have done for me and the people of Assayita," Lema replied. "But as I said, I'd better leave now."

Mr Lema began walking back with Ali.

"When will we have our car back?" Yared asked.

"We won't be travelling by car anymore. Don't worry, I have something better," my father replied.

Confused and angry, Yared asked, "What?"

"For now, on foot, but that won't be for long," Abba explained calmly.

The thought of walking on foot seemed unbearable. What was this secret means of transportation Abba had in mind? I wished it were a helicopter so the pain of losing our country would not drag on for days.

"Yes, on foot. We have no choice. You all have to be strong. If everything works out according to plan, we should be in Djibouti in three days." Abba rolled his sleeves up. "We cannot wait for Ali here, we are too close to the checkpoint."

The stink of the dead camel was still with us. Asrat's face was calm, without a trace of fear or anxiety. Yared was still frowning. If things hadn't happened so fast, he probably would have chosen to stay in Ethiopia to continue the life he knew.

Asrat looked at me kindly. "Don't worry, I will help you all the way. Three days is not all that long, you'll see."

I took in a deep breath of the wretched air. My thoughts raced out of control, fearing the unknown. If we had finished five litres of water in just a few hours, how much more water would we need for the entire journey? If we stumbled onto soldiers, would they let us go? Looking down, next to my shoes, I saw a sharp white bone jutting out from the sand. I bent over and reached for it.

I thought of my mother, Tetye. How would she learn of our escape? She would be devastated.

I thought of our dog Metew. My father had got her in Kaffa when I was six, to keep all of us, especially my mother, company. When she was a puppy, my brothers and I used to hide from her in the cornfield and we loved it when she came looking for us. We would go further and further into the field to see if she was still able to sniff us out. But she always did. Our arms would be cut by the sharp edges of the corn leaves, but the pleasure of being found by Metew was worth it. She would jump all over us and we would rub her fur, telling her what a good dog she was to have found us in the deepest part of the field.

We found out that Meskerem had arranged for her sister, Mimi, to look after the house while we were "on vacation." Would she take care of Metew? Even if she did, I knew that Metew would miss us terribly. If it was just a three-day journey, I thought to myself, why didn't we bring our dog along? And my thoughts raced on. What about school? Could we continue in Djibouti?

"How long are we going to stay in Djibouti?" Asrat asked finally.

"Until the situation in Ethiopia improves," Abba replied.

"And then we will go back to our country?" Yared demanded.

"Yared, we must focus on the road ahead," Abba said firmly, looking at my brother directly. "We will have plenty of time to talk about this once we cross the border."

Meskerem added, "The road won't be so bad. We've hired the best guides."

"We don't know about that. I've never done this before. Have you walked on foot to Djibouti?" Yared shouted at Meskerem, tears still streaming down his face.

"Yared!" Abba shouted. There followed by a long pause. He closed his eyes for a moment and let out a loud sigh. "We've hired the best guides, Yared. I could have navigated using a map, but there are dozens of things that are not on a map that we need help with, like guerrilla fighters who would undoubtedly question us in languages we don't understand, wild animals, or even clan leaders who might wonder why we are here."

Hussein's eyes switched back and forth between Abba, Meskerem, and Yared and he finally said quietly, "This hollow space is actually a good place to stay put, but it would be even better if we move a little further from the bad smell. We should stay as quiet as possible, but we cannot start the journey until dark."

Abba, Meskerem, and Yared were silent. Yared's face was still tight, tears pouring down his face. I feared that he would go back.

Once Hussein had everyone's attention, he stood up. "Follow me," he said. We all got up from where we sat and started following. "As you know, fighters from all fronts roam this region. Also, do not forget there are minefields everywhere. We have to be extremely cautious. We—"

Before he could finish, there came the sound of loud gunfire. We stopped, and fear crept over us. I rushed to Abba. Yared and Asrat looked terrified. My father was waiting for Hussein to continue and he appeared to be thinking hard at the same time. My body was covered with sweat.

Then Hussein's voice filled my ears once more. "Keep walking. We will find a good spot where we can stay until it is safe to start our journey. At night we will be less visible to the aircrafts or soldiers on foot, but we must be extremely careful, anything can happen."

"That is why we hired you. To get us out quickly and safely," Abba told him.

"You have my word. I am experienced in this," Hussein confirmed, and then suddenly stopped without warning. "This is a good place. We can wait here."

———◆◆———

We sat in a circle and ate dry *injera* with meat sauce, and later Hussein rationed water from a container. It looked like there was just one more container left, enough to last another day. We lay under the shadow of a bush and waited for more instructions from Hussein.

Meskerem asked Abba, "How will Hussein know if we are nearing a minefield?"

Abba was quiet and looked as though he would never smile again.

Just then we heard a fluttering sound close by. My father took out a pistol from his back pocket and carefully placed his finger on the trigger. I knew Abba carried his gun whenever he went on dangerous assignments, but the appearance of it here, so unexpectedly, frightened me more than the noise.

Hussein cautiously approached my father and warned him not to fire. It could be farm animals, very common in the area, he said. "I will go take a look. You wait here." While Hussein went to investigate, Abba squatted with his gun cocked. My heart was pounding. I hoped for it to be a wild dog or even a wolf. Yared was no longer crying. Asrat sat motionless, his mouth open.

Meskerem pleaded, "Please, no matter what, don't fire."

"Shhhh . . . just keep quiet," Abba whispered.

The noise sometimes seemed to get closer and at other times farther. We stayed motionless, holding our breaths, only blinking our eyes. In a few minutes, Hussein returned and confirmed that it was some birds eating rodents. We felt safe enough to start whispering. "The best way to deal with desert animals is to leave them alone. Don't be scared of them, don't fight with them and don't play with them. Just let them be and they won't bother you," Hussein cautioned.

My father tucked away his gun. Seeing that the weapon was out of sight, Hussein promised that our escape would be safe and quick.

My brothers and I sat silently, paying attention to everything Hussein was telling us. I had mixed feelings about him. Sometimes his lectures sounded bossy, and at other times they were comforting. Though skinny, he was well proportioned, and his gestures were swift. I wondered if he had children and where his family lived.

"How can we avoid the landmines?" my stepmother inquired.

"In the daytime, I can recognize the tip of the fuse in the sand," Hussein replied with confidence. "There are colourful ones that are placed barely under the surface." He turned to my brothers and me. "Don't pick up anything from the ground."

"It is difficult to see anything in this dust, especially at night," Meskerem persisted.

"Only God can protect us from unseen danger," Hussein replied vaguely, sifting the sand through his leathery fingers. Then I noticed for the first time that he had been walking on bare feet all along on the blistering hot, rock-filled sand. I was stunned. Not once had he complained about the heat or the rocks. And he was not bleeding. As for my brothers and me, we wore brand new Adidas, yet we still found the heat unbearable. My father was still in his black dress shoes and Meskerem in her flip-flops.

We made ourselves as comfortable as we could for a much-needed rest. I took off my shoes and felt some relief from the heat. Hussein took out a bunch of qat from his bag, and with the cigarette my father gave him, he found a spot where he could relax.

Qat is a green, mildly addictive bush that grows in the Dire Dawa valley. Its fresh leaves are believed to give more energy than food and they have a hallucinogenic effect. Hussein wiped clean each qat leaf. He looked at it lovingly before depositing it into his mouth. He would chew on one side of his mouth until he had made a thick paste which bulged out from his cheek like a Ping-Pong ball. He chewed on what he had until he had sucked all of the juice out of it. He did this for an entire afternoon before the paste was spat out. The qat was clearly what kept him going. The rest of us snacked on *kolo* (roasted barley).

Nightfall came and we decided to start our journey without Ali. Hussein pointed towards Dire Dawa, saying, "We must walk in the opposite direction from the city." At night, lights enveloped Dire Dawa in a deep crimson halo, and there was noise all around us. Jets roared, hyenas howled, and insects buzzed as if competing. But the hot, strong wind raged louder than all.

As we trudged on, I kept looking back at the lights of Dire Dawa, the city that my brothers and I had embraced with adventurous spirit just a few days ago. I let my mind wander to the popular juice bar Elaine had taken us to, where we sat on the bench outside and chatted about all the things we had seen. I had sipped a passion fruit juice while Yared enjoyed a guava mix and Asrat licked the spoon from his pineapple and banana mix. It seemed so far away now. It was hard to believe that I would not be returning to school, to my friends, my home, my mother, and to my dog. I didn't even know where we were going. I realized all over again that my old life was gone forever and with that came the strange feeling of rage and confusion.

Once we were over the hill, the landscape looked flat and mysteriously white. The bright full moon illuminated the terrain in such a way that the ground appeared transparent, light glowing underneath it. I had never seen anything like it. Hussein, usually such a talker, offered no explanation. He marched briskly, like a commander in charge, carrying a large bag, having informed us that the night was our best chance to get out of the area. Without even turning to look at us, he shouted an order: "You need to walk in single file so we don't risk being detected by Ethiopian fighter jets." We straightened up quickly into a single file and followed an invisible path to keep up with Commander Hussein. Most of the time, he seemed oblivious of our presence. With qat in his mouth, he kept up his vigorous pace.

"Keep walking. It won't be long before we rest," my father encouraged us.

Now and again Hussein looked to the sky and studied the stars. He seemed to trace their positions with his eyes. I looked up to the sky splashed with stars and wondered how he could tell which stars would guide us to Djibouti. We kept trudging on, one minute through an open field of white sand, and the next only to be tangled in a scratchy bush, and then out into the open again.

I was walking second to last in line when I heard an ear-splitting cry followed by a loud thump even before the echo had disappeared into the dark night of the Danakil. We came to a sharp halt.

"What happened?" My voice came out thin and high.

"Don't move. Don't take even a step."

My father, right behind Hussein, stood still, his hand held up. "I think Hussein fell into a hole."

He inched his way forward to investigate. The rest of us huddled together like a flock of lost sheep. Now we could hear villagers' voices and saw lights approaching. But after some moments they withdrew.

Cautiously, Abba moved to the edge of what looked like a cliff and called out: "Hussein, Hussein!" But there was no reply. We sat on the white sand under the moonlight. The shrubs and rocks protruding from the landscape looked alive, like a family of ghosts. I was terrified. My father called Hussein's name over and over again as loud as he felt was safe. Meskerem convinced Abba to stop shouting lest the villagers heard us again.

I couldn't help but wonder how the moonlight had created the illusion of a flat ground, so that Hussein had fallen over. We sat in silence, eagerly awaiting our guide. The desert floor radiated heat like a sauna. Yared and Asrat gathered rocks and logs for us to sit on.

"I can't just sit here and do nothing," Yared broke the silence. "I have to go and help."

"I'll stay here," Asrat said as Yared got up to go.

The night was more frightening without Abba and Yared. I was certain Asrat and Meskerem could hear my heart thumping.

Suddenly we saw a silhouette moving. It was like a blob of darkness the moon had failed to illuminate. Had I imagined right? Were there ghosts here? I felt numb.

"See, I knew he would be back," Meskerem whispered.

"Who?" I managed to ask.

"Shhh, let's see who it is before we move," Asrat said, moving closer to me.

To our pleasant surprise, it was our other guide, Ali. I felt my shoulders relax.

"You walked too far, why didn't you wait where we had agreed?" he said in a tired voice. "It took me hours to find you."

"We were too close to the farmers, we still are, but Hussein wanted to make some progress in the night and he said you would know how to find us. How *did* you find us?" Meskerem asked.

"I followed your tracks. Your new shoes make deep marks in the sand."

Ali had been gone for so long that I had almost forgotten about him. He had taken our car to a garage. He laughed, "They said we can pick it up in a week." No one had suspected anything.

"Hussein fell into a hole," Asrat said breathlessly. "Abba and Yared went that way to look for him. Could you please go help them?" He pointed.

Ali was confident. "Don't worry. Hussein is made of rubber, nothing will happen to him. I will find him." He ran quickly in the direction where Abba and Yared had gone.

In contrast to Hussein, Ali was chubby, with a smooth coffee brown skin, and spoke a much thicker Somali-accented Amharic. If Hussein was the guide, then Ali, I reasoned, would be the assistant guide. He had told us his wife operated a family store and their three children attended a school in Dire Dawa. Hussein, however, had not mentioned anything about his family.

In minutes, Ali and Hussein rejoined us, followed by Abba and Yared. Hussein was leaning on Ali and hopping like a chicken with a broken leg. Ali was right. Aside from being tired, the only damage Hussein had sustained was to his ankle, which Ali was quick to tie up.

"There are a lot of big holes in the desert. The wind blows the dust so much sometimes that it hollows out huge holes that become traps," Ali said.

"We just slid down the wall of the gap and there we found Hussein struggling to climb out," Yared said.

Our commander took a big gulp of water and said, "I knew this side of the desert was treacherous, but it is one of the few routes less popular with the soldiers and the villagers. It is best if we stay the night here and leave early in the morning."

"But you told us we should begin our journey when it is dark to avoid the military. Now you are telling us to wait until morning? We can't stay here," Abba said.

"But how can I continue? I need to let my leg rest for the night, but by daybreak I should have no trouble walking," Hussein pleaded.

I could see the glowing lights of Dire Dawa in the distance. And I could hear cows mooing and dogs barking, which meant that the Derg's army was not too far away either. Like my father, I wondered whether Hussein was all that intelligent. Or was he just being lazy? In that instant, we heard several shots piercing through the night and instinctively fell flat to the ground.

Hussein said nervously, "It is a very unusual night, sir. The soldiers on the ground must be on alert."

"Look at the sky," Ali added in support. I lifted my head and observed the thick dark clouds that had suddenly replaced the clear sky.

"The rain will make everything slippery," Ali said.

Eventually, Abba agreed to camp out in the open for the night.

I wished Abba had picked better guides, a better day, or even a better season for our escape. But as far as he was concerned, the rainy season was the coolest time to travel. For the other three-quarters of the year, it hardly rained in this region and temperatures reached well over 45 degrees. He had picked the best season.

The rain came pouring down. Our blankets were not for covering our heads but for sleeping on after the rain. We sat under the deluge and got soaked.

All the strange noises around me made me jumpy—the gunshots, the insects, the thunder in the sky. When I looked ahead, my eyes would fix on something in the distance, and I imagined a man with a gun, or a hyena.

"Do you see something moving over there?" I asked my brothers, pointing to a phantom.

"No," they both said. "There is nothing there."

"What is that dark thing?"

"Those are shrubs. Don't be scared of that, Beth. Nothing will happen to you with us here."

Under normal circumstances, Asrat would not have been so kind. Anywhere else but here, he would have laughed at me for being so scared.

The rain stopped. Asrat and Yared were quick to squeeze out the water from their clothes.

"What a waste of money, don't you think, Beth? To have our hair done just to have it rained on like this," Meskerem said.

I took out the pins and hand-brushed my hair for fear that it might permanently get all tangled up.

Abba, Hussein, and Ali prepared the area where we would sleep. It was flat and wet but they still had to remove shrubs and rocks before stretching out our dry blankets. We could build walls with the brushwood and rocks, but there was nothing for a roof to protect us from rain. When I sat down on the blanket it felt comfortable.

"Let your sister sleep in the middle," Abba said, sensing my fear.

Just then it started to rain again. Hussein came fast, pulled out the blanket from under me, and folded it just as quickly, putting it back in his bag so it wouldn't get wet. The rain was beating down on us and there was nothing we could do about it. I missed the warmth of my home, the laughter of Mamma Truye and Alganesh, the comfort of Metew's fur in my hands. My stomach grumbled. I pictured the dinner table in our home with every imaginable dish covering it from one end to the other, the aroma filling up every room in the house. My brothers were seated on each side of me. Yared was upset all over again.

"They didn't have to drag us through this. We could have managed on our own as we always did," he said. This time even Asrat and I were on his side. "We could have quit school and worked to feed ourselves," Asrat went on.

Finally the rain stopped and Hussein handed back our dry blankets. The sand was still too wet to put the blanket on the ground, so I covered myself with it and waited. The sand soaked up the rain faster than I expected. In about an hour, it was dry and warm once again, and I lay down to rest. I couldn't help but remember a popular children's story about how a hyena would know if a child was afraid, one of the clues being that the child slept in the middle. And in the story, the hyena ate the child in the middle.

The Land of Fire

———————◆•◆———————

WHEN I AWOKE THE next morning, I saw that everything blended together in the desert—the camels, the shrubs, and even the sky. Covered by sand, even we blended into the landscape. There was something sad and lonely about the sun as it peaked over the horizon. It looked like a delicate orange bubble ready to burst as it slowly rose between two hills. I loved the morning sun in Addis, as its gentle warmth filtered through the eucalyptus trees. But here in the desert the sun was in full view and too close. "You shouldn't have any problem finding water underground, with all the rain. I knew the first night would be hard, but we survived. Only two more nights and we will be in Djibouti," Abba reminded us.

Yared and Asrat followed Hussein as he limped about, collecting shrubs to make fire for the morning tea.

Hussein was optimistic. "I feel much better. We will continue with our journey after breakfast," he said, as he proceeded to reach into his bag and take out the kitchen box, which included a pot, pan, and kettle. I couldn't believe how many useful items he kept in the bag.

Abba and Meskerem were whispering to each other, and I sensed that they were secretly talking about Ali and Hussein.

Ali poured water into white tin cups and passed them around. The water was putrid, with algae and live insects. My brothers refused to drink it. Hussein and Ali attempted to filter the water using first-aid gauze, which Hussein pulled out from his bag. The gauze strained out the insects and algae but the water still looked cloudy. I took a sip, and even though it had a bitter and overpowering taste, I drank it because I was thirsty beyond words.

"You will like the tea," Hussein said, attempting to give us hope as he placed the kettle over the fire.

While we were waiting for the tea, we saw two people with three loaded camels advancing toward us. I recognized them as the two men who had carted away our belongings in Dire Dawa at Ato Teshome's home. Now it was clear to me why we didn't pack our things on the drive out of Dire Dawa. What surprised me was that this time the men carried Kalashnikov rifles in addition to the swords tied around their waists. It appeared that our possessions had had better bodyguards than us. The two men embraced and shook hands with Ali and Hussein and exchanged greetings in Somali, then continued to talk for a few minutes. They had found us as Ali had, by following our tracks.

"All your belongings have arrived," Hussein said with excitement.

I looked at the splendid, tall camels with elation. They were tied at the mouth with ropes to help guide them. Their heavy feet looked as soft as dough, and they made deep marks in the sand; I heard their footsteps—*squish*—as they approached us. They smelled like cow dung and were dirty, but despite that, they were graceful and in excellent condition. Their humps were so big and high that I couldn't understand how the Somali men were able to pack our belongings securely on their backs.

"Look at these camels!" Abba said. "Aren't they better suited for this terrain than our car?" There was a wide smile on his face.

I noticed three strange objects dangling from the sides of one of the camels. They looked like headless animals.

"Abba, what are those things on the camels? Are they alive . . . ? I mean dead?" I asked quickly.

"This is how they store water in the desert. Those are goatskins, filled with water," Abba explained.

Abba asked the men to join us for tea and they accepted. Their arrival was a much-needed reassurance that things were going as Abba had planned. At least we could change clothes when we wanted to, and now we had lots of water too.

Ali handed me a cup of hot tea. It was bluish red, and looked like onion soup. But I could taste cinnamon and ginger in it, and it was pleasantly sweet. Sugar! I would never have been allowed that much in my tea in Addis! It gave me new energy and a feeling of confidence.

Hussein, Ali, and the two new arrivals happily began chewing qat. Everyone appeared relaxed as we chatted on. Hussein cautioned us not to speak too loudly, so we lowered our voices to a whisper. Yared boasted how he had helped start the fire for the tea, but through all this Abba was alert, watching everything Ali and Hussein were doing with the men who had brought our belongings.

"We do have the camels now and the journey will be easier," he whispered to Meskerem.

"You are right. We should get out of here as quickly as possible," she answered.

Ali and Hussein must have sensed my father's suspicion. They broke up their small conference, and after my father paid the two men, they wished us a safe journey and left.

"We should start moving," Ali said.

It was late morning when we finally resumed our journey. The desert was littered with straw-stemmed vegetation with umbrella-like canopies; some were as tall as five feet, and others grew flat on the ground. There was nothing friendly about the bushes of the Danakil terrain. They appeared hungry and thirsty. Their brown, thorny branches reached out as if to grab me, they broke off easily and stuck to my clothes. I moved slowly, lifting my legs carefully to manoeuvre through the vegetation, but I could not help falling behind. Yared and Asrat were all scratched up too, but they marched on without complaint. Abba and Meskerem were nearly as good as our guides, and even with an injured ankle, Hussein still managed to be way ahead of us.

As we covered more ground, the sounds of the planes and gunshots became less frequent. Abba no longer felt the need to force us down to the ground whenever we heard the jets. Hussein was consistently assuring us that the route we had taken was as safe as it could get.

"The sun wouldn't get as hot here as it would if we were up near the volcano. Up there everything is just fire. The wind is like a flame, and the rivers are made of lava. The lakes are so salty that there are hardly any living creatures in them," Hussein said casually.

"That is true," Abba agreed. "Erta Ale is the hottest and oldest volcano on the planet. Its lava lakes flow all over and everything is fire there."

"That is why," Hussein said, "this was the land of fire," and he marched on.

Now I understood why Abba had to keep an eye on everything—if we made a wrong turn, we would surely end up scorched to death. For me, it was a miracle that I was tolerating the heat at all. At times it felt as though we were walking on fire, even with our shoes on. But, bare-footed Hussein was the true fire-walker.

It seemed that we had walked for three hours before we cleared the thorny shrubs. My body was covered with cuts and they burned. It was a relief when Abba finally announced that we would stop for a rest. When I showed him my wounds he sat down by my side and applied a cotton ball soaked in rubbing alcohol to my injuries. He was sweating profusely.

Asrat and Yared were not overly concerned by their injuries, which might have been worse had they not worn long trousers. Meskerem was more concerned with something else: when Abba wasn't watching, she threw away her malaria pills. When I asked her why, she replied, "I don't like pills. They make me vomit, but I don't want Terrefe to know."

"But you might catch malaria," I said.

"I grew up in Dire Dawa, so I am immune to it," she answered.

"You can never be immune to malaria," I argued.

"Do you think Ali and Hussein take malaria pills?" she asked.

I liked my stepmother more in the desert here than I did in Addis, because there was no need for her to get involved in disciplining us, and we were the only two women in our group. For the first time it occurred to me how close in age she was to my brothers and me. She was in her early twenties.

I noticed Hussein staring at me, then at Meskerem as well. He finally approached me and blurted: "Anyone can tell that you are from the city."

"How can they tell?" I asked.

"No one in the desert dresses like you."

"Like me?"

"All of you need to change your outfits. If you look like the Afar, your journey will be much easier. You need to pass for merchants."

He quickly marched over to one of the camels and unloaded a heavy bag. Then he and Ali handed out *shirits* and T-shirts to Abba and my brothers, and two long, Arabian-style dresses (*drees*) to Meskerem and me. The dresses were cut in long rectangular shapes in a one-size-fits-all style, but they were so thin I could see through them. Meskerem wore hers over what she had already on, and I copied her.

I noticed then Meskerem's eyes fill up with tears. I moved closer to her and asked her what was the matter.

"My breasts hurt so much. They're full of milk. I would have nursed Kalkidan many times by now."

I didn't know what to say and couldn't even imagine what she was going through, so I just stared at her silently as she wiped the tears from her eyes.

"We have rested enough, let's get moving," Hussein declared abruptly and started walking towards the camels. We hurried to catch up.

Abba was walking beside Asrat and I saw him hand something to my brother and speak furtively to him. Asrat looked surprised, but my father ran ahead to join Ali and Hussein. I trailed behind Asrat and asked him what he was carrying.

"Be quiet. It's a bundle of money I have to hide under my belt. Just act like you don't know anything about it."

"How much is it?"

Yared joined us. "What's going on?" he asked anxiously.

"I don't want Abba to see us talking about it. Abba gave me some money to hide. Just keep walking," Asrat said nervously.

"We don't know how much it is," I added.

"Well, then, lets count it," Yared demanded.

"We can't. Abba will be very upset." Asrat glared at Yared.

"I am tired of not knowing anything," Yared complained, not even trying to lower his voice.

Abba glanced behind at us, stopped and waited for us to join him.

"I don't want you guys falling so far behind," he said.

"How come you don't tell us anything, Abba?" Yared demanded.

"I have good reasons for what I do, and everything I am doing is to protect you. Everything I am doing is for you, my children. I will tell you everything once we have crossed the desert, when it is safe to talk about all of this. I don't trust Ali and Hussein." Abba ran off to catch up with them. Meskerem had already gone ahead and was talking with the guides.

"I want to go back!" Yared shouted.

Abba stopped and turned. "You want to go back?" he shouted back. "Do you know what you would go back to?"

"I have friends I can stay with . . . " Yared's voice trailed off.

"Which ones?" Abba came towards us and stopped a few feet away, both hands firmly planted on his waist.

Most of Yared's friends had been in and out of jail for failing to participate in organized progovernment activities.

"It wouldn't have been long before the Derg came after me, and all of you would have been drafted soon after. Don't you see?" Abba shouted. "Who would have raised you had I left you in Ethiopia by yourselves? Your friends? Asrat, please give me back the item I gave you. I have decided it is not safe for you to carry it," Abba demanded and Asrat quickly gave it back.

Yared began crying helplessly. My stomach knotted up, but I controlled myself. I knew exactly how Yared felt. *Why couldn't I just go back and say goodbye to my mother and my friends?* I asked myself silently.

We continued walking. The afternoon sun rose high overhead, blazing over the vast land of few trees and no water. The sun gave reward and punishment. At dawn it looked beautiful; it was hot but tolerable. But now it burned bright red, and fierce waves of heat blasted down on us as from a furnace. I desperately wanted to hide somewhere. Behind us were dry bushes, and ahead of us the path was a cascade of loose stones and dust. Far into the haze I could see a scatter of black mountains. Everything looked surreal.

Three hours after we last set off, we came upon a huge red ant-hill. It had holes all over it and tiny ants hurried in and out. It created enough shade for my family to gather up under it. When I leaned against the anthill, the dust rubbed off easily and stained my dress, but I didn't care because the shade was worth it.

We were given a cup of water from the goatskin before lunch. The water tasted like game meat, but I was terribly thirsty and dehydrated; I had to keep drinking. We ate spicy, chewy meat with sauce and rice. I had to pour powdered milk over the meal to disguise its taste. After lunch, we sipped the delicious tea while Ali and Hussein unwrapped their green qat leaves from a moist cloth and began chewing, making me wish that I had brought my favourite cinnamon-flavoured gum with me.

While I was enjoying my tea, three tall, skinny men materialized before us. They were carrying AK-47 rifles and wearing black tire sandals and old discoloured *shirits*. They did not bear swords like the Afar and the Issa and had no camels to suggest that they were headed somewhere. My father concluded that they were Somali men, not just because they did not wear swords but also because their greeting with Ali and Hussein was familiar and loud and they headed straight to the pile of qat without waiting for an invitation. Ali poured tea for them and they talked with such animation that I feared a fight would break out. They glanced at us from time to time with narrowed eyes.

"They must have followed our tracks," my father concluded. Abba didn't want to miss out on the loud, excited conversation. He approached them, a teacup in his hand, with an offer of a cigarette. They did not speak any Amharic, but each eagerly took a cigarette. Ali and Hussein interpreted.

"They belong to the Issa clan," Hussein said of the visitors. Hussein belonged to the Issa clan as well. They were nomads of the Danakil Desert, grazing their cattle wherever there was rain, either in the Somali region or in Ethiopia.

"Where are their herds, then?" Abba inquired.

"They have not been with their animals for two months now because they joined the Somali guerrillas. They are fighting the Ethiopian army for this land, but the war was taking too long so they escaped. Now they're heading back to their families in the Ogaden region in Ethiopia," Hussein explained.

"How far is the Somali army?" Abba asked.

After one of them had spoken for a while, Hussein translated. "Well, they are in hiding places all over the desert, in the same way the Ethiopian army is operating. If you walk along the edge of the land of fire you are less likely to meet with either of the armies," he advised. "There are no soldiers camping there."

Abba explained that we might encounter more visitors in the desert because it was easy to follow our tracks, especially since we could not walk barefoot. We had to find a better strategy to deal with curious visitors. One suggestion was to let Ali and Hussein do all the talking to strangers so they wouldn't hear us speaking Amharic. Somali and Afar were the most common languages in the Danakil, followed by Arabic. The other idea was to choose our camping sites very carefully. The guides agreed to all of Abba's ideas.

My father suggested we should start walking, even though Ali and Hussein looked reluctant to part from the qat. From the looks on the visitors' faces, it appeared that a new topic was brewing.

Finally, Hussein lowered his voice and said that the visitors wanted to ask something from us.

"What is it?" Abba inquired.

"They want you to give them some money because they have nothing to take to their families," Hussein replied.

"As you know very well I am not in a situation to be handing out money," Abba said with a sardonic smile.

Hussein, never at a loss for an explanation, didn't even translate what my father had said before replying with an ultimatum. "If you don't give it to them, they'll go to the army base and report our whereabouts to the Ethiopian soldiers."

"Who told them we were escaping?" Abba glared, first at Hussein, then at Ali.

"We had to tell them that in order for us to get information regarding the best route," Ali said, trying to repair the damage.

"How could you do that?" Abba thundered. "You know this is a life-and-death situation. You can't tell anyone what we are doing. Didn't I explain this to you very carefully before I hired you?"

A silver-grey lizard peeked out of one of the ant holes and peered from side to side. *If that lizard could talk, maybe it would share its knowledge of the desert,* I thought. Abba was also staring at the lizard, a beseeching look on his face, as if it would advise him whether to give the men money or not. The lizard froze, its two front legs gripping the dusty wall of the anthill. A religious silence hovered over our party. I looked from Hussein to the Issa men, sensing the next words spoken would either close a deal or, in less than an hour, put us in front of the Derg's firing squad. Dire Dawa was behind us, and the war planes that flew overhead told us soldiers from every front were within firing range.

All eyes on him, Abba reached into his pants' pocket and took out some birr and counted to eighty in tens, which was an exorbitant amount, and gave it to Hussein. We were relieved when the men took the money and disappeared.

"You see, it is much better this way. Now they are gone and they won't bother us again," Ali said as he quickly began loading the camels.

We began walking. The sun was still grilling hot but there was a camel's shadow to walk under. A few hours later, we approached the black mountains, which I had seen earlier. They were rectangular in shape, and extremely rocky and steep. Luckily there was no need to scamper over them, our camel train followed a winding path up and around the side.

We travelled for another seven or eight hours, taking a few short breaks in between. We climbed over a mid-size mountain, which proved to be more hazardous than it had looked when we began. Asrat and Yared followed behind me, pushing me up the hill. Luckily for them, I weighed only ninety-five pounds. By the time we reached the other side of the mountain, it was sunset and the sky was getting dark. "I can finally smoke," Abba said as he pulled out a cigarette and lighted it. He sat behind a rock where Hussein and Ali joined him. The rest of us lay flat on the ground.

Not even a minute passed before we heard the now familiar crackling, pop, pop, ratta-tat-tat, pop sound of gunshots. I stayed flat, too nervous even to move. The sounds came so unexpectedly that what was intended to be a restful camp turned out to be a terrorizing moment.

"These shots are not from the military," Ali announced.

"How can you tell which shots are fired from the army and which ones are not?" Asrat asked.

Hussein said the soldiers used machine guns and other big guns, while the villagers used rifles and small handguns. Usually, around this time of the day, the villagers fired them to chase the hyenas away from their cattle. So it was not the army, but I still felt chills knowing the bullets could hit and kill us, or that we could become a hyena's supper.

Our much-needed rest was over before I even felt rested. We started on our dark journey to a different campsite. As we began walking, Ali announced that he couldn't find the flashlights. "We can't make it through the night without them," he said. He had to go back to the village, to his relatives' house, and bring us lights. We remembered what had happened to Hussein the night before, and agreed. Hussein told Ali where to meet us, and Ali took off.

Oasis

———◆———

THERE WAS A STRONG WARM wind blowing that night. We had only walked for about ten minutes when suddenly Hussein commanded us to stop. "We can't travel without Ali. We need the flashlights," he said. Abba was furious. "This is our second night. We won't arrive in Djibouti tomorrow or even clear the army base if we don't continue walking. We cannot wait for Ali."

Hussein insisted that it would be impossible to find our way without the flashlights. My father and Meskerem were apprehensive. They became suspicious that Ali would go to the soldiers to inform them about us. It seemed too much of a risk to stay where we were.

"We will go without you if you refuse to take us," Abba threatened.

Hussein didn't have much choice. When I got up, I felt my legs burning. The cuts were bleeding and the rain water had stained my clothes with blood. It was dark, but the white sand under our feet glowed like a fluorescent light. Hussein shouted an order to walk with caution, there were deep holes, we should walk in single file.

We were still in the vicinity of the peasants' dwellings and I could hear the villagers from a distance and a hyena's deep howl.

Hussein said there was one steep hill in the area, and once it was cleared we could sit and wait for Ali. He marched up the hill far in advance of us. Then, all of a sudden, we saw flashlights at a distance behind us.

"What if it is the Derg's soldiers?" Meskerem asked. "How would they know where we are?"

My father was convinced that it was the Derg's soldiers, led by Ali. He was shaken and agitated.

As we climbed the hill, Abba said, "Now I see ten flashlights."

I prayed for them not to find us. We all knew that our escape was considered treason by the government and that if we were caught we would face a firing squad. It was the period of the Red Terror, when thousands of children, some as young as nine, were shot on the streets for sympathizing with opposition groups such as the Ethiopian People's Revolutionary Democratic Front.

As the flashlights drew nearer, Abba began to act strangely. He was holding a stick in his left hand and a loaded gun in his right, prowling behind us, beside us, and in front of us, murmuring, "No family of mine will surrender. Don't worry, I will get them before they get us!"

As usual, Hussein and the camels reached the top of the hill before us.

"Hurry," Hussein shouted. "It is much cooler up here."

Abba, in his frantic state, caught up with Hussein at the hilltop. Meskerem, my brothers, and I followed. Abba, with his gun still pointing in all directions, asked Hussein, "Who are these people that are following us?"

"I don't see anybody."

My father was surprised. "The people with the flashlights, who are they?"

We could see much better from the hilltop. There were several flashlights and I stood still, terrified of the danger we were in. All around the hill were lights shining between the scattered trees. If we were being followed, then it must be the whole army of the Derg that was after us.

Calmly, Hussein replied, "The lights are from the farmers' compound. Sometimes the peasants light a fire outside their houses to keep the lions away from their cattle."

Abba looked around a moment, then, satisfied, he tucked his gun under his belt. We were relieved, but in the back of my mind I was hoping he would know what to do in case we encountered the lions.

The cool wind blowing on the hilltop soothed the throbbing cuts on my body. The night was filled with animal sounds—crickets, birds, and even bigger creatures. Hussein walked around to see where we should wait for Ali. He decided on the other side of the hill, where there was a flat rock to sit on.

He began unloading the camels. When he pulled at their ropes, they lowered themselves, first onto their front knees while holding their long necks straight, and then bending their back legs forward, until they were down on four bended knees, their stomachs flat on the sand. They spent the night this way, chewing whatever was in their mouths. They hadn't been washed for a long time. Dry dung stuck to their legs and they smelled awful, but I was happy we had them.

Abba gathered shrubs to make a fire.

"No, no, sir, don't light a fire," Hussein called out. "The villagers might wonder where this new fire is coming from and it would make us a target." *How could our fire be any different from theirs*, I wondered. This meant we would not be having tea.

Hussein proceeded with chewing his qat. He put a couple of leaves into his mouth and looked up to the sky. It was a clear and still night. All the stars were out. After studying the sky for a moment, he put more leaves into his mouth and continued chewing.

"Why do you chew so much qat?" Asrat asked.

Hussein replied that if he did not chew qat he would see bad things happening to him.

Abba took out his cigarette and, remembering Hussein's instructions not to light a fire, he hid behind a rock to smoke.

"Like what?" Yared was now curious.

"Every time I close my eyes, I see things in my head. I see hundreds of human creatures the size of your thumb coming to get me from my hut. I hear them asking me to give them qat. I can't focus without it, and it makes the long hot days easier to handle."

"Qat is very bad for you," Abba cautioned. "Once you are addicted to it, you won't be able to do without it."

A few hours later Ali came back carrying two flashlights. At that point we didn't need them, and so we stayed curled up in our blankets and slept. Our second night in the desert and Djibouti was nowhere in sight.

We had tea and dried bread for breakfast the next morning. I realized that my stomach had become used to small meals. The elastic waist of my skirt was loose, which is how I knew I had lost weight. But at least I was not ill. I looked at my family one by one to see if others had lost weight. All I could see different was that their hair was covered with dirt. I turned to look at the camels, thankful that we did not have to worry about them. They ate whatever shrubs they could find and didn't have to drink water as we did, and indeed they were the best means of transportation in the desert, way better than a car.

We began our journey down the other side of the hill. It was slippery, but we reached the bottom quickly. The air began to dry and the familiar dusty desert wind soon came upon us. We rarely spoke when we walked. I stayed under a camel's shadow, otherwise there was no escaping the sun.

It felt like an inferno. I didn't deserve this. My thoughts raced. Could have I been a better daughter, at least to Meskerem? A better student? I didn't know my stepmother very well; I didn't know what her childhood was like or the types of things she liked other than getting her hair done. Would everything be okay if I resolved to be the best person for ever and ever? Asrat was a saint. When Abba was away on business, he took over the responsibilities of the house without being told. He helped the gardener, bought milk for breakfast, and made sure we were well taken care of. Yared was a rebel. I couldn't help thinking that all of this was Abba's fault; he was always making drastic decisions like divorcing my mother and deciding to raise us on his own for six years. He was always away.

Abba was born during the war years when the Italians invaded Ethiopia, and he grew up watching his uncles die fighting for freedom; when freedom came, it was every adult Ethiopian's duty to put their country above their own family. Whatever the Emperor asked them to do, they did wholeheartedly. They built roads, schools, hospitals, banks, factories, bridges. Young adults were sent overseas to get educated in science and medicine. It was this patriotic duty that Abba firmly believed in, that had him leave his family for long periods. No matter how difficult his assignment, he never refused it. In fact, the harsher the environment, the more eager he was to get involved. I realized how difficult this journey must be for him: to abandon his Ethiopia and vanish with his children.

"It will get hotter than this at times," Abba warned. "But just remember, people like the Afar live in this whole area, including near the volcano. They mine salt, trade in business, and raise their families all over the land. They have been doing this for hundreds of years. I would never have picked this route if it were not tolerable."

"Hotter than this?" Yared was already furious again.

"You can handle it. There are babies born here and they get accustomed to it."

Looking ahead I saw a small black lake. I couldn't believe my eyes. As we got nearer, I could see tall palm trees swaying—an oasis! We ran toward it like newborn impalas, weak and shaky but happy to have found a new life. My eyes cherished the colours that replaced the sameness of dust and sand that we had endured for three days. The ground was green with thick grass, and large-leafed plants grew everywhere. There was a fresh wind, it smelled sweet, unlike the dreadful desert wind, and it carried no dust. Rainbow-coloured butterflies fluttered in the moist air. Water from the pond made some of the area slippery. The rays of the sizzling sun were softened by the canopy of the trees.

The camels were unloaded and led to the pond. Our guides jumped in together with the camels to bathe and drink. I too ran and fell into the pond. God had made this oasis appear in the middle of nowhere. I couldn't get enough of the coolness of it on my skin or believe how refreshing it was.

As we were bathing, we heard voices coming from behind the trees. A caravan of twelve men was loading their camels. They had seen us. Two of the men came to the pond and spoke with Ali in Somali. They listened attentively and nodded as they looked at us. They both wore sandals, the straps of which were made of cow skin.

I held my breath and tried to pretend not to notice them by concentrating on washing my arms. After one experience the other day when Abba was forced to give money to desert visitors, I sensed that the rest of my family was tense as well. However, these men went back to their caravan and returned with ten cans of milk for us. Ali must have told them that we had run out of food. I heard their camels gurgling as their caravan began its journey onward.

I was relieved, but Abba still looked tense.

As we got out of the pond, he warned us, "You have to keep an eye on Ali and Hussein. I don't trust what they are saying to these nomads in their language. Better yet, I will talk to them so that they know we are watching."

Abba sat next to Ali and Hussein and squeezed the water off his shirt. "We have relatives in Ethiopia who know that you are guiding us," Abba began.

"They will be happy when you arrive safely," Hussein remarked as he untied the goatskin. He took a sip directly from the neck of the goatskin to rinse his mouth.

"But if anything happens to us, they will come after you."

Hussein spit out the water. "Those people are businessmen and they asked us if we had heard about the condition of the road ahead."

"Is that why they gave you cans of milk?"

"I asked for the milk because we need it for lunch."

I knew Abba would be happy if Ali and Hussein didn't talk to strangers at all, but it seemed unavoidable.

We gathered for a lunch of rice with milk sauce that the caravan people had donated. The milk was thick and sweet. I was happily full for the first time since we began our journey three days ago. Now as we sat under the trees, all life seemed wonderful. We were sheltered from the piercing midday sun by the tall trees, and the light dimmed by the leaves made it a perfect place to nap. Every breath I took carried the fragrance from the pond, the trees, and the plants. Every one of us was in good spirits except for Meskerem. Whenever I glanced at her she would be deep in her thoughts. I knew that she was thinking about her baby.

It was decided that we would rest here for the night. Ali and Hussein convinced Abba and Meskerem that it was the best place to camp and wait for other merchants, from whom we would be able to buy enough food to last us for the rest of our journey. That was how I learned that we weren't on schedule at all. I could handle two more days but I wasn't sure if I could survive any more.

But the oasis was a perfect place to dream. As I lay back, in my mind I saw Djibouti, the country where exiles and their children found refuge. I thought that if we were escaping through fire from a country that was violent, we must be running to a country that was peaceful. I eventually fell asleep, and in my dream I was standing at the top of a mountain in Djibouti, and when I looked down, I saw a city of white houses nestled in a valley. Strawberry fields decorated the riverbanks, along with mango and papaya trees. The river was rich with their juices. From where I stood I could smell ripe oranges and when I drank from the river, I felt so quenched that I was sure I would never be thirsty again.

It was evening when the swooshing of the wind in the trees woke me up. My heart pounded with fear. A disturbing thought raced in my head: what were we still doing in the desert? I said nothing and sipped my tea as I watched Ali and Hussein chew qat while they talked in Somali.

The sky was clear and still. There was a bright full moon and the stars were shining. The moon had made everything visible, which somewhat eased my fears. I could see the reflections of the trees in the pond and even the shadows of the camels. Hussein studied the sky again for a few moments. Under the moonlight, I could see the muscles of his jaw tighten.

I got up and went over to join Meskerem, who had come up with the great idea to comb our hair. "Come. Sit here." She pointed at a place beside her. As she took out my braids she said, "Oh, my Lord, there is so much dust in your hair."

Yared joked with Asrat, "With all the dust out, Beth will be as light as a feather and the wind will toss her like a balloon."

"Let's organize our belongings and make sure everything is in place," Abba called to Yared and Asrat before they made more cracks about my hair.

Meskerem had just as much dust and dirt in hers.

Abba and my brothers opened every load and rearranged all that we carried. I saw Abba stacking our picture frames between some clothes for protection. Much later, Hussein and Ali served dinner, which was the same as lunch, rice with milk sauce.

I woke up just before dawn to find everyone else still sleeping. I felt anxious to continue our journey. The moon was gone, but there was one bright star left in the sky. At first I thought it was an airplane and I stared at it for some time. It did not move. I concluded that the star was a guiding star and it would take us to Djibouti. Only if I could tell it apart from the other hundreds of stars that came out at night! When I looked harder, I saw a smaller star directly above it, slightly to the left. I realized why our guards gazed up at the sky from time to time. I decided to look for the star with them and see in which direction they decided to walk. And then I would know the way to Djibouti, I thought to myself before falling asleep again.

Waraba

I am a woman. I do not like war. However, I would rather die
than accept your deal. —EMPRESS TAITU

THE CAMELS' GURGLING SOUND woke me up from the sheet of
sand I slept on. I lifted my head just in time to see the break of dawn.
I could hear the guides' and my parents' voices. A young woman in a
long black dress came to the pond carrying her son, who wore only
a cotton shirt that came up to his knees. After filling up her goatskin,
she placed it aside and went to join Ali and Hussein for breakfast.

"It is strange that she is dressed in black. Somalis and Afars love
colours, especially red," Abba commented. "I can tell from the way
she wears her hair that she is an Afar."

Her hair had been plaited into a multitude of little braids and
smoothed over with butter. She wore colourful beads around her
neck.

The young mother kept looking in our direction and seemed to
be talking about us with our guides. There was a look of concern on
her face, like a woman who has found her child in trouble. "Don't
worry, desert woman, everything is okay," I wanted to tell her, so

she would not worry for us. She didn't appear to want money from us. Perhaps she just wanted to rest.

"Afars are always curious about strangers travelling through their land. Our very presence here is the hottest news for this lady," Abba remarked.

Though it was late morning, we had not yet moved. Usually we began walking before the sun got hot, but Ali and Hussein went on talking to the woman, which made Abba more angry.

"What are they waiting for? I will go and see what's going on," he complained.

Anxiously, Abba walked over to Ali and Hussein and their desert guest, and I followed him, hoping to take a closer look at the baby.

"*Aninay.*" my father greeted the woman in one of the few Afar words he had learned while working in Aysa'ita.

"*Negay,*" she responded, eyes turned downwards.

Ali and Hussein were surprised that my father spoke some Afar. They explained that she had simply come for the water in the oasis, as she frequently did. She lived in the Danakil Desert. Her husband had gone to the market in Harar to sell goats and buy what they needed at home.

The baby, who had brown curly hair, was almost the same age as my sister Kalkidan. I wanted to hold him and take him with us. I thought of what Meskerem had said about her breasts filling up with milk and all the aching and the need to nurse Kalkidan. Sometimes I wondered how she could even take a step without crying. For the first time since our journey, I admired Meskerem's strength.

"Have you gotten any new information about the road conditions from this lady?" Abba inquired.

"She said the route is packed with caravans so there should be ample help," Hussein said.

"But why does she look so worried?" Abba fired his question suspiciously.

"She does not look worried to me."

Just then, the woman broke her silence and spoke in a very low tone, not in Afar, but in Somali.

"What is she saying?" Abba had sensed the urgency in her voice.

Hussein paused, but Ali picked up the conversation. "She is saying that her child is hungry and she had better get going." The boy was playing contentedly in the sand, but when Ali said something to the woman in Somali, she snatched up the child and departed hurriedly without a response.

"I am sure of it. Ali told her to leave," Abba said when he returned to us.

"She did look frightened," Meskerem agreed.

Abba walked back to Hussein and said angrily, "Why, God knows, after three days are we still wandering in the desert?"

Hussein insisted, "We must wait and get some food because the desert is extremely dry. We can't find water even in the water holes. The water is too deep under the sand." He tried to work things out with my father. "I don't want these children to die. It's better to take our time than risk the minefields."

Abba was not satisfied, but the mention of minefields had silenced him. I had forgotten about them completely. How could we know where they were hidden? I didn't see Ali and Hussein with metal detectors.

"The merchants should arrive any time," Hussein said.

It was about two o'clock when we saw seven men, wearing only fine cotton sarongs around their waists, trickle into the oasis on foot without any camels but with machine guns and bullets wrapped like chains round their muscular sunburned bodies. They crushed the plants with their sandals as they advanced. Once they were close enough to us, five of them stood stiff and still, while two headed straight for Ali and Hussein.

Abba looked concerned. I was frightened. Why did the strangers approach Ali and Hussein and not Abba? They looked as though they had been trained in an army, and I wondered if they were Somali guerrilla fighters.

"These are businessmen, not the merchants we are waiting for,"

Ali called out to Abba, giving us an explanation before he was even asked. "They are going to Dire Dawa for trade." Soon, however, their intentions were made clear as Ali approached my father and told him that the men were asking for money to help them when they got to Dire Dawa.

My father dropped his hands in frustration. "This is not good. This is not good at all." He turned to Meskerem in despair. "I should never have let the guides see we had money and I should have never given the others any. How could I forget how fast news travels in the desert?"

"Just tell them we don't have any money," Meskerem suggested.

"I'll try. But they already know," Abba said, looking defeated.

"They don't want a lot of money. I will make sure they give us information before they leave," Hussein placated him.

"We are not in a position to give money, as you well know," Abba replied edgily.

Ali went back to the men. They talked for about an hour, seated in the same place. I saw them make a few small holes in the sand and place tiny rocks inside, which reminded me of the game of gebeta which my brothers and I played at home. They studied the holes. After a while Ali returned to us again, together with one of the men. The man stared at us one by one; his eyes were fiery red and he looked skinnier than my brothers. When he spoke in Somali, he was loud, sounding like a warrior.

"What does he want?" my father said, glaring back at the man.

"They are not convinced that you don't have money," Ali said. "The holes in the sand are filled with rocks, which means you are carrying money. So he came to see for himself."

"Rocks in the sand!" Abba shook his head in frustration. "They are looking for any reason to get money. How much do they want?"

Ali interpreted. Then he and the Somali went back to join the others, who looked ready to advance upon us. They began to negotiate.

All seven men then came to us.

"They want fifty birr each," Ali announced as the men surrounded us.

"I can only give them each thirty birr," Abba uttered, looking straight at one of the men.

Abba pulled out his wallet and counted the money and gave it to Ali. They surrounded Ali like vultures. Shouting in Somali, they fought over the money and somehow sat down for further discussion with no apparent sign of leaving. I prayed that the merchants that Hussein and Ali had mentioned would appear and chase this pack of bandits to the ends of the earth. But they made themselves comfortable and got busy gathering shrubs to prepare rice.

Abba gestured for my brother Yared to follow him, and told the rest of us to stay alert. They went behind a tree and disappeared from our sight.

The smell of cinnamon, cumin, and chilli peppers filled the air. The wood the Somalis used was wet so there was a great deal of smoke. I was getting hungry.

"You wouldn't believe what we saw," Yared said when he and my father returned.

"What?" Meskerem's eyes opened wide.

"Empty trenches."

"Where? Here?"

"Just outside the oasis."

"They are long and narrow like empty riverbanks," Yared said with excitement. "Look what I found there." He showed us a part of a gun loaded with bullets. "I am keeping it as a souvenir."

"Can I go see?" Asrat asked.

"Me too!" I joined in.

Abba flatly refused. "It's going to get dark soon and we still have these men to deal with."

"I guess the war on this side must have ended," Yared said. "Or the soldiers left and have been ordered back." There was no way of knowing if the trenches belonged to the Ethiopian or the Somali army.

Just before sunset, the Afar woman and the child came back and she talked to the men. She seemed restless; she got up, then sat down again, and looked in our direction. The child and I made eye contact briefly and he gave me a hint of a smile. I wanted to play with him the way I did with Kalkidan. I covered my eyes with both hands and then took my hands off, but before I could whisper, "Ayehuh," I saw three of the Somali men pointing guns at us. This couldn't be real. I moved closer to my brothers.

"The men are saying the money is not enough and they want to search and see for themselves," Ali said, having followed behind.

"Search?" my father shouted. "They don't need to search us! We have already given them money enough to take to their families!"

Not waiting for permission, the men went and opened our bags and suitcases. Holding my breath in disbelief, wide-eyed with fright, I saw my dresses and shirts and my family's things inspected and flung around without care.

"Let's talk about this and find a way to resolve this," Abba said quietly to Hussein.

The men laughed when they saw things they did not recognize, like the statue of Cleopatra and the framed pictures that Abba had neatly packed. One of the men was looking at a picture of Abba wearing a hat and holding a diploma in his hand.

Hussein shouted something in Somali but the men paid no attention.

One of the Somali men held up Abba's picture for the others to see. His companions gathered around to study it and then turned to look at my father.

I searched Abba's face to see what he would do to stop them. His eyes were red and fixed on the scene, his fists clenched tight as if to manage the blood steaming under his skin. "Don't worry, they will find nothing, I have taken care of everything," he told Meskerem. He instructed Meskerem and me to take off our jewelry and hide it.

"Move a little behind me and take your earrings off," Meskerem said softly and moved slowly in front of me. My hands were shaking as I removed my earrings and then Meskerem told me to put them in her hands, which she held behind her back. I don't know how she did it, but she had already removed hers. I saw her placing the pieces in the sand and covering them.

Every single bag was opened and the contents spread out on the ground. But, the men found no money. Ali and Hussein did nothing but watch. The intruders decided to take some of my father's and brothers' clothes. One of them pulled up his sarong and comically struggled to put on my father's beige pants while still wearing his cow-skinned sandals. He laughed and the others watched. They fought over the clothes, pulling a shirt or a sweater from each other. It was as if we did not even exist.

Abba called out to Ali, who came running almost out of breath. "If they take any more things, I will shoot," Abba announced.

"What are you saying, Terrefe? You will get us killed," Meskerem said, shaking her head.

In a flash, Abba took out his gun. I couldn't stay silent. I told Yared and Asrat about my idea of hiding in the trenches.

"What if they see us running?" Yared said.

Meskerem sat holding her knees and crying. "Please hide the gun. If they see you armed they will kill us. Let them take everything. The children are scared, please, please," she begged, choking on her words.

"We have left our country; we've got nothing without our country. I didn't escape from the Derg to come here and get defeated by a pack of bandits. And my name is not Terrefe if I give in to them." Abba held his gun firmly and fought back his tears.

Hussein and Ali begged Abba to put away the gun. "Think of your children; if you fire, your children will be killed."

Eventually one of the men saw Abba. He came charging toward us, screaming and shouting. The others followed, shouting as well, and aiming their guns at us. Abba was yelling too and randomly pointing his gun at them.

One of the men came closer to Abba and stretched out his hand, demanding the gun. I was in my worst nightmare. As dangerous as my father's actions were, I couldn't understand why he didn't seem scared.

"Tell them," Abba said to Ali. "I am not afraid for my life. I am only doing this for my family."

The man ripped the gun out of my father's hand and shouted and fired it up at the sky. The others started firing too. My ears were ringing and my eyes became blurry. I shut my eyes and opened them. Everything was quiet. I saw two of the men looking at each other and then at Meskerem and me. They came toward us and motioned to Meskerem and me to follow them to the back of the trees.

"They are not taking them anywhere," Abba said flatly and came and stood next to me. The men pointed their guns at my father.

I heard Hussein begging my father to stay put. "They won't harm them. Please stay put. No one has to die. They just want to see if they have jewelry or anything hidden under their bras like most women do."

I felt as if my insides were giving out and I struggled to take in air. "Stay close to me, Beth. They will not harm us. We will cooperate, it is better than dying," Meskerem said confidently.

"I am staying with you," I said, looking at Meskerem's back.

"Scream if they do anything to you," Abba shouted from behind us in Amharic as we followed the men. Then all of a sudden my stomach settled and my fears disappeared. My face felt numb.

The men stopped. They smiled and came closer to us. Their teeth had decayed like a dead animal's and their smell reminded me of the stench of the dead camel on the first day of our escape. They poked at us and pulled our dresses sometimes with the tips of their guns and sometimes with their fingers to suggest a body search. I followed their commands. Meskerem was undressing from top down. As they circled around, one pulling my dress even higher, the other pushing Meskerem's further down, I prayed under my breath to the God of my mother (as she was the most religious person in my family) to make them disappear, not to harm us in any way, for none of us to die away from our home. God, let it be over before my father and brothers jump on them. Please, God, don't let us be like the bones of the dead animals we saw along the way. The men peeked through our clothes to look at our breasts, underarms, and stomachs, and at every step of the search they would giggle. A few minutes later, the search was over and they marched back to join the rest of their gang. Meskerem and I fixed our clothes properly and quickly reunited with our family, who were relieved to know we weren't raped and were still alive.

"You're okay. I didn't know you were this brave, Beth. We were watching them the whole time and we would not have let anything happen to you," Asrat said, putting his arm around my shoulder, but I couldn't stop shaking.

"They should just take everything," Yared declared.

"Please don't talk. They will leave soon," Abba warned.

As they were leaving the oasis, one of the men stopped to pick up another framed picture and stared at it. His back was toward us and I could see my aunt's smiling face. The man abruptly threw the photo on the ground and it hit a rock and shattered. Then he fired a few shots at nothing in particular and shouted in Somali *"Laag! Laag!"* The rest of them, including Ali and Hussein, ran toward him quickly, and they all started pulling out money from behind the broken photo. They broke every framed photo and took the hidden money. My family and I sat together staring at the drama in disbelief.

Out of nowhere, the Afar woman reappeared, carrying her child. She had a hand raised to the sky and screamed, *"Hoyo, hoyo,"* repeatedly, which I later on learned meant "Mother, mother." Hearing her strange scream brought back my fear. Blood rushed to my face. My eyes became blurry and I could not see clearly. Yared had his lips shut tight and a strong frown marked the middle of his forehead. He was worried about what Abba would do. "Let them take everything. It is better than dying," I heard him say.

Ali and Hussein were right in the middle of everything. I couldn't tell if they were helping the robbers steal our money or telling them to stop. A couple of men turned toward us and fired in our direction. The bullets hit the ground in front of us. They kept firing. I saw dust rising up, and my father shouted to us to lie flat on the ground. I heard the woman's cry closer to us, and when I looked up I saw her standing between us and the robbers, her child in her arms. His wailing mingled with the sounds of the firing. She put the child on the ground a few feet in front of me, and I saw her black-clad figure running toward the men, hands waving. The horrified boy screamed unceasingly, and I felt the urge to crawl up to him and put his head down. When she reached them, the bandits stopped firing and began to stuff whatever they could back into the suitcases. They trotted toward us and, with Hussein interpreting, ordered us to sit up and held the guns close to our faces. They asked if we had anything else hidden. They warned us that if they found we were concealing anything else, they would kill us. Without any hesitation, Meskerem and I dug out our jewelry. They took the jewelry, the suitcases, and our money and disappeared into the desert.

The woman picked up her child and stood in front of us, her face covered in dirt and tears. She nudged at Hussein and spoke to him urgently in Afar. Abba understood and translated for us. She was saying "Hide them! What are you waiting for? Hide this family in the ground." She marched ahead, pulling Hussein's hand, and instinctively we got up and followed. We walked through thick vegetation toward the outskirt of the oasis to drier ground covered with pebbles and rocks. I could not believe where we ended up—in the trenches. "Jump in and wait for us here. After we make sure there is no other traffic, we will come and get you," Hussein instructed.

The gunshots and the child's screaming still echoed in my ears. My brothers and Abba were confused. It didn't make sense. They should have hidden us before the bandits found us. What was the point of hiding, now that we had nothing left?

Sensing the confusion, Hussein said that the bandits could come back to kill us.

"They know we can't report them. You are scaring the children," Abba responded.

They were our guides after all; handpicked by my father for their experiences in situations like this. We followed their orders and jumped into the trenches at once. We remained there for a long time, covered in dirt and too tired to move.

I heard Abba muttering to himself, "I should have known better. This is all my fault. I shouldn't have carried any money and definitely not a weapon."

"How could you have known this would happen?" Meskerem asked.

"How could I have packed so much stuff for this journey knowing that the nomads who live here don't have much? Who needs all those clothes anyway? What was I thinking?"

"We need clothes, Terrefe."

"Not as many as we brought! Besides, it is too hot to wear so many clothes, we should have packed light. I should have known better."

Abba sounded as though we had brought a house full of stuff, when the reality was that what little we had brought fit on the backs of just three camels. We didn't bring the cozy cow-skin rug that warmed our home or the beautiful starfish that brightened our walls. We didn't even bring my sister.

"In the Danakil Desert, no nomad packs this much stuff just to walk from one end of the region to the other. The money would have been enough, and I should have gotten rid of it at the first sign of trouble," Abba continued in frustration. "Then we would not have attracted all the attention we got."

"We are not nomads. We are not nomads," Meskerem whispered. Abba fell silent.

My brothers and I knew better than to open our mouths.

In the evening, when all was quiet, Ali and Hussein came as

promised and said it was safe enough to pull ourselves out of the trenches.

When we were out, my father scolded them: "How could you let this happen? Could you not have known they were bandits? We trusted you and the worst happened. We got ambushed."

"These wanderers usually go away with a little money, like the others," Hussein tried to explain the unexplainable.

Ali added, "These were *waraba*." Hyenas.

The ambush had left me confused, the screaming and the gunshots were still reverberating in my head. Nothing was making sense. My mind was swirling like the wind. I kept hearing the woman's voice calling out to heaven, *"Hoyo, hoyo."* The heaven she called to was near. How else could we still be alive? I realized I may have just witnessed a miracle. All of us were still alive!

"Well, there isn't any more money to worry about, is there?" Abba said as he searched with his eyes for the camels, who had dispersed during the shooting. Instead, he found the Afar woman in the black dress guarding our hiding place. As soon as she saw us, she came running and gave a bundle tied in a brown fabric to my father. Then she turned and hurried into the darkness. She had left us *yezengada nifro* (boiled barley seeds). We shared it and kept some in reserve. *Yezengada nifro* was one of my favourite snacks.

Abba explained that the bandits, who were of an Issa clan, couldn't have killed us in front of her because she would have been a witness and spread the news to her clan. The Afar often complained to the authorities about the Issa. So the news would have warranted a hunt for the murderers. Regardless, the news of the ambush would still spread far and beyond, but Abba didn't explain further how the news would affect the perpetrators and my family.

"What if they come back?" Yared wondered.

"Don't worry, they have taken almost everything; there is nothing else they can take. They won't be targeting us again," Abba reassured us.

The camels had been gathered up by Ali and Hussein. Now the

two of them were helping us pick up whatever was left scattered about—our water cans, Meskerem's and my dresses. Most of my father's and brothers' trousers and shirts were gone. The frames and photos were broken. We began wrapping the remains of our lives in the dresses.

"If it were up to me, I would leave all the clothes we don't need in the dirt," Abba said. "We will be okay. We don't have much time left until we reach Djibouti."

What was left could now be loaded onto one camel. Hussein and Ali, effortlessly piling up our belongings, tried to convince us that they were still the best guides my father could have found, because we were still alive.

———◆◆———

That night we travelled some fifteen miles in less than four hours. We climbed up and scrambled down hills strewn with large rocks and loose pebbles and shrubs. Miraculously it began to rain. We walked through the tropical downpour as the rain got sucked into the sand. None of us spoke. I thought we were nearing Djibouti when I noticed crimson lights resembling the ones we had seen when we left Dire Dawa. There was no other city in the area to radiate such lights. The rain stopped and Hussein and Ali too stopped. My shoes were soaked, my feet were wet and aching, and my dress was glued to my skin. We looked as though we had just finished a long swim and began to squeeze the water from our wet clothes. Ali and Hussein said we were out of the danger zone and we could sleep the rest of the night here.

I could feel tiny cuts and rough bruises all over my feet, and I wished I could plunge them into a bucket of ice. I rubbed the wetness between my toes and wondered how much of it was blood. There was a gentle breeze; the rain clouds had moved away and the moon was not yet with us.

After we had eaten the rest of the *nifro* the Afar woman had given us, Abba told us about his involvement with the Afar people of this region. The Derg had given my father the job of finding a way to settle the Afar in a single area so they could get health care and education easily. My father did not agree with the plan to force the Afar to abandon the way of life they had known for ten thousand years. He wanted a program that complemented their lifestyle. Then, at least, they would begin to understand what education and modern medicine could do for them. Since the Afar people were nomads, they moved freely across Ethiopian, Somali, and Eritrean Liberation Front territories. Once, the Derg had ordered the mass execution of one hundred Afars for spying. My father did the unthinkable: he told the prison director of the Assayita region that a message from the Derg had been received and the Afar prisoners were to be released. The prison director went ahead and released them.

I was glad I didn't know about this when we were in Addis. What else had Abba done against the orders of the administration? I knew that his work with the Emperor's government counted against him in the eyes of the current leaders. Officials associated with the monarchy had long been persecuted, and many had left the country for fear of being executed. Had my father not been studying in Israel during the coup, his life might not have been spared.

"Ethiopia is not safe. I couldn't continue working there," Abba finished.

"But you had said Ethiopia still needed educated people to develop the country," Asrat remarked.

"We are fighting one another. Nothing is working and nothing is making sense. I couldn't leave you and go to the far end of the country to work like I used to. I just couldn't. That's why we are leaving Ethiopia."

We took turns sipping water, and the last person to drink was Asrat. He used the goatskin for a pillow, while I used my wet shoes. We were exhausted, and just like that we each fell into a deep sleep.

Alone

—◆—

"ABBA, ABBA! WAKE UP ABBA! Meskerem!" Asrat's cry woke us up just before dawn. We had not had enough rest to recover from our six-hour trek the night before.

"What is wrong?" Abba opened his eyes.

"I don't see the camels!" Asrat shouted.

Abba jumped up and looked around. Ali was sound asleep between some shrubs, but Hussein was nowhere to be found. My father called for Ali, and when he did not respond, he went over to the sleeping figure and tapped his shoulder.

"Ali, wake up. Where is Hussein?"

Ali sat up, confused. His hair was covered with dust like the rest of us.

"I don't know." He slowly started to get up.

"Could he have gone ahead?"

"Maybe he went to get water." Ali rubbed his eyes and looked around to see if he could spot Hussein anywhere.

"With our camels?" Abba asked angrily.

Maybe he got eaten by hyenas along with the camels, I thought.

Abba began walking around, looking for a clue. He stopped for a moment and then began walking very slowly, studying the ground. Ali hurried over when Abba found footprints in the sand. He was now convinced that Hussein had abandoned us.

"Should I follow the footprints?" Ali asked.

"How could you not have known he was going to abandon us? Please tell me?" Abba demanded.

Ali backed away.

"*Wolahi*, by God, I don't know anything!"

Abba turned to Meskerem. "They said '*Wolahi*, we didn't know they were robbers' when we got ambushed in the oasis. How can I trust what he is saying now?"

"Why don't we just wait? He might come back," Meskerem responded.

"What are you saying? I know he is gone." Abba lowered his voice. "Ali is waiting for his turn."

"Please, Terrefe, let's just sit and think for a moment."

We sat on the sand, waiting; a strong wind was blowing, drying out the wet clothes we wore. My eyes became so dry that tears were rolling down my cheeks. We were facing east and the break of dawn came in an explosion of red and yellow. A great ball of golden sun rose between two distant black mountains, but still no sign of Hussein.

Abba whispered to Meskerem, "I know Hussein has abandoned us, but we can't let Ali do the same. He is our only hope and we must watch him at all times."

It was hard to believe that Hussein would disappear with three camels and not leave us anything other than Ali. I was already thirsty. How could we find water, let alone the way to Djibouti, without our guides? How could things get worse?

"I should go look for Hussein," Ali suggested. "I don't know the way around the desert, especially to Djibouti, without Hussein."

"You can't leave us," Abba told him. "We will wait for him together."

Ali paced back and forth thinking of what to do next.

Abba whispered to Meskerem, "He thinks I have chicken brains. I know he will not come back."

We had not had anything to eat since the handful of *nifro* yesterday afternoon at the oasis, and we had no food left. There was very little water in the container Asrat was carrying. But I was too tired, confused, and scared to be hungry.

Abba had to make a decision quickly because the sun was getting hot and the wind was scorching, and there were no trees around. An hour passed, Hussein and the camels had not returned. Abba decided that we should start walking, hopefully we would find a caravan to help us. We began our journey, walking in the shifting sand against the wind. We felt completely lost.

Ali was still insisting on leaving us to get help. "I could go to my relatives and get some guides for you for free. The last time I left, didn't I come back?"

"No one will come here with you for free!" Abba said flatly.

"I feel very bad about what happened. I will tell my relatives and convince them to help you out of goodwill."

He was determined. If he could not escape in daylight we were convinced he would try when we were asleep. My brothers said they could take turns watching Ali, and if he tried to leave us they would tackle him, but my father didn't take them seriously. Ali's offer to find new guides was our only hope and therefore worth the risk.

"Promise us in the name of Allah that you will come back for us even if you don't find anyone to help!" Abba pleaded with Ali.

"I promise. I will come back. At least I could be your translator," Ali assured us.

My father was quiet for a long moment. And then he said to Ali, "I have one cheque in my wallet. I will sign it and leave everything else blank." Ali flashed his brown teeth with excitement.

Abba brought out the cheque from his wallet and signed it. He gave it to Ali.

Abba went on to explain. "You can write whatever amount you feel is necessary to give to the new guides, up to a maximum of five thousand birr. When you find the guides, tell them to send some-one to Dire Dawa to cash the cheque."

"The money will help a lot in convincing someone to come with me," Ali said, looking at the cheque in his hand with a smile on his face. "I will hurry."

I couldn't help thinking that Ali must feel sorry for us. He couldn't just let us die in the desert. I was hopeful.

When Ali left, Abba and Meskerem started arguing.

"Why did you let him go when you know he will not come back?"

"Please don't shout. I don't want the children to get scared. How could we have watched him all the time?" Abba said softly.

"But why did you let him go now?" Meskerem said, with tears in her eyes.

Abba moved closer to her and spoke in a low voice, "I wanted to give the children some hope."

Meskerem couldn't keep her voice down through her sobbing. "We're in much more trouble than we have ever been."

"Could you please keep it down?" Abba begged.

"Let the children know. It's too late. They might as well know everything. We dragged them into this and the least we can do is tell them what a terrible mistake we've made."

Abba asked us to come closer to him for a special meeting.

"I sent Ali with the cheque knowing that I was taking a big chance. If we are lucky he will come back for us," he said.

"What if he gets caught?" Yared asked.

Meskerem half turned to Abba to look at him from the corner of her eyes. The look meant, *See, they already know what is going on.*

Abba remained calm. "The officials won't know about us for at least a month because I am supposed to be on vacation."

"I want us to walk in this order." Abba continued. "Meskerem, you stay right behind me." She nodded in agreement. "Yared, follow Meskerem, and Beth stay behind with Yared. Don't be afraid, Asrat will be right behind you."

How did Abba know I hated being the last in line? I was afraid that something would grab me from behind. We walked in that order in single file. My father's steps were slower than Ali's and it was easy to follow him.

"I don't know where we are heading or which way to go. I feel like my legs are broken. I know to the east is the Red Sea and to the north is the Danakil Depression. We should be okay if we walk east in the direction of the sun," Abba said.

Abba had explained before that the Danakil Depression was a stretch of land running alongside the East African Rift Valley, where summer temperatures could reach 50 degrees Celsius or more, and the land itself was 371 feet below sea level—one of the lowest places on the earth's surface. The volcano Erta Ale, "smoking mountain," was within a few days' walk; it was supposed to be the hottest volcano on earth and was the most active in the region. Although we were a fair distance away from it, we could still feel the volcano's intense heat riding the wind. It felt as if we were being slapped by fire. The black mountains in the distance, and the white sand and deep cracks on the ground at our feet were a constant reminder of just how close we were to the "badlands" of the Danakil Depression.

"Close to two million resilient Afars call this land home," Abba said. "They go about their business of herding their cattle, trading in salt, and from time to time selling cattle to buy soap, coffee, and qat. They use sticks, rocks, pieces of fabrics, metals, and just about anything as a sign to communicate to other clan members where food is hidden, where there is water, and if there are enemies in the area. We must pay attention to anything that seems unusual."

For me, the few days we had been wandering in the desert had been unbearable. Ethiopia borders Sudan, Kenya, Somalia, and Djibouti. I could not understand why, of all the routes we could have used for our escape, my father had chosen this land of crumbling mountains and cracked earth. A land choking with bandits and landmines. He made little effort to explain why he had led us in this direction instead of another. We thought it was perhaps because he knew the way.

Meskerem had no idea either how bad it would be, or she would not have left Dire Dawa or paid all that money to get her hair done so beautifully the day before we began this journey.

I stayed strong since Abba was strong. He was determined to get us to Djibouti on his own, no matter what, and there was no doubt in his mind he would succeed. After Abba and Meskerem's argument, the only person talking was Abba, and mostly to himself. I could sense that, in spite of his determination, my father was showing signs of cracking. He would repeat over and over that he was not named Terrefe (Survivor) for nothing. As an infant he had survived the Italian invasion in a mountain cave, with nothing to eat for days while bombs fell from the sky.

"We completely trusted Ali and Hussein and even paid them in advance. We are all alive and that is all that matters right now and we just need to keep on moving," he mumbled to himself.

"It doesn't matter if we meet up with robbers, because we don't have anything they can take from us. If anything, they might help us. That is the best thing about having nothing."

We found ourselves once again among scattered vegetation in the lava fields. After some time in these fields, we came upon white, brown, and black goats, nibbling on the bushes and grazing between rocks. Soon after we saw a man tending them. There were about forty goats, all scattered about. My father signalled to us to stop, and he himself marched forward. The man stood stiff as a bone with a stick in his hand and a *gile* tied to his waist. His long hair was braided evenly and reached as far as his jaw. He watched attentively as Abba approached him. My father greeted him in Afar and the man responded. Then Abba turned and motioned to us to advance. The man was thin and as dark as the men who had robbed us in the oasis, except he was an Afar. When I saw my brothers next to him, they looked just like him, thin and sunburned. His face was smooth and kind when he looked at us.

"Hanike' geda?" (Where are you going?) he asked. Abba tried to communicate in the little Afar he knew before trying his luck in Amharic. The man spoke continually in a low, soft voice in Afar but all the words were lost on us, though they sounded pleasant to my ears. My stepmother, who had been born and raised in Dire Dawa, was able to speak some Oromiffia, a trading language spoken in the region, and she attempted that.

Surprisingly the man did speak Oromiffia. Meskerem explained what had happened to us. Abba, pointing in the direction we were heading, said, "Ask him if that is the way to Djibouti." Meskerem and the man conversed for a while, stopping only when my father interrupted to inquire what was being said. Meskerem said he was asking how we were and what we were doing in the desert.

My father suddenly remembered the long-winded, detailed way of Afar greeting and calmed a little, but encouraged Meskerem to get the information quickly.

She continued speaking with the man and then turned to us in shock. *"Amlake, Amlake, Woy Gudachin!* Oh my God, what big trouble we are in! He says we are heading toward the Ethiopian army base! If we had walked just a little further we would have seen the army's tents and might even have run into soldiers."

Ali and Hussein had delivered us right to the Ethiopian army's doorstep! The man was speaking again. I saw Meskerem shaking her head.

"Are you going to tell us what he is saying?" Abba said, frustrated.

I didn't want my father to get upset, having seen him in the oasis waving his gun. I was glad the bandits had taken his gun.

"What is he saying?" Yared asked.

"He keeps asking for money and I am telling him again and again what happened to us and that we have no money," Meskerem replied.

The man turned away to tend his goats.

"Wait, wait!" Abba shouted. "Here, have a couple of cigarettes."

When my father flicked the lighter for him, the man held the cigarette between his dry, chapped lips. He then took the cigarette out of his mouth to look at it with loving eyes, before exhaling the smoke.

"I don't doubt that you really intend to cross the Danakil Desert." He looked at my father directly in the eye and continued, "But I am advising you to abandon this dangerous plan and turn back to Ethiopia, get some food for your family, and try your journey at a different time, perhaps through Tadjoura. There, it is easy to hire someone with a boat to take you to Djibouti. That way you are more certain your children will not die."

When he saw my father looking at him as if he were a madman, he wished us a safe journey.

Nothing was making sense. How could he expect us to walk back for four days without any food? How would we answer the Ethiopian border officials? And we didn't even know the way back.

Sensing our confusion, the man said, "You are just a day away from Ethiopia."

Shock could not begin to describe what we felt. We were defeated. Just a day away from Dire Dawa? All the walking we had done thus far was just to circle the same area. We concluded that Ali and Hussein had planned for us to get robbed and to wander around the same area to tire us out.

The Afar asked for more cigarettes and Abba gave him a couple more and thanked him. After we had walked for a few hours in the opposite direction to before, I saw Abba look behind and squint. "I feel like someone is watching us. What is that blurry thing over there?" He pointed further back. We all looked but saw nothing.

"Run, run this way!" he shouted and pulled my hand and I started running. "Meskerem, Yared, all of you run as fast as you can before we are spotted. I see a lot of soldiers in that blur, run!" I thought I would collapse any minute. We ran for what seemed like forever. But then I started coughing and collapsed at the edge of a rocky valley. Asrat fell next to me, and I could hear Yared not too far behind.

We struggled to catch our breaths and calm our hearts. All around us were rocks, trees, and dry grass. It was a relief to see some greenery again. We got ourselves up and sat on a few big rocks under some trees. Abba was still furious and upset with himself for trusting Ali and Hussein and for foolishly packing so much stuff. He had developed the new habit of talking to himself. "We will follow the sun and take a northeast direction only," he said. "This way we are sure of not going back to Ethiopia. If anything, we will end up at the Red Sea or in Somalia."

I did not want to arrive in Somalia by accident. There had been endless fighting between our countries. Djibouti was our dream; at one time it had belonged to Ethiopia, then the French had acquired it and it was called French Somaliland; later it was renamed the Territory of the Afar and Issa. In 1977, three years before our escape, Djibouti became an independent nation. In Djibouti we would be safe.

Abba suggested that we should call each other by Muslim names whenever we were in the company of desert strangers. What difference was that going to make? So far no one had asked for our names.

"We will introduce ourselves with our Muslim names to get them to believe we are from this region."

I became convinced then that things would never be the same again. Ethiopia was ceasing to be my country even though I was still walking on its ground. Now Abba wanted us to use Muslim names.

"I know some Muslim names," Meskerem volunteered. "Ibrahim, Abdie, Samir are suitable names for the men. For women, Medina, Zeynab, Kadija are all popular."

"Don't look so sad!" Abba said, pulling me toward him and kissing me gently on the forehead. "Don't you know this is all for now?" I held on to his shirt and cried. I cried until my eyes were burning and my stomach was trembling. Abba kept holding me close.

Yared was digging the sand with a rock, his head turned down.

When he looked up, his face was covered in tears.

"You have to be strong," Abba ordered.

"Yes." Yared replied sharply and looked away.

Asrat had stayed strong. He sat by Yared's side. "Everything will be okay, Yared. Please don't cry." He put his hand on Yared's shoulder.

"Look," he then exclaimed, pointing. "I see monkeys. Do you see them?"

Our attention was shifted and we concentrated on spotting the monkeys in the valley. There were about fifty baboons, jumping noisily from rock to rock. They had camouflaged themselves so well that we hadn't spotted them before, but they had been there all along. It seemed odd for their bottoms to be so red while the rest of their bodies resembled the rocks and the sand.

"We'll use the Muslim names only if we need to," Abba said.

"Do you know why their bums are red?" Yared asked, wiping his tears.

"That's how they are born," Asrat replied.

"Not these ones," Yared said, and then he began to tell us a story, the way he had done, at bedtime back in Addis Ababa.

For an instant, I felt as if I were safe in my bed and realized I was too sleepy to cry any longer.

It was around noon, the sun was intense overhead, and we had long abandoned the idea that Ali would return. I had lost all strength and my throat was as dry as the land. Unable to speak, I tried to clear my throat by spitting. What came out of my mouth was as dark as charcoal. I knew I was not sick, but just heat-stricken, hungry, and thirsty. When the water container was passed around, we were told to take just one sip. I sipped my share and passed the water to Abba, but just as he got it close to his mouth he pushed it away.

"Here. Drink some more and pass it to Yared to carry." He gave the container back to me. I took huge gulps and almost choked.

There was a little bit of shadow under the thin acacia trees, but not enough to cover my whole body. Still, it would be a long time before I found a better spot. I lay down in the shade. My entire being dreaded the journey ahead. I missed the camels, the shadows they cast and their comforting gurgling noises.

After we had rested for a while, Meskerem came up with the idea of moving around the area, as our chances of finding someone was better that way. Everyone slowly got up, except I.

My body felt numb and my muscles were beyond my control. I was starting to fall into a deep sleep under the sizzling sun when I heard my name. I saw Asrat standing in front of me and holding both my hands to help me get up.

"Get up, Beth. We must be going."

"Why?" I said.

Abba came and told me to wake up. I tried to open my eyes, but the powerful sunlight made me to shut them. I tried to put my hands on the ground to push myself up, but only gathered enough effort to move some rocks around. I felt chained to the sun. "I need to sleep, please, just for five minutes more."

"Do you want us to get killed?" Abba said forcefully.

"No," I replied with a huge effort. I was drifting in and out of consciousness. I knew there was something important to be done, but the sun was pinning me down. I kept hearing my name and being ordered to get up. Every now and then someone would place a hand over my forehead.

Finally, I gathered enough energy to say "Leave me here, I will catch up with you later."

I heard Abba's voice. "Okay, we are leaving, but the vultures might think you are dead and start eating you."

I heard their footsteps moving away from me.

The next thing I remember was looking at the clear sky with my head upside down. Someone was carrying me. I turned my head down to the ground and saw Yared's Adidas. "Put me down, I am awake," I said.

Yared held me up and I slowly stood on my own two feet. Asrat quickly gave me some water, and I began walking slowly.

That day we walked for a long time, and along the way we saw vultures in the sky, lizards scurrying on the rocks, and the white skeletons of dead animals on the ground, but no humans. Meskerem had been quiet for most of the journey, and I sensed she was keeping a secret. We had lost the malaria pills with the camels and none of us was protected. She cried when Abba was not watching and I asked her why she was crying. Meskerem said her breasts still hurt as they continued to fill with milk. She squeezed out her milk onto the sand and that helped. But, every time she did that, she thought of Kalkidan. I missed Kalkidan, too. Still, leaving her behind seemed the only good decision my father had made.

At some point, we had finished the water, and Asrat was carrying an empty container. He wanted to know how long humans survive without water.

"Very long," my father assured us.

"More than a week?" I asked.

"Yes."

I was happy. In a week God would send someone to help us.

Suddenly, we stopped walking. "I don't want to walk in the dark. We will get lost," Abba cautioned. We didn't bother looking for a special place to sleep overnight. We just sat down where we were. The soft sand beneath us felt hot, as if it were releasing steam. None of us complained as we lay down on it.

Before we went to sleep, Abba said, "Tomorrow we will rise with the sun and travel east in the direction of Djibouti and we will rest when we need to and walk again until the sun sets. As long as we continue to stay in the Afar territory, we will be okay. We will be on the right track before we know it and we'll be able to find other travellers once we are on the main route. Sleep well." He closed his eyes for a quiet prayer.

Abba's words had a powerful effect on how my brothers and I felt. At that moment we were all excited, as if nothing out of the ordinary had happened to us. As we were falling asleep, we whispered to each other.

"We will be in Djibouti tomorrow."

"Not tomorrow. First we have to find people to guide us."

"Hopefully, we'll find Afar people, not the Derg's soldiers."

"We will get there even if we don't find people, because Abba is going to follow the sun."

"I can't wait until I eat fresh *injera*."

"When I get to Djibouti, the first thing I will do is take a long shower."

"What about you, Beth?"

There was nothing in the world I wanted more than a clean, ice-cold glass of water.

———— ◆•◆ ————

A noise woke me up in the middle of the night. I sat straight up to see which direction it was coming from. Abba and Meskerem slept a few feet to the left of me and my brothers, and no sound came from their direction. The full moon appeared like a window in the big sapphire sky. I heard a small chuckle coming from straight ahead, and saw the shadow of some animal. And then I saw a pair of glowing eyes and more glowing eyes behind those. With my heart beating loudly and gasping for air, I was sure the animals would find me. I prayed rapidly in my heart for God to make us invisible. Suddenly, I could see them clearly, and I realized what they were. There, right in front of me, was a pack of hyenas like the ones I had seen in children's story books. I froze, speechless as a cold stone while they growled and surrounded us. "Hyenas eat those who are scared of them," my mother's soft voice echoed in my head, and I slowly lay back on the ground where I remained stiff, afraid to breath.

About half an hour later, I realized my family and I were still alive, and I lifted my head to look around: from my angle, the land was clear, no trace of hyenas. I slowly sat up to make certain they were all gone.

I could not fall back to sleep so I stared at the sky in search of the big star I had seen at the oasis. The more I stared at the sky, the more I felt I was dreaming. I asked myself who I was in an attempt to understand what was real and what was not. Who would believe me if I said I had slept surrounded by hungry hyenas in the middle of the hottest desert on earth? I said my name was Beth, short for Bethlehem. I knew for sure I was an Ethiopian and had two brothers, Yared and Asrat. That much seemed real. Out of nowhere a question popped into my head. Was Ethiopia still my country? Was I still on its soil? I closed my eyes shut again in a final attempt to make all this a dream that I would wake up from. When I opened them, I was still where I had been all evening and it was all real. This was never going to be a dream, even if I opened and shut my eyes a hundred times. The best thing to do was to keep my eyes shut until I fell asleep, because I knew that sleep brought peace. I moved closer to Asrat and held on tight to his sarong. I placed my other hand on Yared's shoulder and when I felt calm enough, I fell asleep.

Caravans

———◆———

IN THE DISTANCE WE COULD see something moving. I tried to make it out but couldn't. We walked cautiously towards it, fearing that we might be close to the Ethiopian army camp. As we got closer, Abba told us to lie flat on the ground. I lay motionless.

Abba squatted down and studied the scene ahead. Moments later he said, "Get up, get up. It's a caravan." As we gazed in the distance, we gradually discerned a line of camels silhouetted against the pale blue sky; there were at least nine of them.

"I am sure of it. Come, let's go see."

We were now able to make out two men leading the camels, a few walking in the middle, and a few more at the back of the caravan. Then we saw that all the camels were fully loaded except one.

"This is what business people look like. Not like the ones we encountered in the oasis," Abba said.

When the men saw us, they slowly brought their camels to a halt. The camels were twice the size of the ones we had before. Their loads were heavier, and the ropes tied to their heads were beautifully decorated with red and purple fabric with gold trim. The men were dressed the same way as the caravan men we had met at the oasis, wearing sarongs. A few had cloth turbans around their heads, and all were armed with rifles and machetes. The soft wind filled out their sarongs so that they looked like the exotic flags of new nations fluttering in the desert wind. The men looked much bigger and stronger than Abba and my brothers, and when they moved toward us, their steps were quick.

They began speaking in Afar. Abba limped a few inches closer to them, and they stopped talking only to gaze at him with concern.

"Please help us," Abba gasped in Amharic.

One of them seemed to recognize Amharic and said, "Habesh, Habesh," and walked closer.

"We are on our way to Djibouti, but we have lost our way. Could you please guide us?" Abba said.

The man came closer and said, in broken Amharic, "I understand some Amharic, but I prefer not to speak it." His teeth were brown like Ali's.

"I am sick and my children are hungry. We've got nothing," Abba said.

I had never heard Abba sound so desperate.

The man turned to his companions, who were watching us intently, and spoke with them for a few minutes. To our surprise and disappointment, they walked back to their camels and resumed their journey, leaving us standing where we were.

"Oh God, our Father in Heaven," I heard Meskerem cry. "Let's follow and beg them again."

Abba agreed, but when he tried to run after them, a sharp pain paralyzed him and he fell down defeated. My brothers and I rushed to his aid, but Meskerem kept running after the caravan, screaming in Oromiffia.

When they heard her voice they slowed down, but only the man who spoke with my father was ready to speak again. And then I heard Abba trying to speak Afar. Meskerem was gesturing with her hands as she spoke and the man glanced at the caravan moving ahead.

He then shouted, in a voice loud enough to be heard for miles. The caravan came to a halt.

"Abba, they stopped," I said.

Meskerem hurried back to tell us what had happened.

"He speaks Oromiffia and I asked him to help us just for a few hours. He said the caravan has to arrive in Djibouti in two days for an important transaction, and they will be delayed with a sick man and a woman and children with them. Regardless, they have agreed to take us and show us a track we could follow on our own."

The man had a pleasant face and said he was happy to hear my father speaking some Afar. Abba was quick to realize that if there was a time to impress anyone it was right then. So he said a few words in Afar and then asked Meskerem to translate in Oromiffia.

"Tell him this," Abba said to Meskerem. "My name is Terrefe and I was the manager of the Assayita State Farm and Settlement Program for four years."

Meskerem translated.

"I am an agricultural scientist and have worked diligently in the Afar state for four years. My hope is still to utilize all of the 700-kilometre stretch of the river to give life to everything along its path: purifying the water for healthy drinking, planting trees to prevent soil erosion, and creating an irrigation system for year-round farming. The desert does not always have to be where the scorching wind ravages the land."

My stepmother translated in Oromiffia.

The man was curious and to my surprise he paid close attention to what Abba was saying.

Could what Abba had said make any sense here in the middle of nowhere? Would they believe him?

"I am the only one who speaks Amharic and Oromiffia," the man said, "But, I prefer to speak Oromiffia"

The water they gave us was cool. There was plenty of it and it filled me like food.

The men warned us that if we couldn't keep up with them, they would go on without us. We had no doubt that they meant it.

Abba said it was a very good sign that they gave us water because in the Afar tradition once they are kind to a stranger, it meant they were willing to protect us. "But I have a feeling there are some Issa people travelling with them, otherwise the Afar don't generally call us 'Habesh' in a discriminatory way. But we are moving, so that is good." He explained further, "To the Issa, Habesh means 'Highlander,' and that means people different from them in religion and culture."

The men were not walking but running, and so were the camels. We trailed behind for as long as we could, but the unyielding heat was difficult for my ill father to handle. Abba even allowed my brothers to support him. From what the man had said, it would be two more hours before we rested for lunch. Abba was staggering, and Yared and Asrat wobbled under the weight of his sliding body.

"I'm going to beg them to let us rest for a while," Meskerem said, coming up behind the man who spoke Oromiffia. After they spoke, he approached us with a can of milk for Abba. Abba drank the milk, but he was still too weak to get up.

"I asked my friends to stop for a few minutes to help him and they have agreed," our interpreter said, looking at my father. "But we will have to continue with our journey."

One of the men opened something tied with a piece of cloth, and I saw him take a pinch of what looked like black pepper. He mixed it with camel's milk in an empty can. He came to Abba and said, "This is a good medicine for your illness and you must drink it at once."

Abba took the can and looked at the mixture; he smelled it.

"What does it smell like?" Meskerem asked.

"Ash."

Abba was pouring sweat. When the man saw Abba shivering, he started a fire and began boiling tea in silence.

Abba finished the medicine in one quick gulp and placed the empty cup on the sand. The tea boiled in seconds and after the man had added spices to it he gave Abba some to drink.

I knew Abba was in no condition to be walking, especially with the sun fully out, but we did not want him to get agitated. Yared and Asrat lifted him up and he started moving his feet slowly. The caravan men were up and running once again and in minutes they were far ahead of us.

One of the men who had been talking to Meskerem stopped and waited. Once we caught up with him, he told us we were close to the scheduled rest stop and he would stay behind and walk with us. The other men continued with their run, speaking to each other in voices that sounded like shouting, and firing shots at nothing in particular, as though celebrating something. The wind blew towards us the dust that they raised.

When we trailed in at last at the destination, we found that every camel had already been unloaded. Tea was served and rice was cooking. On another fire, there was a big pot, and as we approached, I saw two of the men carrying fresh meat and tossing it in. Two goats had been killed and the aroma of the stew was mouth-watering. We each received a cup of sweet tea. I could not wait to eat.

"Look," Asrat said, pointing straight ahead.

A short distance from where we had camped there were what looked like three huts. They were in the unusual shape of giant bubbles, brown as dust, and so completely covered that it appeared they had no doors or windows. Around the huts were thorn barricades.

Abba explained that it was the custom of the Afar not to remain long in one place. For all we knew, the huts could have been constructed less than an hour ago. When it was time to move, the materials could be taken apart, folded up, and packed on a camel's back. The Afars call the huts *ounga*. The covering is made from a very green tree, named *oayba*. The *oayba*'s thin long leaves are woven beautifully into a covering the size of a carpet, which is draped over the wooden poles, giving the huts their hemispherical shape.

A tall man of medium build, with a face as dark as Addis coffee, approached us. He had emerged from a hut, carrying a long stick that he used to chase the goats out of his way. His hair was grey, his beard red. There seemed to be a place of respect reserved for him in front of the fire between the two tallest caravan men. The man slipped off his sandals before seating himself. He had soft eyes and a smile to match, wore no weapon, and seemed friendly. We learned that he was the uncle of the two men he sat next to and that all the huts, the animals, and the camels, belonged to him. It became clear why my father was not allowed to sit on the camel that had not been carrying any load; the nephews had just bought it at a market near Dire Dawa and they wanted their uncle to see it in its superlative condition. He listened to his nephews whisper to him, and I was sure it was about us. Moments later, he got busy with fixing the fire and helping with the cooking. My father was quick to explain that this was a sign that he was not threatened by us. In fact, he had accepted us as his guests, which was a huge benefit for us. Soon he went about to inspect his new camel.

According to Abba, nomads have superior abilities in reading peoples' faces and can know much about them before any words are exchanged. That was why the man didn't concern himself with firing random questions at us. He could tell that we were harmless; he could also tell from the dust we carried on our feet that we had wandered around for some time. The first thing he would give us was something to eat, and then he would ask where we had come from, where we wanted to go, and so on.

"When you decide to become hospitable to strangers in the Danakil Desert, you are not one hundred percent sure of what kind of people you're hosting. Murderers are known to roam about, not to mention the endless wars that have been waged over this land between the Afars and Issas, and everyone else in Ethiopia. So this man is trusting us and risking everything, and in turn we must be polite and leave at the earliest possible moment," Abba said.

"I think we should rest here as long as we are permitted and gather some energy before resuming our journey," Meskerem put in.

A beautiful young woman in a long red and green striped dress stood inside the thorn-barricaded compound and looked at us curiously, but did not come to join the party. Her hair was braided in single strands, ending just above her shoulders. I had never seen this kind of hairstyle before. I was sure it had been soaked in pure fresh butter; how else could it be so thick and healthy?

We drank fresh milk with our meal. I was not sure if it was camel's or goat's milk, but it felt thick on my tongue, almost as though it had some rice powder in it. On the fire, I noticed some ribs being barbecued and later, to my delight, we were given our share of the meat.

As we were eating, a few of the men looked at the sky. I couldn't tell what they were studying at high noon, when not even vultures were flying around. I was thankful that the uncle had put up a woven mat, which he attached to one of his huts, for us to camp under. In the Danakil, the shadow of a mat saves lives. One of the men in particular kept glancing up in an apprehensive way and then I saw him talking to the uncle. Just after our meal, the caravan men marched, as if under instruction, to the area where they had left their loads and returned with two sacks full of qat. The qat had been wrapped in damp cloth to keep it fresh. They each took a bunch, then they rewrapped the remainder and placed it back in the sack. I was glad the circumstances favoured rest. Abba fell asleep on a cow-skin mat and the rest of us were given flattened parts of cardboard boxes.

When we woke up, it was late afternoon. The man who spoke Oromiffia told us that they had learned that there was a strong wind on the route to Djibouti, so they would delay their journey until tomorrow morning. We could not have been happier at the news. Abba was given more of the medicinal tea and he slept until dinner time. Yared volunteered to help care for the camels. Asrat, however, chose to walk behind one of the huts and disappeared from view. When he was gone for too long, I became concerned.

"I'll go look for Asrat," I whispered to Meskerem, careful not to wake up Abba.

Asrat had retreated behind a hut and I found him seated with his legs crossed. When he saw me he was startled and tried to hide what he was holding in his hands.

"What are you doing here?" He glared at me.

"I came to see if you are okay."

"Who else knows I am here?"

"I told Meskerem I was going to look for you."

"Go back. I'll be there soon."

Asrat and I had been rivals growing up, and the only time we had not had a fight was here in the Danakil Desert. We had fought about everything, and Yared would be the impartial judge. Asrat and I would call each other names. I called him Eucalyptus Tree, because he was so tall, and he called me mosquito. Now I thought of dashing forward to check what he was hiding. But I turned back.

What was he hiding from us?

———◆•◆———

That night I fell into a deep sleep. I was dreaming I was in Abaya, a cotton-farming area in central Ethiopia where my brothers and I had once spent our vacation. In the dream, we went fishing. Yared told Asrat and me to sit on the bank while he went into the water. He had a long rope with a hook dangling at one end of it. He tied the other end of the rope to a big rock and started to walk into the river. I watched him as he walked further and threw the rope in a circular motion and into the flowing river. As he stood waiting, Asrat and I saw the other end of the rope turn into a snake. We screamed, and then I woke up to find my stepmother screaming, "Snake, snake, snake!" One of the men had caught a black snake.

The night was warm and pleasant. I could hear a crackling sound as of flies burning in an outdoor fire, one by one. I heard Yared coughing and Abba tossing and turning.

I wanted to tell Yared the dream I had and how the snake was real. I whispered, "Yared, Yared, are you listening?"

He replied right away, "Yes."

"I can't sleep."

"The desert moon is so bright," he said.

When I told him about my dream, he thought it was strange how Meskerem's scream entered into my dream. As we lay on our backs we could see the shining stars. They were never this bright in Addis. Soon I discerned something strange moving about in the night sky. It looked like a swirl of dust the wind had picked up from the desert floor, but what was it doing way up in the sky and why was it moving?

Now I was thinking of my mother—how at a complete loss she would be when she heard that her three children had vanished! But I couldn't talk to Yared or Asrat about her as long us Abba and Meskerem were with us. I didn't want to give them any clue that I was thinking about finding a way to tell her that I was okay once we reached Djibouti. Yared and Asrat never mentioned our mother, either.

The next morning I awoke to the sound of children playing; a small girl of about four years old, with the same hair style as the woman I saw yesterday, and a boy who looked a little older than the girl were running in circles and laughing. The boy had no clothes on, the girl wore a wrap below her waist. They were running around in between the huts and chasing a lamb. I wished we had reached the end of our journey and this was Djibouti. I wanted to stay where we were. Abba could continue his farming project with the Afar people he respected so much, and we could help tend the animals and welcome travellers every now and then. Although I still could see planes in the distance, I felt safe and secure.

Abba was still weak and it took him long to get up. "I didn't sleep at all," he gasped.

The men gathered at the back of the house to wash. I thought we would eat breakfast when they returned, but instead, they each rolled out a small, colourful mat and stood in a single row and faced the rising sun. With their hands lifted just to their chest, they bowed down in synchronized motion to kiss the ground and worship Allah. The women were praying next to the huts.

I had seen them pray during the day and in the evening just before we slept. None of my family prayed as they did. Even Ali and Hussein did not pray like them. From time to time I saw Abba close his eyes and pray in silence. I also prayed in silence, especially at night. "Please, God, don't let the animals find us." I prayed at other times, depending on how scared I was. Would God hear me and respond faster if I prayed with gestures?

Breakfast was as lavish as dinner. There was leftover goat soup and it tasted delicious with the homemade bread someone brought out from the hut.

After breakfast, the men began packing. Two of them were sitting next to us. As one tied the goatskin water container with a rope, the other, who spoke Oromiffia, said, "It will take just one more night to reach Djibouti, but we have to walk fast." He looked at my father.

"We are ready," my father said quickly. "I am feeling much better."

He tried to get up to show us how well he was feeling, but sat back down quickly.

"You should stay here until you feel better," said the man. "But the caravan cannot wait. People in Djibouti are waiting for their goods."

"If the caravan leaves we won't have anyone to guide us to Djibouti."

"Our other caravan will arrive here in four days. You can come with them."

We thought about it, especially Meskerem and Abba.

"This is a great place to rest," Meskerem said. "The uncle will give us food if he knows we are staying, and it is good for the children."

And so we decided to stay.

We camped among the Afar for four days. The uncle didn't speak Amharic or Oromiffia, and neither did the women and children. Although we kept to ourselves, the women would bring water and food for us when it was time to eat. By the end of the third day, there was no meat, just bread and milk. My father said that, as strange as it seemed, the Afar in Assayita didn't consume much meat even though their entire lives were spent as shepherds.

It was better for Abba to stay off his feet and eat plenty of goat soup. The uncle expanded our shelter and added more matting to make walls. Here we stayed, protected from the sun and the dust. There was a rough wind that shook the woven mats and dumped sand on the rooftop, but that was all it did.

For the first two days, Abba was in great pain, but by the third day he started to feel better. The other caravan arrived on the fourth day, just as scheduled. It was as big as the first caravan and the men were dressed in the same fashion. They were like an army outfitted with rifles and *giles*, ready to fight the murderers and bandits rampant on the road to Djibouti.

After consulting with the uncle, one of them, who spoke Oromiffia, came and told us we could go with them. He said they would leave after chewing qat for a while and would be travelling without resting as they were behind schedule. They were hurrying to meet with the first caravan because they had extra camels to bring back more goods.

About an hour later we began our journey. From time to time I stopped to empty out some dirt from my Adidas but kept up with the men.

I was happy to be in the company of many people. There was a camel shadow for every member of my family to walk under. My father was one camel behind me and Meskerem was with him. Yared and Asrat were under two different camels' shadows in front of me. When I turned to look at Abba, I saw that he was falling behind. At one point, he stopped walking altogether. Asrat went up to one of the men and tagged him to get his attention. When the man saw my father, he ordered the camels to stop and rushed over to see him.

"Just a sip of water and I will be fine," Abba said.

His hands were shaking as he lifted the big container to his mouth, and the water dripped down his chin. He slowly sat down. His face was sweaty and his eyes were cloudy. He seemed to have turned older.

"We can't wait," the caravan man said as kindly as he could.

"Meskerem, tell them to go. I will rest for a while and catch up later." Abba's voice was weak and he had to clear his throat several times.

I asked him, "Do you think it's malaria?"

"I have had malaria before and this is not malaria. It is the heat. But I know I will feel better once I rest."

His look frightened me. His hands were shaking.

And then he added, "I want you to go on with the caravan while I rest."

He should have known we would not leave without him. He was the one who got us here. Even when we were lost without guides, I knew he would lead us to Djibouti.

"We can't leave without you, Terrefe," Meskerem said, moving to his side. Asrat and Yared agreed. The caravan, on the other hand, had to depart.

"We will give you lots of milk and food to help you until you find other travellers, which I am sure will be before the day is done. This is a popular route to Djibouti," one of the men said.

He stretched out a hand and pointed.

"You are almost there. If you stay on this track, you will arrive there on your own."

There was nothing but emptiness where he pointed. The black mountains, white sand, and scanty vegetation had given way to a brown earth covered in dust. Were we really that close?

The camels started moving.

"You see, I will catch up with you in no time, just go with them,"

Abba motioned with his hands.

"Why are you talking like this? We have gone this far together and we will arrive in Djibouti together. We are just one day away," Meskerem pleaded.

Abba became agitated. "Are you refusing to listen to me?" He glared at Meskerem with his cloudy eyes. "I am telling you to go. Go now and let me have my rest."

Abba was scaring me. I felt that if he still had his gun, he would point it at us and order us to follow the caravan.

Meskerem was just as stubborn, and Abba shouted at her, then paused and held his chest.

"You do whatever you want," he said and took in some air. "But my children are going."

"Please, Abba, let us stay. I am tired, too. We can all rest with you," I said.

"We don't have to be separated, Abba. The man will guide all of us," Yared pleaded.

When Abba heard Yared's voice, he looked at him more intensely than before and tears ran down his face. I could tell there was so much Abba wanted to say, but the words were stuck in his throat. "Please go. Please," Abba said kindly. He then wiped his tears with both hands.

He finally convinced Yared and me to go with the merchants and wait for them at the next camp. He was sure they would make it there by sunset.

My feet felt heavy. My heart sank with sadness because I didn't want to be separated from the people I loved. What evil thing was making all this happen? Yared looked too upset to talk but his pace was quick, as if he were determined to leave our father. I looked back and saw Meskerem and Asrat still seated on each side of Abba in the wide-open desert. I wanted to run back.

It was still morning, the sun was gentle, but I knew we would not stop until it was past noon. Ahead, the sand stretched endlessly on without interruption until it met the blue sky. It looked as though we were walking to reach the sky. There were a few things that I had liked about the desert, including the tea, the oasis, the morning at the uncle's compound, and this infinity. This sea of sand had unexplainable power. It was so peaceful it made me stop walking and stand mesmerized. The sand under my feet was shimmering; when the wind blew across its surface, it rose up and curled and set off as if it had a life of its own. If my own two feet hadn't walked this part of the earth, I wouldn't have believed the story of "Lucy," the first hominid. I wanted to run back to Abba and tell him that the story he told us about Dinknesh was now making sense to me.

"Beth!" Yared was tugging at my hand. "You can't go back. Let's keep moving. We've got to keep up."

I started walking with him again. By tomorrow evening we would be in Djibouti, the city I had dreamed about, with the white houses and strawberry fields and mango trees, mountains with watermelon rocks and grape-juice fountains. But I didn't have the excitement in me to match that dream. I would be without half my family when I arrived in Djibouti, and I feared that Abba, Meskerem, and Asrat might not make it. What if Abba was so ill that he could not get up? What if they got lost again and ended up in Somalia? How would we ever be reunited?

I started to cry and could not see where I was going. I heard Yared calling my name. "I think we'll be resting soon," he said.

We approached a lonesome tree. Its dried, leafless branches made it look like a spider's web. The caravan men unloaded some food and one of them started a fire to make tea. Yared and I sat near the fire while the merchants took out their prayer mats. The tea was quickly prepared, the water boiled in seconds. While the men prayed, Yared and I sipped our tea. After their prayers the men gathered together away from us for their tea. Now and then they would throw a glance at us but no one made an effort to bother with us.

The rest of the afternoon was dominated by an unfamiliar wind. The gentle breeze of before turned into a strong gust. The equatorial sun was at its peak, ruling the sky and everything under it. There was not a trace of cloud to signal oncoming rain. The caravan was moving at a pace I could handle. Sometimes the men would look back in our direction. Once, the tallest among them, with tight Afro curls, came toward me, his Afar knife dangling from his waist. He had a big friendly smile, and his eyes narrowed to stare at me. He spoke gently in Somali before stretching out the water container toward me. I gulped down as much water as I could and passed the goatskin to Yared.

"These men are really kind," I said to Yared, when the man rejoined his companions ahead of us.

"I am sure they will guide us to Djibouti, but once there they will leave us," Yared said.

"What will we do then?" I asked.

"Beth, we can't think about that, we just can't," he said in frustration.

"It's just a day away."

"What is a day away?"

"Djibouti!"

"None of this is making any sense to me—you and I out here all by ourselves with these strangers. Everywhere I look I don't see anything that looks remotely like earth. The land even smells strange. I don't even want to go to this Djibouti," Yared said. He pressed his lips together and clenched his fists and opened them again. The sun shone hard on his forehead and I could see he was perspiring profusely. He looked very dark and skinnier than ever, and all his energy seemed to be directed at moving one foot in front of the other.

I turned to see another Afar walking alongside me. His presence startled me. He was heavily armed, with the Afar knife at his waist and a Kalashnikov slung over his right shoulder; his face was dark and lean. I couldn't tell his age. He wore a red and white cotton cloth wrapped around his head, his shirt was brown with white stripes, his sarong was multicoloured, orange, blue, and grey. I quickly moved closer to Yared, avoiding any eye contact with the man. He came closer and stared at us. Yared put himself between me and the man so the man couldn't stare at me. Just when he was starting to speak to Yared in Somali we heard several gunshots. The Afar abandoned us and rejoined the caravan.

"I wonder if they were firing at birds, because I don't see anything," Yared said. Then he added, "I don't trust anybody in this desert. Just stay close to me."

Late in the afternoon, the camels stopped abruptly. The men gathered together and talked. I couldn't believe my eyes when I saw the man who was supposed to have stayed behind with my family among them. I searched for Abba, Meskerem, and Asrat, but I couldn't see them.

"Where are they? Do you see them?" I asked Yared urgently.

"No."

We went to the man and asked him where our family was. He stood up, tall as a tower, and spoke angrily in Amharic.

"They are resting."

He turned around and joined his companions. Yared and I felt relieved and Yared smiled. But, where were they resting? The man didn't tell us.

"At least they are okay," Yared said.

The caravan began moving. I could not understand why the man who spoke Oromiffia was walking with us when he was supposed to be with my family. Something must have gone wrong. I also felt tired, but if I stopped walking I knew they would continue without me.

When the sun dipped beyond the horizon, we approached a large volcanic rock. From a distance, it resembled a whale on the plane of a shimmering sea, scuffling to swallow an ostrich, but when we got nearer, its bronze outer body looked jagged and its centre smooth and black. It was right here that we camped for dinner.

The man who spoke Oromiffia began stuffing a small pot with the dinner leftovers. The precious food dripped down the sides of the pot beyond retrieval and fell in the dirt. He continued to fork the mushy mixture with his fingers.

"Look at his fingers," Yared said casually.

My eyes popped when I saw them bending forward, backward, and sideways as if they were made of fishbone.

Suddenly he sprang to his feet and leaped forward to where my brother and I were sitting. He could have heard us. With a serious look on his face, he directed us to look where he was pointing. Even though the hand stretched to the east, his forefinger curved up, pointing to the sky.

"They'll need this food," he said in Amharic, heading off in that direction.

"He is going back to Abba!" I shouted with joy.

"We should go back with him," Yared said. "They will be happy to see us."

Yared cautioned that Abba might get upset. But we galloped ahead to catch up with the guide. When he saw us behind him he stopped and motioned to us with the hand holding the food to turn back, but we kept following him.

He shouted in a broken Amharic, "Why are you following me?"

We had to think fast.

"We don't want to go to Djibouti. We want to be with our family," Yared said.

"Don't follow me."

"What should we do?" I cried to Yared. "I don't want to go to Djibouti. What would we do there by ourselves? Maybe one of us should go—he won't be angry with me."

I had been the only girl in the family for a long time and Abba constantly instructed my brothers to be nice to me. I often got to sit in the front of our car, I could have two desserts, and I could get anything else if I begged for it. With this assurance, I followed the man with the strange fingers.

Yared stayed with the caravan.

"Don't lose him," he shouted, "stay behind him."

The man was walking fast. When he turned around and saw me

following him, he yelled at me in Afar and I stopped, shaken, but he didn't chase me away. He turned around and moved on. I continued to follow him.

I hadn't expected that it would get pitch dark so soon. I was scared, more scared than I had ever been. The night was filled with the familiar insect noises and the grunting of animals, sounding nearer than they'd been before. My ears picked up an unusual thud, the sound of a drumbeat over my head. When I looked up I saw hundreds of small black birds flying erratically, as if their nests had been robbed. I then tripped over something, lost my balance, and plummeted down to the ground. I jumped up quickly. I had not noticed the birds before and I was overwhelmed with fear, not because they could attack me but because they could be bats. If they were bats, I would be doomed. We were told as children that if a bat flew directly over your head it was bad luck, and this was not just one bat, but hundreds. I tried to protect myself by covering my head with my dress. I was shivering and I couldn't stop. I knew that Abba would be upset that I had not stayed with Yared. I felt my face and ears getting hotter as I moved my feet quickly to keep up, but I stumbled and fell again on my face. Before I realized, the man was right there, pulling at my hand, helping me to get up.

I hadn't noticed the dark clouds that hung above the swarming bats until I was slapped with large raindrops. The warm sensation of the water soothed my burning body. Then the man unfolded a piece of cow skin from his bag and put it over my head like an umbrella, saying, "Hold it like this." It covered my head and shoulders. Even after the rain stopped, I continued to hold onto the cow skin like a shawl. I noticed that the bats were gone.

The man stopped to look at the stars from time to time, but he was growing impatient. He raised both his hands to the sky and dropped them again. He was looking for the star that I had seen before at the oasis. And then there it was. He saw it, too. After that, the star was always ahead of us and to the right.

I sensed that the man was looking for my family. They were not where he had left them. We walked in circles for several minutes, but saw no sign of them. We settled for the night in an area that was flat. I knew that my family was somewhere nearby and in a few hours we would find them. I prayed for God to reunite me with them. I thought of Abba. I appreciated him for not escaping from Ethiopia without us and for picking this desert route and not the forest. Had we travelled along the Kenya border and wandered for as long as we had, we would have been eaten by lions or attacked by other animals.

The man didn't make me walk any faster than I could. Soon he sat down and untied the water container from his waist and gave me some to drink. Then we rested. In my loneliness that night, I realized that I had had everything when I thought I had nothing. My family was everything. My fear was intense, as I imagined the horrible things that could happen. The only salvation I had was sleep. I just wanted to sleep away the scary night and wake up to the morning.

The morning was cold and I felt damp from the night's rain. The slightest breeze made me shiver. I jumped up, looking for the man and saw him walking a distance away from me. I raced, abandoning the cow-skin blanket I had found myself in, to catch up to him.

He had a folded mat in his hands and said, "I'm going to pray. Stay here." His voice was gentle, almost musical, enough for me to trust him. I sat down but still ready to sprint like a cheetah if he went away too far. He rolled up his sarong above his knees and sat down, then poured water over his head and washed his hands and feet. He rolled out his mat to pray.

Later, trailing behind him, I asked, "Where is my family?"

He spun around. His face was unusually thin and it was tense as he shouted in reply, "I am looking for them!"

Why, all of a sudden, was he mean to me? He continued walking and began humming.

"But you speak Amharic," I insisted.

"Be quiet!" he shouted back in Amharic and continued humming.

It was a relief to hear him humming, however, because I figured he would not be doing so if we were in a bad situation. This lifted my spirits.

I started chanting, choosing a melody that was on the music charts for a long time when we lived in Jimma: "My neighbour's a beautiful girl, my city's Addis Ababa," the song went. Was it a song about Addis Ababa or about the beautiful girl? I was three when we moved from Addis to Jimma. I liked Jimma a lot, but many things I heard about Addis made me proud to be from there. I told my friends in Jimma, "We have bigger streets in Addis Ababa." And when I heard about the cinemas in Addis, I told my friends about them as if I had actually gone to the movies myself. And there were definitely more cars in Addis than in Jimma.

But these thoughts stirred up my emotions and once again warm tears ran down my cheeks.

———◆◆———

We soon caught up with another group of traders. Their caravan consisted of six camels and three men in turbans. I stood behind my guide and peeked to see if my family was among them. They were not. The others conversed with the man and glanced at me from time to time. Soon they moved on in one direction and we in another.

We stopped to eat rice porridge. As I was munching, the wind became strong and dumped sand in my food and blew it into my eyes. It became necessary to gulp down the food as quickly as possible before the meal turned into dirt. I heard the man's voice. He was already up and walking. I tried to follow him, but I could not see where I was going through the clouds of sand. The man turned and grabbed my hand and pulled me along and I trotted beside him.

We came up to another caravan, which was a sure sign that we were near Djibouti. There were two men and an older woman wearing a long Somali dress. They all seemed to be in a rush. It was a long caravan. The man let go of my hand and went to help load the caravan and I found myself standing next to the old woman. Her face was a soft brown and looked as though she used a special oil.

I thought we had arrived in Djibouti, but I was not quite sure where Ethiopia ended and Djibouti began. I picked up some sand and poured it down on the ground and asked the woman, "Djibouti?"

She glared at me for a minute, and I repeated my question. "Does this sand belong to Djibouti?"

She smiled and spoke to me gently in her language. But the next thing I knew the earth had turned upside down and I found myself caught in a spiralling dust storm. I could see nothing. I felt a tight grip on my hand, a force pulled me down to the ground. Sitting down, I covered my face with my dress, my head between my knees. The storm went on for what seemed like forever. I stayed motionless, the tight grip of the hand on me. My nose and ears were plugged with sand and hot desert air.

Finally I felt hands removing the dust from me. When I lifted my head up and opened my eyes, I could see nothing. I rubbed my eyes over and over, but it was no good as my hands were dirty and made things worse. My eyes burned as if someone had put hot pepper in them, and I began to cry. I felt some relief when my tears washed out some of the dirt. Moments later I could see the blurry figure of the old woman standing next to me, but I couldn't get up. When I tried to move, my legs felt limp, all the energy had been drained out of me. And then I realized that I was buried from the waist down, my legs were stuck deep in the sand.

With the help of the old woman, I released myself and removed the dust from my dress. Suddenly I remembered where I was, and I was overwhelmed with fear. Frantically, I ran in search of the man I had come with. I saw the camels, and some of the men, but with their hair covered with sand, they all looked alike. They were fixing their loads. I ran from one man to another and looked at each one carefully. I realized that unless he recognized me, it would be impossible to find him on my own. I seemed invisible to them, because no one paid attention to me as they continued fixing their turbans and tending to the camels, eager to get going. And then I saw a smaller figure running towards me. At first I thought it was the man, but as he came nearer, he looked thinner and shorter. It was my brother Yared. I thought I was dreaming. It had been only one night since we separated, but it felt like years. He slowed down when he saw me. I felt God had sent an angel.

"I wasn't sure if it was you," he said. "From a distance, your figure looked very small, and I prayed that it would be you."

I cried. "It was a scary night, darker than all the other desert nights. It rained and rained and the man didn't want to talk to me and there were bats."

"When you didn't come back, I got scared. I blamed myself for letting you go and I regretted it. Next time, no matter what, we should never separate."

All of a sudden I was filled with energy; I thought I could walk to Djibouti and back again. So when the caravan began moving, I was marching right along with everyone else. The wind had ceased and the ground was covered with fresh, unmarked sand, making it look incredibly flat. It looked as though no one had ever walked on it before, and we had just witnessed the birth of a new earth.

I soon spotted the man I was looking for walking with the caravan. It seemed that he had given up the search for Abba, Meskerem, and Asrat. How were they going to arrive in Djibouti on their own, especially since the trails they were to follow had completely been wiped out?

Night had fallen and we still had not arrived in Djibouti. The men began unloading the camels for yet another night in the desert.

The next morning we rose with the sun. We ate a good breakfast, which included the sweet and spicy tea, which Yared and I called the caravan tea. I had watched it being prepared several times to see what went in it. While the water was boiling, fresh ginger was added, followed by loose tea, cinnamon sticks, lots of sugar, and dried peppermint leaves. The tea filled me with energy and was more a dessert than a tea. No tea would ever taste the same because it would miss the main ingredient—the desert water pulled out from under the sand and stored in goatskin.

The camels were loaded unusually quickly, and we resumed our journey. The landscape had changed dramatically. There were endless piles of small, round volcanic pebbles, looking like shiny flat marbles arranged in perfect order, sometimes resembling little tables, and under the sun they reflected the colours of the rainbow. I walked in awe of this beauty, thinking that this would be the last time I was seeing it. The flat desert and the wonders of the landscape preoccupied me for a while, but soon the piles of pebbles were behind us. There were now larger rocks and the land was difficult to negotiate. My shoes slid on the rocks, twisting my ankles more times than I can remember. The camels were not spared as they stumbled over big rocks, the soles of their feet toiling against the hard surfaces.

The caravan jogged along as fast as before, regardless of the conditions, and Yared and I kept up with it. I had developed a scheme that I introduced to Yared in order that we should not lose each other again. We would trail under the shadow of every single camel until the last one, then we would scramble our way back to the lead camel and begin again. After several miles of this, one of the men approached us. He stopped and pointed, directing us to walk in that direction. The caravan itself was headed in the opposite direction.

"Djibouti," he said.

Just like that. Yared and I had reached Djibouti.

Borderline

———————◆———————

"DJIBOUTI! DJIBOUTI!" HE REPEATED from a distance and left with the caravan.

"How come they are walking in the opposite direction?" I asked Yared.

"I don't know."

We felt abandoned and vulnerable without food and water, but to our relief, as we squinted into the distance, we saw the blurry movement of people. Two women and two men waited for us to join them. The women had freshly braided hair and their clothes were pristine. To our great surprise, they were Ethiopians and spoke perfect Amharic. They looked older than us, and maybe were in their early twenties. They sensed right away that something was not right with us. We did not look like desert dwellers.

"My name is Foad," said one of the men. "And this is Kassim, this is Zeynab, and she is Nora."

We introduced ourselves.

Foad had a twinkle in his eyes that attracted my attention right away. He was almost as tall as Yared.

"You look like you escaped on your own. Did you?" he said

with astonishment.

They were Muslim Ethiopians from Dire Dawa and had been involved in a student political movement there. They had run away from the Red Terror after their friends were detained. It was not only in Addis Ababa that there was repression, throughout the country young people were being tortured, locked away, and killed for one reason or another.

"Do you know what to say to the officials?" Foad asked.

"We will tell them what happened to us," Yared replied truthfully.

"Don't tell them that you thought this was a vacation," Foad said with a smile.

The others laughed too. Foad was a bit chubbier and had a dimple when he smiled. Looking at him, I became aware of what attracted my attention to his eyes. Under both eyes he had scars in the shape of tears, their precise matching shapes suggesting that they were tribe marks. I had known people in Addis Ababa from different regions of Ethiopia, bearing traditional cuts above their eyes and ears. But I had never seen cuts under the eyes.

"What should we tell them?" I asked.

"You want to convince them that they should let you stay in their country. So you have to tell them that you and your family feared for your lives and if you go back to Ethiopia, you will be killed."

How could we, a fourteen-year-old girl and an eighteen-year-old boy, convince the representatives of another nation, standing on their sand, that the Derg would kill us if they deported us? What stories would we tell?

"Tell them your parents died in the desert," Kassim volunteered a solution.

It was the wrong thing to say.

"They are not dead," Yared said emphatically, glaring at him.

"I know that. I was just trying to help you."

Yared and I quickly tried to rehearse a better story. We went back and forth with different ideas. I suggested that since the Derg had killed Emperor Haile Selassie, the King of Kings, the most respected person in Ethiopia, they would be capable of killing children as well.

Yared said my idea was not convincing because they detained Haile Selassie after they overthrew him in 1974, and he died in 1979, and still no one was certain how he died. The military hadn't reported that they had killed him.

"What about all the gunshots we heard day and night? A stray bullet could easily have killed us." The conversation with Foad and his friends had given me permission to keep talking about the situation in Ethiopia without fear.

I recalled an afternoon in Addis Ababa when, as I was listening to the Amharic music countdown on the radio, I heard gunshots close enough to be in our backyard. I turned the volume down. When all was quiet, I crept outside, careful to stay within the fence. There I heard a woman's high-pitched voice, "My son, my son," followed by uncontrollable wailing. I usually stayed inside during gunfire but the woman's cry was so wrenching that I could not ignore her. Nervously I opened the gate and stepped outside. A small crowd had gathered around the woman. She was holding her head with both hands and shaking violently as she continued to scream. "They killed my son, these *buda*! Oh, my Lord! . . . " A man had his hand on her shoulder and was telling her not to get herself killed by calling the government *buda*.

"They're listening. It is best not to call them evil. Please, please, be quiet. Your other children need you."

The woman looked familiar, but I didn't dare push through the crowd to find out who was lying dead, the gravel road soaking his blood. I went back inside.

I recalled the mass executions of November 1974, a few days after the Derg overthrew the emperor. Derg soldiers had executed former government ministers, high-ranking officials, and military personnel, including the Oxford-educated prime minister, Endalkatchew Makonnen. The Derg replaced him with General Aman Andom overnight. If ever there was a way to shatter the spirit of an entire nation, this was it.

This was five years ago, I was nine, and I remember exactly where I was when we heard the news over the radio. At the breakfast table, shafts of sunlight poured in through the window where Abba sat at the head, my two brothers to his left, and I on the right. It was one of those rare and happy moments because Abba was home. The announcer read the council's statement between intervals of martial music: "The decision to carry out the executions was one of policy." And something about corruption, bad administration, and officials making themselves rich at the country's expense.

Abba had stopped eating and turned the volume up, and was listening attentively. My brothers and I did not move. It felt as though time stood still as I heard the names of the dead and watched my father's frozen posture. A few minutes later, a startling sound brought me back to myself—the scraping of a chair against the hardwood floor. Abba was at the doorway, on his way out. "Finish your breakfast." And he was gone.

As for Emperor Haile Selassie, the people of Ethiopia would never see him again. Endalkachew Mekonen, among the executed, had attended my parents' wedding, and he was expected to become the next United Nations' Secretary General. He was a favourite relative of my mother, and she risked her life to visit him in jail knowing very well that the Derg had forbidden visitors.

As soon as she learned about his capture, my mother took a taxi to the prison on the outskirts of Addis Ababa where the ministers were being detained. As the taxi approached the compound, ten armed soldiers swiftly surrounded it. One of them shouted, "Did you not know there are no visitors allowed?" My mother replied, "No." Then they said, "We will let you see him, but if you ever come back again you will be in great danger." They led her in front of a closed window and once it was fully opened, she saw Endalkachew

Mekonen in dirty brown pyjamas looking at her with a pleasant smile. He requested a pen and paper and wrote a note to her, which all ten soldiers read before giving it to my mother. The note read, "I may not be able to return this favour, may God bless you."

———◆◆———

Foad and his friends knew a lot more about Djibouti than we did. They had been planning their escape for a long time. They told us that Djibouti's population was only 250,000 while Ethiopia's was 26 million. Djibouti had gained its independence from France in 1977, just two years before. Most Djiboutians were multilingual; they spoke Somali, Afar, French, and Arabic. Foad and Kassim told us about all the things we could do in Djibouti.

"We could work at the railway station; this way we get all the food from home." Kassim said enthusiastically.

He was referring to the Ethiopia-Djibouti railway that gave the countries access to each other's resources. Djibouti received leather goods, fresh fruits and vegetables, and qat, along with other goods. In turn, Ethiopia was given the use of the port on the Red Sea. The railway was completed in 1917, and had been highly successful in its mission.

"It's such a balanced system," Foad said. "As long as they get their tea, Ethiopia will have access to the port." We all laughed. I laughed more in the short time we were with Foad and his friends than in the fourteen days we had spent wandering in the desert.

I looking behind, hoping to see my family, but the sunken plain stretched forever.

"You must not worry," Zeynab said, looking at the desert. "They will arrive soon." She held my hands.

"They are all alone and our father is very sick," I said to her.

"When we last saw him, he couldn't even walk," Yared added.

"I have an idea," Foad said quickly. "Once we clear ourselves and we tell them about your family, we should ask the officers to send someone to find them." Yared and I promptly agreed.

We walked slowly, and thoroughly enjoyed each other's company. As we walked I noticed the ground had more greenery and vegetation and fewer bumpy rocks.

"Look," Kassim said and pointed ahead.

We saw a white watchtower surrounded by a wire fence.

"We've made it, we've made it! We're free to say whatever we want about the Derg." Foad started jumping all over the place and kissing the ground.

His friends joined him in the excitement, kissing the ground and hugging each other. Watching them made me feel alive. I had survived all the elements of the Danakil Desert. What Yared and I had endured was nothing short of a miracle, but I did not kiss the ground.

Foad and his friends darted toward the wire fence and we followed. Inside we saw four men dressed in military uniforms and carrying machine guns. They were seated in the shade of a tree that looked quite out of place; it was huge, and the leaves were dark green. I hadn't seen a tree that big since the oasis. I thought to myself they must water it and shower the dust off its leaves to keep it so clean. I saw a young man singing in a clear voice in Somali, and when he stopped another man took over. I heard the laughter of men in the background. There was nothing threatening about life on the other side of the wire fence.

Inside the fence, built on piles of volcanic rocks, was the watchtower. On each side of the tower were five small white houses. We slowed down and walked closer. When the singing stopped, the men began to converse in French. I did not expect to hear French so soon, but it was a relief, especially from Somali. It made me feel hopeful about our situation.

"Let's go and report ourselves," Foad said.

"What if we did not report?" Yared replied.

"Our guides told us it was best to report,"Nora said. "This way we get permission to enter and they give us a paper, then we can tell any police officer in Djibouti that we were given permission from the border officials to enter."

We followed Foad and approached the gate. Within seconds an officer was standing in front of us, his feet wide apart, his black military boots planted in the sand. His brown uniform was wrinkled from sweat and his cap had the blue and white single-starred flag of Djibouti.

He shouted something to the others and studied us one at a time. Then, putting his finger on the trigger of his rifle, he said loudly in Amharic, "Go back to your country." He shoved Foad with the butt of his rifle.

Foad did something quite unexpected. He fell on his knees and begged. "Kill me if you like, but I can't go back. Please hear our story." The officer kicked him with his boots.

"Get up."

"Sir, please," Foad protested in a weak voice.

Another officer, much taller than this one, came to the scene. He stopped what would have been a severe blow to Foad by reaching out and holding back the arm of his companion. He had a cigarette held between his teeth and a rifle dangling on his side. The other man stepped aside.

Yared and Kassim helped Foad to his feet. I moved closer to Zeynab and Nora. Foad had strength enough to tell his story, which the officers assumed included Yared and me.

We were led into the compound and stood facing the rest of the officers, who were sitting lazily on their chairs, not surprised to see us. Obviously there were other Ethiopians who had arrived before us in the past. At the door of one of the offices, under the shade of a large mimosa tree, we saw about ten or more tired-looking men and women waiting in a line. We were taken to an empty doorless room with an earth floor and brick walls and told to wait there.

While we waited, Foad said, "They are going to keep us here for a while and make us work."

"How do you know?" I asked.

"Our guides told us that may happen, if we are not lucky."

"What kind of work will we do?"

"I don't know. Maybe mop and sweep."

I did not mind working, but how long could they keep us here? They could do anything they chose, even kill us, and no one would know about it. This was an office compound in the middle of nowhere, staffed by armed men, with a thin road that snaked out from the gate to only God knew where.

A large truck loaded with sacks arrived and the driver jumped out. Soon one of the officers brought for us some Somali-style food and a litre of water in a goatskin and told us to eat. I was hungry and we all ate from the same corroded tray that gave the bland rice and sauce a rusty flavour.

"Should we ask them to send help for Abba?" I whispered to Yared.

Before Yared could reply, an officer barged in and snatched the empty tray. "You, you, and you," he ordered, "on your feet, follow me. I have work for you."

Yared, Foad, and Kassim followed the officer to the truck, which stood in the centre of the compound, and were told to unload it. Foad jumped onto the back and began lifting the sacks. He placed one on Yared's shoulders and one on Kassim's. They carried them to one of the empty rooms where they were instructed to store them neatly and bring the rest.

Soon their shirts were drenched with sweat. Stripping off their shirts, their bodies shaking, they continued to carry what must have been seventy pounds of rice and powdered milk on their shoulders, back and forth under the sizzling sun. There were no less than fifty sacks in all. Yared was the tallest and the skinniest. His ribs showed and his body wobbled as if it were about to collapse. I thought to myself that if Abba were here the soldiers would not have made Yared work in the sun like this. The officers were making the boys do their jobs, while they lounged in the shade of the trees, talking in French and singing in Somali, their mouths filled with qat.

They stopped singing and began whispering. It wasn't long

before two of them stood in front of us girls with friendly smiles wide enough to show the green qat in their mouths. One of the men looked at Zeynab and gestured with his head for her to follow him. At first we did not understand his command, but when the second one joined in and spoke to her in Somali, she translated what he said and their intent became clear.

"He is saying they have work for me, but I will not go. I have an idea what they plan to do," she spoke softly in Amharic.

The second man was looking at Nora. Even though they had friendly smiles, their fingers were toying with their rifles.

"He wants Nora to help too, I am calling Foad. Foad! Foad!" Zeynab screamed at the top of her lungs.

Foad was just finishing loading a bag when he heard his name. He looked our way and, suspecting trouble, came running, followed by Kassim. Yared looked my way and then he too was running toward us.

I thought Foad would ask Zeynab why she had called him, but he politely asked one of the soldiers for water. Kassim also pleaded for water.

Yared sat by my side and asked if everything was okay.

"Something is not right. Stay here," I whispered.

Foad and Kassim collapsed next to us from exhaustion and the soldiers had no choice but to go and get us some water.

One of them brought the water and as he began to leave, Foad spoke.

"Excuse me, officer."

The man stopped and turned.

"We've all worked so hard, we are too tired to help you any more. Thank you for letting the girls rest. Would you be kind enough to let us continue with our journey? You don't have to show us the way or give us food and water. We are very grateful for all your help so far."

The man walked away without replying.

Foad had been polite, and Kassim spoke to him angrily. They

began arguing. Yared and I took turns nervously sipping water out of the white jerry can the soldiers had left for us. There came the ongoing chatter of the men under the tree.

Yared was too tired to move and curled up on the floor. I pressed my back against the mud wall and could feel my bones grinding against it as I closed my eyes.

"Beth, Beth," I heard my name and when I opened my eyes I found my face pasted to the earth floor and my lips covered with dirt. I sat up quickly, rubbing my face, and found Yared looking anxiously at me.

"It's morning."

I heard chatting and the sound of trays and pans.

"They are gone," Yared said in a shaky voice.

Zeynab, Nora, Kassim, and Foad were not with us.

We stepped outside. The bright sun was blinding, but once my eyes adjusted to it, I saw that the officer who spoke Amharic was seated on a flat rock washing his feet under the shade of a tree. He was not wearing his military uniform but rather a grey and white sarong and no shirt. Seeing him in bare feet and alone, Yared and I decided to approach him.

"Good morning," Yared got his attention and the officer greeted us.

"Can you help us?" Yared went closer, and I followed.

"What is it?" the man asked, rinsing his mouth and spitting on the ground.

Yared looked at me, surprised that the man was talking to us. "What should I say?"

"Tell him how sick Abba is," I replied quickly.

The officer scooped water with both hands from a big metallic bowl and splashed it on his face. We watched the water run down his hands onto the sand.

Yared told him about our lost family and the officer listened patiently, nodding his head and saying, "Hum, hum" every now and then and rinsing his mouth. When Yared was done, the man said, "I must go pray now." He picked up his folded mat and stood up.

Yared and I had no choice but to head back to the room. I felt discouraged and also angry that we had forgotten this was the prayer time. But at least the man was not mean to us.

Before we reached our room, we heard people talking and headed in their direction. To our surprise we saw Foad, Kassim, Zeynab, and Nora with two officers. The officers didn't seem as authoritative as they were yesterday, and the next thing I knew, our four friends had gotten permission to leave the border and go to Dikhil, where they could obtain papers to stay in Djibouti and passes to go to the capital, which was also called Djibouti. There it was possible to find work or apply to immigrate to the Middle East, Europe, or North America.

They stopped to talk to us.

"I told the officers about your family," Foad said kindly.

"What did they say?" Yared asked.

"They didn't say anything about your family, but they said you could leave with us."

Yared and I hesitated. We were free to go and we even had friends this time. But it was not right. We had to stay and wait for our family. We decided not to go.

Nora spoke to me as they prepared to head off. "Don't separate from your brother," she said in a sharp tone, sounding more like my mother than a person I had met only yesterday.

Before I even had a chance to say "I won't" they set off on their journey. Yared and I watched them, Foad's arm on Zeynab's shoulder, on that thin road that snaked its way to somewhere.

"I am glad we're staying," I said.

"Me, too. I am too tired to walk," Yared replied.

Back in the room, which was not as hot as I had expected, Yared slept on the cool floor, and I decided to stay up and act as guard.

The silence did not last long. I heard fighting. Some Amharic words and Somali words. Yared woke up.

"Are you okay?"

"Yes."

When all was quiet again, we stepped out to look and saw two refugee men limping along the road to the watchtower. I could tell from the blood on their foreheads and their swollen eyes that they had been badly beaten; they looked terribly skeletal and their heads had been shaved.

We heard them whisper in Amharic as they sat outside, close to our room.

"Let's go talk to them," Yared whispered.

They told us they were caught attempting to escape to Dikhil after four days of languishing here.

Their names were Paulos and Mesfin, two friends from a beautiful city in Ethiopia called Debre Zeyet, famous for its fresh fish.

Like Foad and his friends, Paulos and Mesfin were involved with the student movement and had led protests against the Derg throughout the country. They told us it took them only three days to reach the border, but that didn't explain their skeletal look and shaved heads.

"You've got to be crazy. You want to wait for your family here?" Mesfin was shocked when we told him. "You can't trust these people, they will have you working again tomorrow and drain every bit of energy you've got left, and we know what they could do with a girl like your sister. If you've got a chance to be free, go. Go now."

"Did they shave your heads?" I asked nervously.

Mesfin frowned, looking at his elbow. I noticed it was dripping blood. He grabbed the bottom part of his sarong with one hand and bit a piece of it and tried to tear it, without success. Without hesitation, I ripped a piece of cloth from my shredded dress and gave it to him. Paulos helped tie the cloth around Mesfin's elbow.

"No, they didn't shave my head." Mesfin offered no other explanation.

"No matter how young or how careful you are, you still end up being dragged into politics—because a friend asks you to read a mere flyer, or something," Paulos said.

Paulos was the less bruised one but he had old scars on his face, hands, and legs.

When we saw one of the officers walking toward our room carrying food, we left Paulos and Mesfin and ran to receive our breakfast.

After a few days of waiting at the border, Yared and I became convinced that it was not the best place to wait for our family. We had learned that the road to Dikhil was short, only two hours on foot.

Yared and I chose our freedom and after our breakfast, we thanked the officials and told them we were leaving. We started walking, and they said nothing.

Refugees

———◆●———

A HOT WIND SWEPT THROUGH the valley, sending its red dust high over our heads and exposing the roots of the shrubs. The volcanic rocks of the area felt sharp under our feet.

As hostile as the land seemed, there were small shanty houses along the road. We saw families and children once more, and we felt happy. Within a few hours we were in Dikhil. The outskirts consisted of more shanty houses, densely packed. Yared and I had learned a lot about Dikhil from Foad and his friends. There were three kinds of settlers in Dikhil: those who had come for a short period, those who were planning to move on to the bigger world beyond Djibouti, and the Djiboutians who had jobs and beautifully painted brick houses. Most of those who stayed temporarily were nomads of the Danakil. When the desert became intolerably hot and dry, they moved here, occupying the abandoned shelters and supported by clan members, until they felt the urge to wander again. The permanent residents hosted relatives who came from the capital to buy qat or camels. Sometimes families came to meet eligible men for their daughters. Djibouti was theirs—the language, the religion, the culture, and the tradition—it was where they belonged.

For the time being, Yared and I belonged in the refugee camp, which was located just outside Dikhil. We had managed to make our way to a small tin-roofed shelter. The walls were made from piles of rocks and the floor was earth. The room was bare with no windows, and the entrance had no door. The insistent cries of children pierced through the walls; when one child stopped, another took over. It seemed as though there were more children than adults here.

The camp was clearly overpopulated. Dusty hills stood like walls all around. Rows of tin-roofed shelters with rusted corrugated-aluminium walls stretched out in all directions. Rusty pots and pans were kept outside these homes filled with dusty brown water. It was not only barefoot children who were coming in and out of these shelters, but also sheep and goats.

"I don't hear any dogs barking," Yared said.

"Maybe there are no dogs allowed in Dikhil," I replied.

I remembered Metew. Her name meant "let it be." It was a male dog, but we called it she. My father used to say she was like his fifth child, and yet we had abandoned her without a goodbye. Metew had come to us when she was a puppy, a surprise from my parents. She arrived on the back of a pickup truck, buried among sacks of potato and spices. When the truck stopped, she bounced off onto the green grass. She was a sheepdog, a perfect dog for children growing up in the wilderness of rural Jimma.

Metew and Jimma were happy thoughts. It was the thought of Jimma that made it hard to believe I was actually where I was. Once more I closed my eyes tight and opened them again to see if I would wake up from a nightmare. Had I ever lived in Jimma, the name synonymous with rainforest, where coffee, sunflowers, and bananas, pineapples, strawberries, and oranges grew wild? Everywhere you looked you saw light green, darker greens, and then richer greens.

"What do you think happened to Metew?" I asked Yared.

"Maybe Mamma Tiruye will keep her. But I know for sure she will miss us."

When I closed my eyes, all I could picture was life in Jimma and when I shut my ears I could hear the tat-tat sounds of fresh coffee roasting.

A rock protruding from the wall I was leaning against hurt my side and called me back to reality. I wished I were anywhere else. Even the warm soft sands of the desert floor had been more comfortable, and the air was much sweeter. Tears came to my eyes, and I wept.

"Let's try and sleep. Tomorrow morning we will look for the local market."

Sleep made me forget my hunger, but the heat inside the shelter was unbearable, so Yared and I decided to sleep outside.

The next day, when I opened my eyes, I saw a sheep's legs near my face. I saw more sheep in our shelter. Yared stood up and cuffed and pushed them out one by one. Somali children and women with squirming faces were saying something, but I heard only *"dilo, dilo"* as they passed by our dwelling. I could tell they did not like us.

We left the shelter in search of the market, not giving the rest of our neighbours a chance to wake up and repeat *"dilo, dilo."* We had not walked very far when we heard someone calling us: "Yared, Yared!" We turned around and saw Foad.

"When did you leave?" He asked, evidently happy to see us.

"Yesterday. Where are the rest of your friends?"

"Remember I was telling you about a family friend who had a shop at the market? Well, I found him. But his shop is his home because he is always on the road with a caravan. His family lives in Dire Dawa. He has room for just one extra person, and I sleep in the shop for now, but my friends are staying with his aunt. Nora and Zeynab will probably work there, as the aunt has three small children and is pregnant. Kassim doesn't want to stay, but he has no choice for now."

"Where do you get your food?" I asked.

"Oh, the food is free. The line-up is long, though, unless you go early in the morning."

"How come it is free?"

"Because it is for refugees like us. It comes from the United Nations." It was a relief to know that we would not starve to death. And we didn't have to work for the food or do anything. All we had to do was line up to receive our ration of powdered milk and rice. "The food you receive is based on your family size," Foad explained. He promised to take us to the United Nations office the next day.

The last time I had heard about the United Nations was when my uncle left for Paris with his family to work for it and we had all gone to the airport to say goodbye.

There was a long line of people waiting at the UN office the next morning. Most were Ethiopians, the rest Somalis. When our turn came we registered our names and said that our parents and brother were on their way. The officers were Djiboutians and spoke Amharic. They told us that they had to be registered once they arrived, meanwhile we received a sack of rice and powdered milk. The white sack of rice and the brown bag of powdered milk were marked with the letters UN in blue.

A chaotic market was the centre of Dikhil. Today it was market day. We had to ask what day of the week it was and learned that it was Tuesday. The Afars called the market day "Talayto." In a large city like Dikhil, the Afars came to sell their cattle. In a village, the Afars would trade in smaller items like salt, corn, dates, handwoven baskets, grinding stones, and spices.

Long colourful Arabian-style print dresses, the kind worn by every woman in Dikhil, were on display by the hundreds. I was still wearing what I'd worn for fourteen days in the desert, a miniskirt, a shirt, and my blue-and-white Adidas. No one would believe that my skirt was once bright orange and my shirt yellow. I had washed them every time I had the chance, in the water holes dug by the caravan men. But with every wash, they turned a deeper brown. It would have been nice to own one of those long Arab dresses.

There were all kinds of spices on sale—red and black pepper, turmeric, coriander, chillies, cinnamon—and each portion for sale was measured with a small white *ciene* (coffee cup). The smell of spices permeated the air, causing me to sneeze from time to time.

I heard the sounds of camels, and my attention shifted to a corner of the market where five or six caravans with about thirty camels had gathered. They had customers, all men, who had their hands stretched out to receive the freshest qat. This green-leaved, short thin branch was the source of life, it seemed. Each buyer walked away with a bundle of qat in one hand and a box of Marlborough cigarettes in the other, all the while muttering something in a language I did not understand.

Rhoda of Dikhil

———————◀◆▶———————

The tastiest food is the one you eat when you are hungry.
—AFAR PROVERB

AND THEN, THROUGH ALL the noise of the busy market, I heard a word I recognized.

"Selam."

I turned quickly and saw a young woman who was perhaps three or four years older than me. She was beautifully dressed and strikingly beautiful. She wore dark eyeliner and a deep plum-coloured lipstick.

"Selam," I greeted her, surprised.

"Are you here to look for work?"

"Work?"

"I can tell from the way you are dressed that you are not from Dikhil."

I turned to look for Yared. He had found some boxes and was carefully flattening them with his shoes. He stood out like a mushroom in a field of grass, the only one in the market with an Afro, and I noticed some boys watching him from a distance.

"I have come from Ethiopia and this is my brother, Yared," I said.

I noticed that she had pulled an edge of her dress up and held it under one arm so it wouldn't drag. It was bright purple with a floral print all over. She was holding a small, brown leather bag in her other, henna-decorated hand, and the multicolour beaded necklace she wore looked as though she had made it herself.

"I was born in Ethiopia, too. My father is an Ethiopian Afar and my mother is Djiboutian. My name is Rhoda. What's yours?"

"Beth." As soon as I said it, I realized that I might have made a mistake. Abba had instructed us to use Muslim names. What if she did not like highlanders?

"I came to Dikhil two years ago looking for work. I work for a veterinarian," she continued, paying no attention to my nervousness.

"Why did you come to Dikhil?" Rhoda asked, looking at the dusty collapsed boxes Yared was holding.

"We had to run away from the fighting in Ethiopia," Yared said.

We told her the whole story of our escape and our father falling ill, and our experiences with our guides. How it had taken us fourteen days to reach Dikhil.

"You are very lucky to be alive," Rhoda said, as she wiped sweat from her face. "That desert is the gate to hell for anyone, let alone children like you."

Two women, whose faces were masked under a yellow cream-like paste, passed us with a small child. The child's eyes were fixed on Yared's Afro. I had seen other women wearing the same yellow cream earlier.

"Do you know where we can get help for our family?" Yared asked.

Rhoda replied forcefully, *"Allah argae."* In the Afar language, "God knows." Yared and I had already informed the people at the UN office about our family, but they didn't seem to care. They considered us fortunate to have been allowed into Dikhil in the first place and to be given food.

"Our father was a very important official in Ethiopia and he has good connections. Once he gets here, he will pay anyone who can help him," Yared said to Rhoda.

"But I don't know anyone who would set a foot in that land of fire to go and rescue him. You need a supply of camels, food, and water. Besides, it is full of *waraba*, you would need an army, and that still won't be enough," Rhoda replied, looking sympathetic. "What about you? Where are you staying?"

We told Rhoda about our shelter.

"There are no showers there. You can get sick from all the stink," she said with a look of disgust.

"There are no mattresses, either," Yared said, bending down to organize the card boxes he had crushed.

I saw Rhoda staring at Yared's hair. His Afro attracted the attention of the local Muslim men and women, most of whom covered their hair. And now I noticed that it was filled with dirt and probably hosting living things as well. I wished he could get a haircut somewhere.

"Would you like to come to my house to shower and wash your clothes?" Rhoda asked, removing a straw from my hair.

I was thrilled. I could not believe our luck, that on our first day in Dikhil we would meet such a nice person.

"How far is your house?" Yared asked. "We don't want to be too far from the border."

"It's very close. Did you see the school on the way here? It's next to the school."

I did not remember seeing a school, but we trusted her. Before we left, Rhoda stopped to pick up some fresh vegetables, a brown square of heavy Afar bread she called *gaanbo*, and some fresh jumbo.

"The *gaanbo*, the dates, and vegetables are very fresh on market day; other days, they sell leftovers," she said as she stuffed her basket with the purchases.

We walked with her through the city centre, past a police station, and a row of nicely landscaped white houses. This was the other side of Dikhil, where the rich people lived.

Rhoda worked in one of these clean white houses. The man she worked for, Ali Wollao, was a Djibouti Afar. Rhoda informed us that about forty-five percent of all Djiboutian were Afar, with links to Ethiopia, and about fifty percent were ethnic Issas with links to Somalia. The rest were French, Arab, and others. The Afars occupied the northern part of the country while the Issas dominated the south. I thought that if Rhoda were stranded in Addis Ababa and I had met her on the street there, I would not have stopped to talk to her. I would have been too busy playing with my friends to notice that she was in need of help.

"This is like my own house. Ali Wollao is away most of the time and I can do anything I want," she said as she took out her key and opened the door. Yared and I had not been inside a real house since we left Ethiopia. We followed her into a dark room that felt strange and eerie, like a cave with a high roof. It was quiet and the air seemed laden with the smell of wet animal skin.

"I keep all the windows shut to cool the rooms. Come in."

She walked hurriedly to a side of the room and opened the shade. I felt the sweat on my body dry away as the air-conditioning cooled my skin. I took in a long, deep breath. We were in a living room with bare walls. There was a mattress in one corner, and a colourful Arabian mat surrounded by colourful cushions was spread out in the centre. From where I stood I could see the kitchen, which had a two-burner gas stove and a chair.

It was afternoon. Rhoda said we should wait until sundown to take our shower, when the water would be cool enough to use. I could see the glaring sun off a roof, beating down on the tar, but not on us for a change. We sat on the bare cement floor, which was much cooler than the room itself, and would be even cooler at night.

A little later, Rhoda came from the kitchen carrying a large tray. She placed it carefully on the floor. I'd never seen a dish of spaghetti served in such a chaotic manner. The noodles were topped with large chunks of kidney meat, yoghurt, cinnamon sticks, and cardamom seeds, all afloat on a red tomato sauce. The strong aroma made my mouth water. I swallowed hard.

"What are you waiting for? Eat," Rhoda instructed as she sat down.

"Okay," we obeyed, not daring to ask for forks.

I was hungry enough to eat the spaghetti with my fingers, but we were eating from the same tray and Rhoda was sitting across from me. I was afraid of making a mess. I noticed Yared also hesitating.

"You just hold the spaghetti with your fingers and twist it between your little finger and thumb until there is nothing dangling and then eat it. Like this." Rhoda demonstrated. The sauce was dripping between her fingers, but she managed to get the food in her mouth and lick the sauce afterward.

Yared and I reached for the food.

Rhoda paused to take a look at me and Yared enjoying her food, filling our empty stomachs hurriedly.

"Do you know what the Afar people think is the tastiest food?" Rhoda asked.

We didn't know.

"It is the one you eat when you are hungry," she answered.

As we were eating, we heard the sound of school children, chirping like birds. It was early for school to be out, I thought.

"Did you go to school in Addis Ababa?" Rhoda asked.

"I was in grade eleven and Beth in grade eight."

"The schools in Dikhil are for boys only. There are French schools in the city of Djibouti where girls are allowed in."

"We don't plan to stay in Dikhil," Yared replied defensively. "Once we are reunited with our family, I am sure we will continue with our education."

"Don't you want to go to school?" I asked Rhoda.

"I have to work and send money to my mother. When I marry and settle down, I will bring her to live with me."

I wanted to ask her where her father was, but instead I asked her something else.

"Do you speak Somali?"

"Yes. Everybody speaks Somali here."

"What does *dilo* mean?"

Rhoda looked shocked. "Where did you hear that?" she asked with a scowl.

"The people at the refugee camp were saying '*dilo*, *dilo*' as they passed by us."

"Those people are mean to strangers."

"But what does it mean?" Yared insisted.

"It means prostitute in the Somali language, but don't let it bother you."

"Why would they call us that?" I asked.

"Because of the way you are dressed. The women here don't show their legs; Dikhil is very different from the desert in how women are dressed. In the desert, the women wear almost whatever they wish, but here it is expected that women wear long dresses." She picked up the tray and left for the kitchen.

I decided I didn't want to go outside dressed the way I was.

Rhoda quickly emerged with another large tray. What I saw in her hands could only have been sent from God. The sight has been etched in my memory for all time. Three large glasses of water, each packed with ice cubes. As I placed my fingers on the cool moist glass, a chilling sensation travelled through me straight to my heart. This was the moment I had dreamt about many times in the desert. With the first gulp of the water, I knew that sometimes dreams do come true even if in the most desolate of places. Moments later, big Ausa dates were placed before us. I tasted one, and it was the sweetest thing I had ever put into my mouth.

Rhoda said we could come to her house to eat or take a shower whenever we wished.

"Ali Wollao won't be back from his business trip for two days. You can come here anytime you want. I will ask him if he can help you," she offered.

I trusted Rhoda, perhaps because she was an Ethiopian and spoke to me in Amharic and knew about our customs, and also because we were close in age. We had nothing to give her in return for her kindness, so the same question kept popping into my head: Why was she so generous to us? Our experiences in the desert had made me too suspicious.

"Do you know how we can get our father to a hospital when he comes?" Yared asked.

Rhoda said Ali Wollao knew a French doctor in Dikhil. We should bring Abba to Ali Wollao.

She prepared a place for us on the floor to take a nap until the water was cool enough for showering. Yared said he wanted to meet Foad again in the market, because Foad had relatives who knew a lot about Djibouti. It was just like Yared to want to hang out in the city, but I didn't want to be separated from him for even a minute.

"You won't find anyone in this heat. You should rest and wait until sundown," Rhoda said.

Yared was restless, feeling perhaps that if we stayed indoors we would miss the arrival of our family; and I was thinking that if Rhoda was the Derg's spy it would give her time to notify them and capture us. So we decided to go.

We had taken not even a step outside the air-conditioned room when we were engulfed by a thick wave of heat; moments later I was already drenched in sweat. Yared's T-shirt was pasted to his body. The streets were deserted. The market was empty and the city silent. It was the quietest time of the day, when every living soul took to the shade. Empty bottles littered the streets, having melted and moulded into abstract art; insects that once buzzed in our faces now crawled on the dirt road; policemen sat on their station veranda, their shirts unbuttoned all the way down.

"I think we should go back," Yared suggested. And so we did.

In the evening we lined up to take our showers. Yared went in first. Rhoda had already prepared one of Ali's clean sarongs for him. For me she brought out a long Arabian-style dress, its colour bright orange as the sun. Since the dress was thin, she gave me an under-garment to cover my body from the waist down.

Yared came out looking like a different person, clean and light skinned. I took my new garments and headed for the washroom. It had a stand-in shower and the walls were grey cement. When I felt the first splash of water run down my skin, I felt so relaxed that I didn't want to come out. I changed my clothes for the first time in weeks. My head felt light, and I was certain that if Abba and Asrat saw Yared and me now, they wouldn't recognize us. Wearing Rhoda's clothes, I looked like one of the local girls. After I was dressed, Rhoda soaked my hair in rosemary oil and braided it such that it looked like the rope the caravan men had used to tie the camels' mouths.

"Next time I will give you something that you put on your face and it will make you more beautiful," Rhoda promised.

———— ◆•◆ ————

It was a magnificent morning with a warm sun kissing our skin. If I closed my eyes, I could pretend I was in a sandhill fortress, my home perched above a beautiful stream abounding in black diamond, dark purple, and orange volcanic stones. We could collect them and dec-orate the entrance to our home. The sparkling pebbles would make it seem that the house was made of precious stones. We might even name it The Palace. Yared and I, the inhabitants, were descendants of the great traveller of the Danakil Desert, Terrefe Asrat. The Palace was our reward for enduring our hardships.

The reality was that our shelter was stuck on a bare hillside, on a dust road leading to a narrow meandering stream that trickled its way down between volcanic rocks. The other refugees, our neigh-bours, trespassed on our property to reach its banks, and thus the whole camp knew about us within a day.

Neither Yared nor I were eager to boil plain rice for breakfast and so we sat outside, with the sun on our faces, watching the pass-ersby. Mostly women and children went to the stream, and some of them stopped to talk to us in Somali. Dressing like the locals had made us more approachable. Two women had tried to speak to us in a halting Amharic, but what shocked me was that they made a reference to our family.

"You will have your father," one of them predicted.

"They all know about us," Yared said after the two women were gone.

We inched our way down the hill and immersed our feet in the trickling stream. It was surprisingly clean and soothingly warm when I splashed it on my face. I took in a deep breath. Reassured that there were no crocodiles in it, I walked in further and washed my arms. We could bathe there just like the others.

"I doubt if there are any fish here." Yared bent down and looked closely at the water.

Eating fish was a luxury. During our vacation in Abaya, Yared went fishing every day and we sometimes ate fish twice a day—Nile perch, cod, tilapia. But now, white rice and powdered milk was our diet. If I had magical powers, I would turn the sack full of rice into a catch of fresh fish.

◆

On our sixth morning in Dikhil, I woke up to see a goat nibbling on my cardboard mat right under my nose. Yared and I were now used to sleeping on flattened boxes, which were much more comfortable than the rocky sand floors on which others slept in the refugee camp. We even found that a smooth rock could be a pillow if placed under the cardboard in the right position. The only problem was that every morning we had to wake up before the goats and sheep were let loose, and hide our cardboard bedding before they ate it.

That morning, having no plan, we decided to stay in our shelter until the afternoon, when we would go to Rhoda's for our showers and naps. However, our day of rest was transformed when we heard a soft voice at our entrance. An old man appeared at the door and said in a low tone in broken Amharic, "Your family is here." He added after a moment's pause, "They are resting by the hill at the outskirts of the houses."

"They are here, they are here!" Yared exclaimed and sprang to his feet. My heart pounding, I bolted out the door after Yared, leaving the old man behind. "Abba has made it! Meskerem and Asrat too!" I screeched, running after Yared, until my eyes blurred with tears. We arrived at the edge of the refugee camp and stopped. At the bend in the road as it passed the last house, we saw some children staring at us. We approached them hoping to find an adult who spoke Amharic and were stunned to see the same old man who had informed us about the arrival of our family. With him were gathered a few people.

"How did he get here before us?" Yared wondered aloud.

"Maybe he took a short cut, but let's ask him where they are," I said, going closer to the man.

As we approached him, to our great surprise, we saw that in the midst of the small gathering were Asrat and Meskerem. Abba was not there. My knees were giving out but somehow I managed to go forward and embrace Asrat and Meskerem. "Where is Abba?" I asked.

"He is right there," Meskerem said, pointing toward a tree. "Let's go. He'll be happy when he sees you."

I almost didn't recognize my father, who was resting with his back against the trunk of the tree. His face had collapsed into a Danakil depression. His brown skin had turned black and was wrinkled like a dying leaf. He had been given water. We approached carefully.

"Abba," I whispered. When he opened his eyes and saw us, his face lit up.

"There you are. My children." Tears filled his eyes.

I fell into his shaky arms and cried some more. I pulled back just to look at him and see if it was all real. Abba was not wearing his shirt and I could see the sweat running down his body. I noticed something just under his ribs when he stretched out his arms to hug Yared.

"The soldiers at the border said they were expecting us because of what you told them."

"Were they nice to you?" Yared asked.

"When they saw how sick Abba was, they let him rest with Meskerem, but they gave me some work," Asrat replied.

"Look how clean you two look," Meskerem remarked, smiling at Yared and me.

I couldn't say the same about her or my father or Asrat. They had been in the desert six days longer. Asrat seemed to have lost half his weight. Yared was two years older than Asrat, but they were almost the same height. They stood side by side, comparing their Afros.

I was disturbed about what I had seen at the base of Abba's torso—a small dark circle big enough to put your little finger in. A bullet, I thought, must have gone clean through, a long time ago. Had he kept that a secret?

Meskerem looked a lot shorter and much darker than I remembered her. I sensed that something was wrong with her. Did Abba know? I stole a second look at her and our eyes met.

"Are you guys going to take us to your shelter?" she asked.

"The Palace," I said, and everyone laughed.

The sun was getting hot and the tree, with its diaphanous shade, was not enough protection for everyone, so it was time to head on, much to the disappointment of the people who were being entertained by our reunion.

A fat oxen or at least a sheep would have been sacrificed for our miraculous reunion if we were in Addis, but Yared and I served overcooked white rice and milk to our family in our shelter. Abba reassured us that since we were all together once again, he felt much better and he promised to get us out of Dikhil. Meskerem explained that Abba had recovered due to the goat soup and camel's milk that a desert dweller from the Issa clan had given them.

"When we encountered him, he was walking by himself and decided to guide us to his hut where he sacrificed a goat for us,"

Asrat said. "At times the journey was very frightening."

Meskerem continued. "Once, we found a man with a gun willing to lead us here, and after we had followed him for an afternoon, he had a change of heart. When it was evening and we were sleeping, he came sneaking to where I was and started to unwrap his *shirit*. I screamed and Terrefe and Asrat woke up. When they realized that he was about to rape me, he pulled out his gun. I then heard Terrefe's voice, 'Meskerem, Asrat run in different directions and scream as loud as you can. He's only got one bullet and he won't shoot if we all run in different directions.' Asrat and I did just that and moments later the man disappeared."

Yared and I related our experiences since our separation in the desert, and we were all very thankful that we were alive.

"I still think he should see a doctor," Meskerem turned to Abba once again.

"I know when I am better and there is no reason why I have to put myself in the hands of some doctors when I feel just fine," Abba responded.

I was convinced that a drink of ice-cold water and a shower at Rhoda's house was the cure to everything. I knew my way around Dikhil and I felt I could take my family anywhere. But I could not picture Abba patiently waiting in line at the UN office for his ration of rice and powdered milk. He was already complaining that he was tired of eating rice all the time. *He's more like his old self*, I thought with relief.

Ali Wollao

———◆●———

We all need each other. The only time we don't need
someone is after we die. —AFAR PROVERB

AS WE NEARED RHODA'S house, it was no longer the quiet
sanctuary I had known. Seated on the veranda were three women,
wearing beautiful dresses like Rhoda's, and two children. The front
door was wide open and I could see the silhouettes of several men
camped on the mat in the centre of the living room. How could I
explain this crowded house to Abba, having told him that the place
was quiet, with only Rhoda there most of the time? What a relief
it was then to see Rhoda step out with a tray bearing small colourful teacups! She noticed us, and after serving the women she came
toward us, dangling the wooden tray at her side. As usual, she was
wearing a beautiful dress, this one with a red diamond pattern on a
white background.

"You found your family!" she beamed. "Come inside, come in
this way." She galloped in front and led us like caravan camels, one
by one, inside. The air-conditioned living room was dark and filled
with white clouds of cigarette smoke. The men in the room had

not bothered to open the shade. Beside each man was a cup of tea. Next to one of the men was fresh qat piled on a tray and, right in the centre was a pile of loose white sugar. Beside the sugar was a large silver teapot. I had never seen a teapot this size before. The men were conversing in Afar and, except for a few glances toward us, appeared undisturbed by our presence.

Rhoda made a brief stop at the kitchen to put away the empty tray and then led us to the door on the far side of the kitchen, which had always been closed on our previous visits. Flinging it open, she cried, "Come in."

The room was furnished with one double bed and the walls were undecorated.

"You should rest on the bed and I'll go prepare something to eat," she said to my father, studying him like a nurse.

"Did you tell her I was sick?" Abba glared at Yared and me.

"This is a real bed, Abba. You should rest," Asrat told him. I had noticed that Asrat had become more confident addressing Abba since our separation.

"I'll sit on the bed only because I am tired of sitting on the floor. Come on, Beth, sit here."

I proudly bounced next to my father while we waited for Rhoda to return. Asrat and Yared never objected to my status when Abba was around. The bed was firm and covered with a single beige-coloured sheet. Positioned diagonally, it looked like a floor decoration. The door to the closet was open and clean sarongs were stacked inside. On the far wall, there was a window. The trim was painted blue and we could see a blue sky through the glass panels.

Rhoda returned half an hour later with rice and meat sauce.

"Today is the holiday of *Jumua* and Ali's relatives usually make a stop here for tea. The food is almost finished," she apologized.

"Is Ali here?" Yared asked anxiously.

"He is on his way with more relatives, and I have to go and cook."

Rhoda stayed with us while we ate. She seemed to like our family.

"Why are so many people here today?" Yared asked.

"Ali Wollao is the host for the gathering, and people usually come when they want. He will not be here until evening, but they have come anyway."

Rhoda explained that it was common for the Afar to gather together to discuss important matters. "As you know, the Afar keep moving from place to place, so they make it a practice to come together to share what has been going on in their family, clan, or what have you. Among the Afar, *dagu* means news. If an Afar heard on a radio that a thunderstorm was predicted for Assayita, he would tell everyone he met on his way, from Assayita to Dikhil, and the news would spread across all the Afar territory in a very short time."

No matter how remote their location and how lacking in technology they were, the Afar stayed informed about most things affecting their lives. To me *dagu* explained how the *warabas* in the desert had been able to locate us, however off the map we thought we were, and why they kept demanding money from us even when we told them we carried none. It was a sure thing that when Ali Wollao's guests departed, they would spread the news that a certain family from Addis Ababa, who had survived the dreadful journey through the Danakil, was resting at his house.

Rhoda explained that the Afar seldom turned to the governments to settle their issues. They had their own laws.

Abba added, "If, the Derg wanted to discuss important matters affecting the Afar people of a certain region, it would approach the sultan of that state. Then there are the *maakabans*, religious leaders, who deal with day-to-day issues. The *kedo abobti* are the heads of the clan, and the elders too settle many disputes before they escalate; events such as weddings and funerals are handled by a group called *fiema*."

"That is right," Rhoda said, smiling at Abba, evidently impressed with his detailed knowledge of her people's way of life.

"Do you know what the word *Afar* means?" my father asked, never missing an opportunity to teach us something.

My brothers and I looked at each other.

"It means 'subdued,'" Abba said, answering his own question.

"Subdued? What does that mean?" Yared asked.

"It means a people who are naturally calm. It could also mean, like a wild tiger, not wild anymore; a crazy person not crazy anymore."

Rhoda returned with glasses of ice-cold water.

Abba was finally convinced to rest his head on the pillow. He took a deep breath and then closed his eyes.

"I can hardly sit up anymore," Meskerem whispered as she slipped next to Abba.

"It is too hot to do anything right now but sleep," I said.

We all took a nap in the air-conditioned room, and my head did not hurt this time.

———◆◆———

When we woke up, Rhoda told us it would take at least three hours before our turn to take showers, because it was time for prayer and the guests had to wash. The mothers wanted to bathe their children as well. When the guests finished washing, it was finally our turn.

After their showers, Abba, Meskerem, and Asrat looked years younger and Rhoda gave them new outfits.

"I can't just sit here and do nothing," Abba said, feeling restless. "I must go and talk to those men and see if I can get some information."

"Can we trust them? Including Rhoda? Yared and I are not sure why she has been so nice to us and why she thinks Ali Wollao will allow this," I confided to Abba.

"They know through their *dagu* that we have nothing. I am sure even Ali Wollao has received the news of us being hosted at his house and he already has given his permission for us to stay," Abba replied. "Now I must go and see what information I can get from the people gathered in the next room." He stood up to leave.

"Ask them if they know of a doctor," Meskerem pleaded.

He stopped at the door. "You are in a doctor's house. Ali Wollao *is a doctor.*" *Seeing a doctor is the last thing on Abba's mind*, I thought. Now that he had both feet on the ground, he was ready to move on with his master plan.

"He is a vet, Terrefe," Meskerem called.

"I know," he replied from the other room.

Meskerem's face was unusually dark; her eyes searched for something on the bare blue wall.

"I am worried that if we don't move quickly, it will be too late," she said.

"It won't be too late. We just got here today, and Abba is going to do something to get us out of Dikhil soon," Asrat comforted her.

"Terrefe needs to get well for him to think clearly. But if he keeps refusing help, then it will take a long time before we can send for Kalkidan. It is already too late for me to nurse her." Meskerem was crying now.

"They will take care of her until we get her," I said, not quite sure how we were going to bring Kalkidan to us now that we had crossed over into another country.

None of us spoke. Meskerem sobbed, and covered her face with the bed sheet. My brothers stayed quietly seated on the floor. We didn't know how to comfort our stepmother.

Once I was sure Meskerem had fallen asleep, I got up to see how Abba was doing in the living room. The door was ajar, and I saw him seated on the floor next to a heavy-set man, conversing in Amharic. He inhaled deeply, the end of a cigarette glowing between his fingers, then he exhaled, sending up a white cloud of smoke.

"Now I know what Abba was wishing for," I said to my brothers, who were still sitting on the floor doing nothing as if they were in jail. "He's finally got his cigarette."

Rhoda brought in rolled woven mats in case we needed them. "I have good news," she announced. "Ali Wollao said you can all spend the night here." It would be crowded but my family could fit in one room. Abba and Meskerem could have the bed while my brothers and I could sleep on a mat on the floor.

"Is he here?" I asked with excitement, as though I were waiting for a favourite uncle.

"No. He has not arrived yet, but the cousin who took my message yesterday is back and told me that Ali Wollao is happy to help."

"Did you tell our father this good news?" Yared inquired.

"Yes, both your parents know," she said. "Don't worry about the guests. They prefer to sleep outside anyway, so you can have this room."

My brothers and I unfolded the woven mats and lay down to rest. My family was finally together under one roof.

───◆◆�───

It was a great disappointment for Abba the next day to learn that Ali Wollao had arrived while we were sleeping, chewed qat all night, heard the daily *dagu*, and then left at the break of dawn.

"Who knows when he'll be back again?" Abba said despondently to no one in particular.

My father's plan became clearer that morning. He wanted to talk to Ali Wollao about getting us out of Dikhil by securing passes or whatever we needed.

"You could talk to him at dinner," Meskerem said.

"You are not in Addis Ababa. The Afar dinner times, if they have any, are not the same as ours," Abba said angrily. "He may eat at his uncle's or cousin's or wherever he happens to be and you could wait here five days before you have dinner with him. I know this because I have worked with them."

"He is an educated man," Meskerem insisted.

"It does not matter. He is not going to change his culture because he is now a vet."

Rhoda was at the door with our breakfast. She said she had talked to Ali briefly and he had agreed to help us with whatever we needed, but since more relatives were arriving in the next few days, there wouldn't be enough room for all of us to stay here.

"You see, Ali Wollao's uncle who lives in Djibouti city is getting married to a woman who lives in Tadjora. She will be his third wife. He travels frequently, and whenever he comes this way he always stops here."

"A wedding is a big event indeed," Abba confirmed.

Yared volunteered to go back to The Palace with Asrat.

"But your father should stay here with Meskerem. It would also be better if Beth stayed here too because she is a girl. The two of you can come here for your afternoon naps, showers, and food any time you want to," Rhoda offered.

"I don't want to stay in Dikhil more than three days," Abba said testily. "I have already wasted enough time wandering in the desert. When you see Ali, would you please get me from wherever I am or wake me up if I am sleeping?"

Rhoda agreed. She seemed to respect Abba as if he were her own father. She hadn't told us anything about her actual father.

She was certain that Ali Wollao could get us out of Dikhil.

If we went through regular procedures, we had learned, it could take months or even years, just to leave Dikhil. The distance between Dikhil and Djibouti was about thirty miles. After walking for fourteen days in the desert, and in my father's case seventeen days, thirty miles to Djibouti seemed like a stroll from my home in Addis to my soccer field.

"We have to get to Djibouti and find a way to contact someone in Ethiopia to let them know we are all right. And after that we should be able to contact my sister in America and my brother in France," Abba said.

So the master plan was to take us out of Africa entirely. My mind filled with all sorts of thoughts. My headache returned and the pain became intolerable. I squeezed my eyes shut for a moment to make it go away. One thing was certain: there would be no Ethiopia for any of us in the near future.

Abba had convinced us that he would find a way to bring Kalkidan to join us. If Meskerem or anyone mentioned Kalkidan, he had one answer. "Didn't I promise you that we will be reunited with Kalkidan? We will find a way, you will see. I am not named Terrefe for nothing."

After a moment he added, "I met a police officer at the qat ceremony last night. He spoke a little Amharic and informed me that it was next to impossible to get out of Dikhil without the proper papers, but as long as we are Ali Wollao's guests, his people will not bother us. But if we dare to go to Djibouti city illegally, then we would no longer be Ali Wollao's responsibility."

Ali Wollao had not met us, yet here we were, his guests. This was nothing short of a miracle. We were safe in Dikhil. Foad had said that the police didn't like refugees and constantly harassed them and threatened to put them in jail.

My father discussed his plans. He warned my brothers and me not to talk to anyone about our situation, or how we escaped. There was still a chance we could be apprehended by the Derg's soldiers.

It was chilly on the veranda, where we had decided to have our breakfast that morning. The outside air smelled fresh, and I took in a deep breath and stretched out my arms. I could smell aromas of cinnamon, cloves, ginger, and tea as I sat on a red and green straw mat, Rhoda's large silver teapot releasing steam, the white teacups neatly arranged on the tray before her. She served us Somali bread called *luh-luh*—flat and thick like a pancake, with a glaze of melted spiced butter and *berbere* (jalapeno powder) coating on top. After serving us, Rhoda went back inside.

"When we get to Djibouti city, we'll need to find a way of contacting your aunt Kelem in Addis. I'm sure she is worried sick by now," Abba said.

"She is the only one we should contact in Ethiopia," Meskerem said. "Even that is risky."

"You know how news travels fast. We don't have any way of knowing how safe we are here and who is watching us. The more people find out about our whereabouts, the deeper we get ourselves and those we love into trouble," Abba replied.

Meskerem turned to us, "It's too early to contact your mother."

Yared shot her a hard look over his right shoulder and their eyes met briefly, then she turned her face away and looked down at her tea.

"She will be interrogated by the Derg's officials, so it is better to wait for things to settle," Abba said gently, looking at Yared.

I was afraid Yared might get up and run away, but I couldn't say a word. I turned to Abba and silently pleaded; *please let's find a safe way to let her know where we are.* I knew rebellious thoughts were running through Yared's head and that Asrat was biting his tongue. Whenever someone mentioned my mother, I took in the words and clenched my teeth until the pain passed. I hoped she would find strength in God to survive the now empty days.

Abba was puffing rapidly on his cigarette.

"Imagine, after all we've been through, to get caught by the Derg's informants here," he said, shaking his head. I waited for Yared to blurt out something like "I would rather die than leave Ethiopia," but he said nothing. Rhoda returned just then to give us cold water to drink and to collect the empty teacups. Abba and Meskerem smiled at her and thanked her for her kindness.

"Why don't you take me to the market?" Abba suggested to Yared.

"We can go now." Yared liked the idea.

Asrat wanted to tag along. Meskerem said she was still exhausted and needed to rest. I decided to stay behind and wash our dirty clothes.

I closed the bedroom door behind me and took the *safa*, a large round metallic bowl used for washing clothes, and headed to the back of the house where there was a flat rock and I had seen people rinse their hands and feet before prayer. I sat on the rock, filled the *safa* with water from a hose, and added some white powdered detergent.

When I got to Abba's pants, I emptied the pockets and found a cigarette lighter that did not work. I was tempted to throw it out, but instead placed it aside. Then I picked up Asrat's pants and, when I felt one of the back pockets, I heard a soft crinkle. I flipped out the pocket and discovered a neatly folded piece of paper along with a Bic pen. I took off the lid and scribbled on the folded paper and to my surprise it was working, so I placed it beside Abba's lighter, along with the folded paper.

When I finished washing, I dried my hands on my pants and carefully picked up the note. Nervousness overcame me as I began to unfold it, so I slowly folded it up again, making sure it returned to its original shape and placed it back next to the pen. But my eyes kept shifting back to it. What could it be? A poem by Asrat? A note? To whom? I started to pick up the *safa* to return to Rhoda, but changed my mind and picked up the paper instead. I sat back on the flat rock and unfolded the paper once again. I opened it entirely. It was a note and when I read the name of the person to whom it was addressed, I was shocked, happy, and confused all at once. I began reading.

Dearest Tetye,

I hope you are well. Aside from missing you very much I am okay. I don't know how much you know, but I hope this letter reaches you before you hear the bad news from someone else. I know you will be devastated either way, but I just want you to know that we are just fine. When I came to lend you my watch I told you my dream, about crossing a wild river and landing in a puddle of mud. Remember? Well, things happened just the way you interpreted the dream. This is all I can tell you for now because of our situation. Please don't say anything to anyone because we will be in big trouble.

How daring Asrat was to write this to our mother! I didn't have a chance to think more about it, because I suddenly heard a movement behind me. I turned and saw Meskerem standing on the steps.

"Oh, you scared me," I stuttered.

My hands immediately began shaking. I grabbed the *safa* with the letter squished in my hand. "I just finished washing and was about to return the *safa* to Rhoda."

Meskerem's eyes were red, and she said she couldn't sleep.

"You were gone for so long I came to see if you were okay." She glanced at me, then stared into space, not appearing to have noticed my nervousness. But, then again, Meskerem didn't let her feelings show. I wondered if she had been spying, and knew that I was hiding something from her. I had been so stunned upon discovering the letter that I wouldn't have noticed if a gorilla had been sitting next to me.

"Here, would you please wash this one for me? I'm so tired." She handed me her dress.

"Are you okay?" I asked.

"I am fine but sometimes I feel dizzy, my stomach hurts, and I want to throw up even when there is no food in my stomach."

"Did you feel like this in the desert too?"

"Sometimes. But it is more painful here."

"I hope you don't have malaria, because you weren't taking the pills."

"This is not malaria. Come to think of it, I felt sick like this before," she said, then paused for a moment. Her eyes had become wide and alert as if she had just figured out something.

"What is it?" I asked.

"A strange thought crossed my mind."

"About what?"

"About why I feel sick."

"What is it?"

"It could be . . . oh dear, let's not think too much now." She went back inside.

I started washing her dress. I tried to think of the last time I had seen my mother. I wished she were with me to hug me and comfort me in a way only a mother could, only then would everything be tolerable. There were just too many things that I had no control over, that kept getting in the way of us being together. It seemed we were getting further apart with each passing day. If our previous separations were not bad enough, here we were, her children, with a plan to leave the continent without her. It seemed impossible to close this widening gap.

———◆•——

A few weeks before our escape, Tetye had taken us to Kokeb Restaurant, on the rooftop of a twelve-storey building. The elevator there was the only one I had known in my life. The restaurant was in a bright room with windows all around it. On one side, there were rows of tables covered with white linen, and in the centre there was a bar that my brothers and I were forbidden to go near. On the other side, in front of the balcony, was a round seating area with hand-carved wooden tables; a large Ethiopian rug covered the floor. Above the seating area hung the straw roof of a mud hut, with all kinds of stuffed exotic birds and butterflies perched on top.

We usually sat at a table on the balcony which had a magnificent view of the Jubilee Palace where Emperor Haile Selassie lived. Often we walked close to the edge of the balcony to spot any of the emperor's lions roaming in the garden. All we saw were ostriches galloping like horses, peacocks dancing, and dogs napping. We could see all of Addis Ababa from this great height, and our neighbourhood, with the houses hidden inside a forest of eucalyptus trees.

My mother never left her seat to join us in the balcony. She sat comfortably on a wicker chair, wearing her dark brown sunglasses, sipping her black Jimma coffee out of a white cup. On her wrist, she wore the gold Omega watch presented to her by the emperor's son, Alga Worsh, when he came to visit her after she gave birth to Asrat. This was the last image I had of her, her hair straight with red henna highlights glistening in the afternoon sun, fresh red nail polish, a red lipstick mark on her coffee cup, and the smell of her perfume, Shalimar, filling the air around her. She was wearing wide-bottom pants and cranberry red platform shoes. That day, she said many times, as she always did, "Please don't go to the edge." But my brothers and I kept returning to the edge because that was where most of the fun was.

Her cup of Jimma coffee in her hand, my mother would tell us stories about the royal family of Ethiopia.

"What is a higher position than that of a king or a queen in Ethiopia?" She asked, as she always did, and after several tries when we couldn't give her the answer, she told us with a smile, "Why, it is that of a monk."

"When Queen Zewditu died, her niece, my grandmother, Tidenekialesh, inherited thirty armed guards, several houses in different parts of Ethiopia, and the best cooks, nannies, maids, and other servants. Tidene's favourite house was the one no one knew about. It was built secretly for no other purpose than for her to use when her husband upset her. She would go there and no one would know where she had disappeared." Tetye paused to take a sip of coffee.

"Tidene believed everyone deserved to share her wealth. Every night, after their duties were done, the servants ate fresh meat with butter and drank *tej* (honey wine) well into the night before another workday began. Tidene sat by the fire sipping *atmit* (a porridge-like drink) and contentedly listening to the laughter coming from the servant's quarters. She was satisfied that all was well, and she had done the right thing with her inherited power and wealth. At night, it was not uncommon for her to hear some of the servants' drunken voices. The log-cutter, Ato Woyna, had a special way of expressing himself when he was drunk. He would walk close to Tidene's bedroom window and shout, 'Tidenekialesh, you have no worries, lying there by the fire, wrapped in your ancestors' blankets.'"

My brothers and I sipped our soft drinks and listened contentedly.

———◆◆◆———

Having spent a whole week in Ali Wollao's house, we finally met him in person. One evening, my family and I were seated on his veranda sipping Rhoda's tea when three men walked past us and went inside. They seemed like yet more visitors. But shortly after, Rhoda came out to call Abba.

"You may come inside to meet Ali Wollao. He is waiting for you," she said softly, with a wide smile on her face.

"Ali Wollao is inside?" Abba beamed as if he were about to see a long-lost friend.

"I don't believe it," Asrat remarked.

I felt so happy. I was certain our situation could only get better now, that Ali Wollao was on our side and would protect us from all the dangers Abba and Meskerem had warned us about. It felt like Ali Wollao had mysteriously landed inside the house, delivered to us from God.

Yared was quickly on his feet to follow Rhoda inside.

As we entered the living room, we saw the three people who had passed us before seated on the mat. Rhoda began to speak in Afar. For the most part, she was looking at the man seated in the centre, who I knew could only be Ali Wollao. I stared at him. He seemed in his early twenties and wore a green polo shirt and a blue plaid sarong with a wide leather belt. Ethiopian doctors in Addis Ababa wore Western outfits even when not at work. His smooth brown skin was like my father's, but his face was square at the forehead and narrow at the jaw. His eyes were small but very dark and attractive and his teeth appeared to be filed into sharp points. Ali Wollao sat cross-legged, while his companions leaned on pillows. None of them was armed. I had wondered how Rhoda, just a few years older than me, was so skilled at housekeeping. And now here was Ali Wollao, a doctor, only a few years older than my brothers. Even Abba was taken aback by the combination of Ali Wollao's youth and mature manner.

"This is Ali Wollao and I told him you are named Terrefe," Rhoda said.

"Aninay," Abba saluted.

Ali smiled and greeted us in Afar. "How are you feeling? I heard you were not well," he asked through Rhoda.

"We are all doing wonderfully. Rhoda is taking such good care of us that we have nothing to complain about," Abba replied.

The good-natured greetings went on for most of the evening. Finally Abba said, "We only have one favour to ask of you. As you are aware, we need permission to enter Djibouti city and to stay there until we figure out what it is we need to do to leave Africa. This favour will be much appreciated and we will be forever in debt to you and your people. We are very thankful for all your help so far, but we can't do anything without the permits."

Rhoda translated, and Ali Wollao listened carefully, nodding and saying, "Ye, ye, ye" to acknowledge. Before he answered, there was a moment of silence, during which time Rhoda went to the kitchen and came back with some water.

Then it was Ali Wollao's turn to speak. His voice was gentle and soft, almost a whisper. We all listened attentively while he spoke and the other men nodded in agreement. We had trusted Ali Wollao's associates with our secrets. Perhaps they too could help. Although dressed modestly, they could be doctors, ministers, high-level religious leaders, negotiators, or even policemen. They all sat quietly drinking tea and listening to Rhoda's translation.

Abba asked Rhoda to tell Ali Wollao again that we had to get out of Dikhil and if he could help us. When she translated, Ali just nodded, saying "Ye, ye, ye" from time to time, and then they were both quiet.

"What is he saying?" Abba asked impatiently.

"He is happy to hear that you are all well, and repeated everything you have just said. He was sad to learn that you had such a rough journey and that it is a wonder you are all alive and not even sick," Rhoda explained.

"What did he say about helping us leave Dikhil?"

"Maybe we should mention that we need to see a doctor," Meskerem interrupted.

"He is a vet, Meskerem. Besides, it is more important that we get out of here and then look for the best doctors in Djibouti city," Abba whispered to her.

Rhoda explained the Afar tradition regarding a discussion of an important matter. "It is their custom," she said softly, "that when someone is talking, everyone listens and no one talk until the speaker is done." Abba nodded in frustration. Rhoda continued, "And then people do not continue from where that person leaves off but rather begin by reviewing everything the person has said. Only then do they say what they want to say," Rhoda finished.

"I know that, it's just that I have a plan that I know will work and need a little help," Abba whispered to himself.

Then Ali spoke.

"This could be it," Abba said, and told Rhoda to listen carefully.

There was more conversation about the desert we had crossed, and what could be done about the robbers, and how lucky we were that we did not run into landmines, and finally everyone concluded that the attackers would receive the just judgment of God. Meanwhile, I was distracted by how much sugar Ali Wollao and his guests were putting into their mouths to sweeten the qat. There was a lot of loose sugar in a container on the mat, and I wanted to reach over and get a tablespoon or two for myself. It seemed such a long time ago since I bought sugar from the store on Tito Street in Addis.

I realized I had never seen women in Dikhil seated with men during chat sessions except for this evening. There were the three of us—Meskerem, I, and Rhoda. I was sure our presence was unusual, but this assured me that it was part of the special treatment we were receiving.

I was getting sleepy and my brothers wanted to head out to The Palace for the night. I walked out with my brothers to wish them good night and the three of us sat outside for a moment. The moon was bright white and beaming. It was a good feeling, knowing that we were all safe and together.

I wished my brothers a good night and headed back inside. I saw that Abba was well settled with Ali Wollao and the others, and appeared to be enjoying their company. I went inside to sleep.

The next morning, I joined my father and Meskerem as they talked over tea. I found out that Ali had finally agreed to use his network of contacts to get us refugee permits. He had also invited us to stay at his house for as long as we wished. But Abba had his doubts.

"I have no doubt Ali Wollao will help, but I am one hundred percent sure it will not be soon. I have to try some other ways," Abba confided in us.

Abba and my brothers frequented the market. Sometimes they would be gone the whole day, returning in the evening. They went to Foad's relative's spice shop and collected whatever information they could about escaping to Djibouti.

Meskerem and I stayed indoors in the cool, air-conditioned rooms, wearing clean Somali dresses and taking showers in the evenings. Sometimes we would borrow Rhoda's *safa* and wash our family's clothes. Since Rhoda had refused to have us help in the kitchen, we sometimes had nothing to do but comb our hair.

One evening as Meskerem and I sat on the front veranda, we heard the sound of music coming from the living room. It was just after siesta, the sun was melting into the sky and the cool evening air brought relief from the stale heat. It was a male vocalist with a guitar, singing in the Afar language. Even though I didn't understand it, the rhythm was soothing and uplifting. As we sat there listening, it suddenly felt as if our life had a purpose after all, and Abba's plan suddenly seemed brilliant. I closed my eyes. The song was speaking to me: "No, little girl, don't despair, don't you see the light shining so bright over the desert sky? Your path in the sand is shimmering with gold, everything will be all right. No, little girl, don't despair . . . "

When I opened my eyes I could not believe what stood in front of me: a green Mercedes, dust covering its four tires, parked a few meters from Meskerem and me.

The driver and the front-seat passenger got out first, followed by two men who emerged from the back. I couldn't help but stare. They must have been influential people to be driving a Mercedes; even Ali Wollao, the doctor, didn't have a car. One of the men was much shorter and skinnier than the others. They were dressed like Ali Wollao and they walked right past us and went inside without a word.

"I think these are very important people," Meskerem commented.

"Was Rhoda expecting them? I mean, did she say anything to you about them? We should go inside. They must be here for us," I said.

Meskerem didn't get up. She smiled at me. "I am sorry but I don't think they have anything to do with us. But I am sure their arrival will attract more people, just look at the car."

"We should go inside and see what's going on anyway. Rhoda will tell us why they are here."

We found Rhoda in the kitchen scooping a rice dish onto a large tray. How Rhoda could cook so much food in a short time without looking tired was always amazing. This rice dish was my favourite: white rice mixed in a goat stew with cinnamon sticks and cloves. Chunks of goat meat piled up on the tray, with the rice, and the aroma was captivating. The music was still playing. The tape recorder was in the kitchen carefully placed on top of a small table but Rhoda turned it off when she saw us.

"There are new visitors in the living room," Meskerem announced.

"Yes, I know. I met them when they came in. They have travelled from Djibouti city and I am getting ready to serve them. The short man you saw is Ali Wollao's uncle, Habib, who is a respected leader in the Afar community. The one with the turban is a religious leader and also a relative; the other one is the driver,"

"They are from Djibouti city!" I said full of excitement. "You must introduce them to Abba. Please."

Rhoda was busy taking out one food-laden tray after another to the guests.

"Why are you taking out so much food when there are only three of them?" I asked.

"If you look now, you will see that there are already other visitors in the living room who have joined them. Habib is never without followers," Rhoda explained.

Habib, I said to myself. The name sounded so nice. I peeked out from the kitchen and saw that Rhoda was right, there were about ten more people gathered now. Habib must be the shortest one, I concluded. I saw the religious leader go out the front door, perhaps to get something from the car. Maybe they had brought sacks of Ausa dates.

I found a stool and sat down in the kitchen. Meskerem began assisting Rhoda by filling cups of water. Rhoda continued going in and out of the kitchen carrying the trays. When she was finally done, she removed the music player from the table and placed a small tray full of food on it. "Iyan Meskerem, Betleen," she invited us, "come let's eat." We ate from this communal tray with our fingers.

"Have you ever been to Djibouti city?" I asked Rhoda.

"Betleen, I think you've asked me that before. I wish I had, so I could tell you what there is to see and do. I have heard that it is really beautiful, and a little more like Dire Dawa. The difference is that Djibouti city has the beach at the Red Sea so you can just imagine all the fun one can have swimming and relaxing there, especially when it gets too hot."

"Why did all these people come here to see Habib?" I inquired.

"For many reasons. He is well known by the Afar people to be generous and helpful. So wherever he goes, people come in flocks. And besides, he just got married."

And then she let us in on a secret.

"He was looking for a third wife for a long time, and finally he found an Ethiopian Afar near the border, in Ali Sabeih. He already has two wives in Djibouti; one of them is a Somali and the other one was born in Ethiopia. Traditionally, the Afars marry their cousins at a young age and the groom's side of the family pays the bride's family, but if you marry outside the family, as Habib did, then you must pay not only the bride's family but also the family of the cousin who was traditionally supposed to marry her. "

"Where was the wedding?" Meskerem asked.

"In Ali Sabeih, where his wife lives now, and where she will continue to live. This means that Habib will be back this way very soon." She giggled suggestively.

"I wish Terrefe would come now so he does not miss the chance to meet someone as important as Habib," Meskerem remarked.

"Do you think he can help us?" I asked.

"Habib is a very helpful man, indeed," said Rhoda. "But this is not a good time to introduce you, with the wedding so near, but Ali Wollao won't forget to find a solution for you."

The food was delicious, but Meskerem didn't take long before she threw up in the sink when Rhoda was out serving the guests. That was when we excused ourselves and headed to our bedroom.

I found out the next morning that Abba and my brothers had returned very late and missed Habib.

We all sat on the front veranda having breakfast, which this time Meskerem and I had helped prepare. While Meskerem and Abba discussed Habib, I told my brothers how Habib had appeared before me like a dream.

"Does he really look like Abba?" Yared asked.

"Not really, he is short and skinny and much darker than Abba."

Just then, Ali Wollao came out onto the veranda. We didn't know he had been inside the house and were surprised and happy to see him. Abba quickly got up and offered him his spot on the mat. But Ali Wollao declined and squatted the way I had seen kids do at the camp.

Rhoda went and brought a cup and poured out hot tea from the pot for him, and I watched as he reached over to the *luh-luh* plate and took a piece. I felt very happy to see Ali Wollao eating with us. I remembered, when we were resting with the Afar caravan in the desert, Abba telling us that if the Afar served you food and ate with you, then they had accepted you as their own.

Rhoda joined us so that she could translate. My father was trying his best to use the Afar he had learned from his fieldwork. The conversation seemed smooth. My father thanked Ali Wollao again for his hospitality.

Ali Wollao responded with hands and face lifted up to the sky. "You are Allah's guest and I am just doing my duty to obey his will. I have heard about your work in Assayita and how you saved the Afars from persecution. My people are indebted to you for that."

"I was in a position to help," Abba replied.

"Please feel free to live here in my home. Rhoda already knows how to take care of you and your family. Please accept it as understood that I too am in a position to help."

"My only regret is that I never achieved my plan to turn the Awash Valley of the Assayita region into a year-round farming area for the Afar nomads of the Danakil Desert. I know the Afar move between Ethiopia and Djibouti, but if they found an environment where they could support their families and cattle, they would settle for longer periods, don't you agree?"

Ali Wollao looked at my father as if he had just said the most brilliant thing on the planet. Being an Afar himself, he was just as passionate about the topic as my father. "The valley is full of nutrients. I have often wondered why the Ethiopian government has not done anything about it."

"It is not just this government, it's the government before this, and the one before that. No one wants to invest in that region. Their excuse is that the nomads refuse to attend schools or go to hospitals, so it would be a waste. But I told them that it would have to be done in a manner that appeals to the Afar and is suitable to their lifestyle."

Abba offered Ali Wollao a cigarette and they both became quiet for a while. Rhoda headed back into the house to do some chores. When the cigarettes were done, the two men had one more round of tea.

As soon as Rhoda returned, Ali Wollao began to talk and she translated. "We consider our livestock more important than land. This is why we are not transitioning to agriculture, although diversifying makes sense for survival. This is the tradition. I became a vet to work with my people, because the Afars are suspicious of Western medicine."

I could sense that Abba's heart was still in Assayita, in the project he had envisioned but never got to finish. Ali Wollao seemed extremely pleased to have found an educated man to talk to who had actually worked in the Afar State.

"How about fishing?" Abba asked. "You have the Red Sea coastline; why can't that be introduced?"

"The fish catch is massive, this is true, but the majority of the business is operated by foreign vessels, so most of the catch is exported. We just never looked at it as our tradition. But we must start to look for other means of survival. Would you like to come and visit my work site?" Ali asked.

Abba hesitated before replying, "I would like to, thank you for your offer."

Ali Wollao shook Abba's hand and held it for a while. "Everything will be okay for you and your family. I will see to it that you get the permits."

"Thank you. Thank you very much."

Then Ali Wollao left for the day, and Rhoda went back inside the house.

I had tried to help Rhoda but she wouldn't allow it, instead she would take me to the market with her. That was how I got out of the house. Meskerem was no fun. She had a lot on her mind that she was not sharing with me, but that was all right, because I didn't tell her how much I missed my mother. The last time I mentioned

Kalkidan we both ended up crying, so I had concluded we were not good company for each other.

It was so hot in Dikhil that outside the air-conditioned rooms, I would sweat profusely. The dust too was extreme, and it was necessary to shower in the morning and at night. My clothes needed to be washed daily. As my mind wandered, I wished I could write a letter to my mother and my friend Seble just so they would learn that I was okay for now and Abba was doing everything he could to make things better. He complained about having to eat rice every day, but he was sure we would find *injera* in Djibouti city, along with a new life.

The things I liked in Dikhil were few, but I treasured them. I loved staring at the night sky while lying on the mat. I felt that I was part of the desert, a bigger world. I felt strong like the nomads. I felt as if I could do anything. When my family and I ate together under one roof and from a communal tray, even though it was always rice, it felt like we belonged.

Ali Wollao managed to convince my father to visit a doctor. Abba went as a sign of respect for his new friend and Meskerem went along, too. The result was that nothing was wrong with either of them; at least that's what they told me and my brothers. I had not heard Abba complaining about his health, but Meskerem still continued to look unwell.

Yared would go to Foad's and spend the entire day just hanging out with him. Although Foad had the means to leave Dikhil whenever he wished, he had decided to stay a little longer to help a relative at the spice shop. Asrat hung out with Foad and Yared. Abba, in the meantime, had discovered the means to escape to Djibouti, but he needed money.

We had been in Dikhil just over one month and nothing had changed about our circumstances. One day my father returned from the market with a proposal.

"I can't just sit here and do nothing about our situation," he began as usual with an introduction. "I spoke to an Afar Ethiopian driver who will be shipping some merchandise to Djibouti tomorrow. He has agreed to hide me in the truck among the goats. There is not enough room for everyone. It would be easy to catch us if we all go together anyway. Once I get to Djibouti, I will work to get you out of here as fast as possible."

My heart broke at the thought that Abba was planning to abandon us. His imminent departure brought back my fears and quickly made our situation seem risky. I put on the saddest face possible and begged to go with him.

"It may seem a short journey to you, but it is dangerous. What the driver is doing is illegal, and if he gets caught he will lose his job and be jailed. I don't know what they will do to me. Besides, the driver does not have enough room for everyone."

"Isn't there another truck that could take us?" Yared demanded.

"Not for another week, and that is what I am trying to tell you. I will get you out before that. I want you to stay right here where I know you are safe, so when I look for you I will find you. If I wanted to leave Ethiopia without you, I would have bought a one-way ticket to France and stayed there with my brother. Why would you now think that I am going to abandon you? I would never leave you; even when I am dead I will be with you."

Abba stared at us intently.

"What if Ali Wollao and Rhoda get offended because you've left us under their care without their permission? They might do something bad to us," Yared blurted out.

"I hope my sister is not holding grudges for leaving Kalkidan with her like that," Meskerem said tearfully.

"We need to focus," Abba said, putting his arm around Meskerem's shoulders. "I know the Afar people. They will not harm you. They have eaten from the same plate as us. If they meant to harm us, they would not have taken this long.

"Stay alert and pay attention to everything. Think of this as a field trip with your school, just open your eyes and learn everything you can. Learn the Afar language and the Afar customs, because that will help you to make friends."

I listened to my father's advice but I still wanted to get out of Dikhil with him. He couldn't just leave us here to figure things out on our own. But for once it wasn't I who cried first; my stomach trembled at the thought of not having Abba with us the next day at breakfast, but I did not cry. Instead, it was my oldest brother, Yared. His face was soaked in tears and his nose was running like a tap. It was always difficult seeing Yared cry, since he was the strongest and the most rebellious. He was desperately upset, and by looking at the veins popping through his face, I knew it would not be long before he devised his own escape out of Dikhil, and out of our family.

Abba continued with his numerous reassurances, but Yared did not speak.

"There is always a reason for something to happen," Abba said. "When we see an opportunity we need to take it. This is how the real world is. We don't have any control over a lot of things. But God will make things happen, and we make the best out of the situation we are faced with. I know you are upset because of everything that has happened to you; and most likely you blame me for it all. But I want you to be able to see the whole picture. I hope you understand what I am saying. If you don't understand now, I hope you will one day. I have a plan for when I get to Djibouti city and I will get us back on track."

He stretched out his arms, and without hesitation, we each fell into his embrace one by one.

When we pulled back I glanced at Meskerem. Her dark face was like cracked glass, and she seemed to have shrunk a size or two. Asrat seemed the least disturbed by Abba's news. He listened to Abba's pleas like a mature adult, and I could see why Abba always picked him to watch out for me. I could hear his obedient voice as he promised to "keep an eye on her," just like in Addis.

Of course Abba had not discussed his plan with Ali Wollao, who had repeatedly advised us against attempting to escape to Djibouti. He could not understand why Abba was in such a hurry, especially when he did not have to worry about where to sleep or what to eat.

That evening, I wished my brothers would not go to the refugee camp. Why didn't I say something to keep them with us? When I closed my eyes and lay down to sleep, my head began to spin. My heart began pounding just like it did the first night of our escape from Ethiopia.

A cool morning breeze on my face woke me up at dawn, and I lifted my head from the floor. I saw that the front door was wide open and I watched as a shadowy figure made his way through the middle of the room before closing the door quietly behind him. I lay still, letting the tears run down the side of my face.

On Afar Time

———————◗◆◖———————

I climbed this tizeta hill holding whatever might be in my
hands but keeping the memory of you in my heart.
—ETHIOPIAN SONG, "TIZETA"

AFTER ABBA LEFT, I became good at staring into space, the way
Meskerem would. When I gazed directly into the soapy water of
the *safa*, just like magic my thoughts would transport me back to
the Ethiopia we had left behind. I was back home, playing soccer
with my friends or chasing our dog across our lawn. Ethiopians
have an Amharic word for this magic trip, *tizeta*.

I had thought *tizeta* was the daydreaming that enamoured adults
would indulge in—staring into space and not eating or sleeping
until they met their lovers again. There was a famous love song
called "Tizeta." No one could say with certainty who had written
the lyrics or composed the tune. Some believed it was a shepherd's
son in a remote part of the country. "Tizeta" became a popular harvest song that was copied by singers in the cities and became known
throughout the country.

I climbed this tizeta hill holding whatever

might be in my hands but keeping
the memory of you in my heart.

Whenever the song played, Ethiopians would get sentimental and tearful, they would remember the times when all was good. After the revolution, many would remember goodbyes to brothers who went to jail; mothers would be haunted by the *tizeta* of their vanished children who took in their last breath all alone in a back alley, under a bridge, on a gravel road, on school grounds, saying, "Mother, this last breath is for you."

———————

Yared and Asrat frequently visited the city centre for any news about Abba. The Ethiopia–Djibouti border was becoming extremely busy with the influx of Ethiopian refugees, and the refugee camp was more crowded than ever. My brothers learned that the police had become extra vigilant of the refugees, and to be careful, and if needed, to hide in mosques. I stayed put at Ali Wollao's house, except on the occasions when I went to the market with Rhoda. I wanted to be sure when Abba came to look for us, that I would be where he could find me. For a person who didn't speak the language and didn't know the customs, there was not much else I could do. The streets did not feel welcoming. Even when I was with Rhoda, people would stare at me.

Two weeks went by since Abba left and we hadn't heard from him. We were not sure what to do, and we constantly worried about him. One evening, before Yared and Asrat headed back to the camp, we discussed the possibility of escape to Djibouti. Since Abba was already there, we figured, he would be happy if we made it easier for him by arriving on our own. Once there, we would ask around among other Ethiopians and find him. But we had no choice but to find a way to leave Dikhil. Yared and Asrat, who went to the market every day, would look for a driver who would be willing to take us to Djibouti.

For three days, Yared and Asrat looked for a driver, and they finally found one willing to take us for fifty Djibouti francs per person. None of us had seen money since the day we got robbed at the oasis. How were we going to find the funds? To ask Rhoda would not be appropriate because she was already doing so much for us. And she would not approve of the idea. Looking for work was not an option since we had no papers. Contacting someone in Ethiopia would get us killed. Eventually Meskerem came up with a brilliant idea.

"I have seen people selling rice in the market, so we could sell the United Nations' rice and milk."

"That would work! I can ask Foad to help us sell the food at his relative's spice shop," Yared said in excitement.

Our UN rations which were stashed at the refugee camp came to a total of eight sacks of rice and ten sacks of milk. We would have had more if Yared and Asrat hadn't given some away to the neighbours.

It took us two days to sell everything. We finally had enough money to pay the driver. He met Yared and Asrat at the market, took the money, and gave them simple instructions about where to meet him for the journey.

We were to go across the hills by the refugee camps where the bathing water holes were, and when we reached the end we would see the highway. We should wait for his green Suzuki truck off the main road, where we should hide behind a tree. As soon as we saw it, we were to run very, very fast to where he would be waiting; the back door of the truck would be open and we were to jump in and hide among the goats and sheep.

I had only one concern: "How am I going to jump into a big truck?"

Asrat was quick to respond, "We will help you and Meskerem."

So all was settled. We slept, waiting for dawn, when we would leave Ali Wollao and Rhoda.

Dawn came and I opened my eyes at Meskerem's insistent tugging. I was already scared. But even if I had a sixth sense and were
able to foretell how the day would go, I would still have risked crossing the river and waiting for the truck driver on the other side. In a
few minutes, Meskerem and I would meet Yared and Asrat at the
refugee camp.

In my heart, I knew Ali Wollao and Rhoda deserved an explanation, a thank you, or at least a goodbye from us. Disappearing
without a goodbye as we did with my mother and my friends in
Ethiopia, I knew, would be hurtful, but there was no other way. I
wanted to cry.

"Hurry," Meskerem said.

At first, I could not find my slippers. I had to dig through the pile
of shoes at the door, left by the guests who had arrived during the
night.

Although the truck was to pick us up around nine-thirty, we had
to leave the house before anyone was awake. The guests were sleeping in the living room as well as on the veranda. After finding my
slippers, I followed Meskerem, who was already out the door. The
streets were eerily quiet and the air was moist. The sky was still
dark, and I was reminded of the times when we went to church in
Ethiopia. If I heard the birds chirping before I made it to church, I
knew I had missed a good portion of the service.

We reached the camp quickly. Yared and Asrat had packed a
large container of water, their old and torn pants, and, to my great
surprise, my miniskirt, shirt, and Adidas. We ate flavourless leftover
white rice.

When it was time to leave, and when we were sure that no one
was watching, we headed out. We walked to the back of the shelter, down the hill in single file, glancing over our shoulders from
time to time. But at the river we stumbled upon some people
who were already up and taking advantage of the coolness of the
morning, bathing and washing their clothes. They were the same
people who had called out *dilo, dilo* to me on our first morning at

the refugee camp.

"Just pretend you did not see them," Meskerem, said looking downward.

As we began to cross the river, the women stopped what they were doing and watched us. I had a bad feeling about the way they were staring at us, as though they were undercover Derg informants and at any moment would jump out of the water and grab me by the neck. Once we climbed up the bank and were out in the open, I felt relieved that no trouble had followed us.

The land beyond the refugee camp was rough with rocks and dust. There were a few trees but the morning sun was already gaining strength, and I began to sweat. We walked until we saw a dirt road, which we concluded was the highway. Cars passed by. We walked back and sat under one of the trees. It seemed that we had arrived too early; the truck did not appear. An hour passed and the heat was increasing by the minute. We saw small cars and some big trucks go speeding by, leaving swirls of dust behind, but none slowed down.

"Where is he? Did he say to wait right here on this spot?" Meskerem demanded.

"He told us to wait by the road in the morning. It is still morning and we are by the road, so we should keep waiting," Yared said defensively.

If he did not show up, would we just go back? He had taken our money and we had no more food to sell and no more food to eat. We would have to explain to Rhoda where we had been and pray she would understand, or we would have to lie about why we had left so early. It felt terrible.

The sun, penetrating through the scattered leaves of the tree, burned my head. I longed for a big green tree with wide leaves to sit under, rest my head just as I had done in the oasis of the Danakil, or to be in the midst of a sea of eucalyptus trees, smelling their sweet fragrance in the air of Addis Ababa. Soon it would be lunch time and Rhoda would notice we were gone.

We were still sitting, waiting, when suddenly Meskerem began vomiting the rice she had eaten for breakfast. I put my hands on her shoulders and attempted to support her while Asrat offered her some water. There came the sound of an engine.

"That must be the truck!" I said with excitement.

"Sit down!" Yared ordered.

"We should all stay down and not move," Meskerem instructed as she wiped her mouth.

Instead of a green truck, a yellow jeep swerved off the main road and drove toward us. Could it be Ali Wollao and Rhoda looking for us? It was a roofless jeep with two people in front and one in the back. The driver stomped on the brake a hair's breadth from my face.

We could not hide. There were three muscular police officers in blue and white uniforms. One had rolled-up his sleeves and reminded me of my father. The driver remained in the jeep while the other two jumped out quickly and marched toward us. I knew that we were in more trouble than we had ever been in when they pushed us from behind and escorted us to the back of the jeep. It was bigger than it looked, with two long benches facing each other at the back. They seated us there and closed the door, offering no explanation in any language.

None of us protested as they drove off. How did they know where to find us? Was it written on a public notice somewhere telling everyone that we were the unwelcome Ethiopian refugees? Foad would never tell on us. Then who could it be? Perhaps the truck driver wanted to keep our money without having to risk being caught smuggling us, or perhaps it was the women at the river.

It did not take long to arrive back at the city centre. Everyone on the street stared at us. The jeep stopped outside the police station.

The officer who was sitting in the front seat went inside, while the rest of us waited outside in the heat. We looked at each other. We were all sweating and kept silent. The driver and the second policeman began conversing in Somali, completely relaxed, as if nothing had happened. About fifteen minutes later, two tall Somali police officers came outside and stood on the steps, looking in our direction.

"What will they do to us?" I whispered to Meskerem.

"Nothing. We didn't do anything," she replied without fear.

The officer who had gone inside came back to ask for our identification. When we said we didn't have IDs, the police decided to take us somewhere else. The jeep travelled along a bumpy road to a remote part of the city with empty streets. Occasionally we saw sand sweepers on the road. We didn't see any houses for a while but saw some camels, before we entered what looked like a wealthy area and the jeep stopped abruptly at the gate of a building. It was the biggest in the neighbourhood, the size of a small school set among white residential houses. We were escorted inside and handed over to a man who was waiting at the gate. Then the jeep disappeared from sight.

"Habesh, habesh (highlanders, highlanders)," the guard uttered before he hurried us to an office. A fan on the ceiling was scattering papers all over the floor. The guard handed us over to a man dressed in a white shirt and a sarong with a mouth full of qat. He spoke very little Amharic. We managed to understand that we had been detained. Meskerem cried loudly and pleaded in Amharic and Oromoffia as he walked us down the hall to where he said he needed to keep us.

"We didn't do anything. What are you doing? Let us go, please let us go!"

The man walked ahead as if he had not heard her, until he met another officer. Yared and Asrat were handed over to him and taken away to a section for men, while Meskerem and I were taken to the women's section. The building was even bigger than it appeared from the outside. The floor was cement and the hallway empty. Up near the ceiling there were windows letting in the midday sun.

Meskerem and I were led to a large room with a high ceiling and a large window that opened to the hallway. The room looked more like Ali Wollao's living room. It had a mattress and a dirty, torn-up piece of cloth on the floor, and brown cubes of brick layered in a corner. It smelled of dust and a faint trace of burnt oil. After the guard left, Meskerem and I found our way to the dusty mattress and sat down, deflated.

A few minutes later, the door swung open. A light-skinned man, whom I thought to be Arab, entered. To our great surprise and relief, he spoke Amharic fluently.

"Selam."

"You speak Amharic?" Meskerem asked, excited.

"When I heard you crying out in Amharic, I looked out my window and I knew you were Ethiopians. You are lucky that they did not lock your door."

"Who are you?" Meskerem asked.

"My name is Greek," he replied. "Everyone asks how I got my name. I am part Greek and part Ethiopian."

"What are you doing here?" I asked after we told him our names.

He glanced out the door to make sure no one was coming.

"Like you, I am a prisoner, and they never run out of work for me to do here. I mop, help with the paperwork, and I even cook. I know what goes on around here," he added with a serious look.

"What do you mean?" I asked.

"We don't have much time before one of them comes back, so I will tell you quickly. You are in big trouble. They are going to try to sleep with you, which they always do with women prisoners. We all know that women prisoners don't stay here very long. The only trick that sometimes works is to scream very loudly like a crazy person. When the male prisoners hear women screaming, they know what is going on. I will tell the men to bang the cement floor with their drinking cups and create a disturbance. The warden lives very close by, so the guards will report the disturbance if you are lucky or the man in your room will leave you alone. I hear footsteps, someone is coming. Don't be afraid and don't try to escape, the heat will kill you before you make it anywhere. No matter what, don't keep quiet if you are in trouble."

He closed the door behind him.

A skinny Somali man came in with a plate of rice with tomato sauce for us to eat. I was worried about what Greek had said. If we didn't scream, would we be in trouble? I felt better knowing that Greek was with my brothers close by in case something happened. But there was no need to scream; the man served us the food and left. We ate what was served.

Afterward, Meskerem lay down, but I sat up as long as I could. The dust from the mattress made my eyes itchy and I kept rubbing them. Whenever I closed my eyes, my head would be filled with disturbing images. Most of the time I saw my father collapsed by the highway having missed his ride, and vultures surrounding him while he lay baking in the sun.

Meskerem's movements brought me back to the present. "Don't worry. I know what to say and do if any man comes in the night," she reassured me.

I finally rested my head on the flat mattress. It felt cool on my cheek. The dust was stronger, but I felt tired and closed my eyes; just when I was about to fall asleep I heard a woman's loud voice and some footsteps. She was speaking Somali. She went on and on for at least half an hour until a door slammed shut, and then all was quiet.

"There must be air-conditioning in this building," Meskerem said.

I wasn't sweating; in fact, the air was somewhat cool and it was already evening. I could still smell the burnt oil in the air. I was resting against the cool brick wall and Meskerem lay close to the edge of the mattress.

"We have to find a way to escape. I can walk in the heat as long as we are where Abba can find us," I told Meskerem.

Then I heard someone fidgeting with the doorknob. I lifted my head and saw it squeak open, very slowly. Did the guard hear what I had said? My heart began to pound. I hoped it was Yared or Asrat or even Greek. But then a short shadowy figure crept in, closing the door slowly. He tiptoed toward us.

I put my head down and tried to control my breathing.

"Stay down," Meskerem whispered to me.

I saw the dark figure find its way to the foot of the mattress and sit down. He then quickly shifted toward the top.

What I heard next was Meskerem's loud shout. "Stop, stop! If you don't, I will scream louder."

"Toss . . ." He put his finger on Meskerem's mouth to silence her.

I sat up immediately and pulled Meskerem toward me. He did not acknowledge my presence, even with my arms tight around Meskerem's shoulders. With Meskerem leaning on my chest, my back was pressed against the brick wall. We turned sideways.

I heard him muttering something as he pulled up Meskerem's dress. She pressed her back even harder on my chest and kicked her legs out like a wild mule. "If you don't stop, I will scream!"

"*Tinish, tinish,*" he struggled in Amharic. "A little, a little."

He pulled away a bit further and attempted to reason with her.

There was a dim light coming from the hallway, making it possible to see, and I spotted the brick cubes I had noticed earlier.

"Leave us alone. I am pregnant," Meskerem continued. "You are scaring my daughter."

I froze where I was as he turned to look at me. He reached out his hand and pushed me in an effort to get me to go back to sleep. I moved further away to the bottom corner of the mattress, preparing to grab a brick. Then he turned his attention to Meskerem. He unzipped his pants very quickly.

"What are you doing? Take me to the hospital if you don't believe me. I am pregnant and I am married," Meskerem shouted at the top of her lungs over and over again, kicking her legs and throwing her hands at him at the same time.

My heart was beating fast, but no words came out of my mouth. I pictured myself smashing his head with the brick, cracking open his skull, blood running all over his face. I held one of the bricks in my hand. It felt heavy but I knew I could lift it up above my head and throw it down hard. But what if he died?

Finally, Meskerem kicked him hard enough to ward him off, and he crawled on the floor like a lizard making his way to the door.

After that, Meskerem and I decided to sleep in turns like we often had to do in the desert.

The next morning, the same creepy animal was at the door with two cups of tea and a French baguette under his arm. He looked orderly in his clean uniform. He placed our breakfast on the floor without glancing at us and left.

I stretched my hands up, but my back was sore from the night's struggles.

We had not finished our tea before a man we hadn't seen before walked into our room. He was dressed in a brown uniform and wore black sandals. He had muddy brown eyes on a face that was soft, and he seemed polite. He introduced himself in Amharic. "My name is Ahmad and I am the warden." It was strange how Djiboutians could speak some Amharic but most refused to speak it unless it was a life-and-death situation.

"You shouldn't have tried to go to Djibouti without a pass," he scolded. "There are procedures set out for refugees and those procedures must be followed."

Meskerem and I did not dare speak.

"But now, seeing that you have already been caught committing a crime, we have to follow a different set of procedures altogether."

All I could think was that we should have obeyed Abba's order and stayed where he said he would find us. If we got deported back to Ethiopia, Abba would never find us. At least I would see my mother in Ethiopia, but not before I received the Derg's punishment. The warden continued. "We keep people who violate our laws in jail for a long time," he said authoritatively.

"Where are my sons?" Meskerem asked.

It was the first time I had heard Meskerem refer to my brothers as her sons. Last night, she had called me her daughter when the attacker came.

"I'll visit them once I am done here." He paused for a moment and continued. "You do have an option though," he said with a smile.

"I am looking for servants to clean, cook, and wash my clothes in my home and I want both of you to work for me."

Yared and Asrat were not offered a job at the warden's house. They were not even allowed to sleep there. We all got released because Meskerem and I had agreed to work for the warden. In turn, he agreed to take my brothers to the city and drop them off at the market. But I did not worry about Yared and Asrat. I knew they would find their way to the refugee camp and settle there like before. But, Meskerem and I had no one to protect us, not a good thing at all for refugee women like us. The warden had said if we tried to leave the house without his knowledge, we would be sure to end up in jail again, and he would not rush to rescue us the next time.

———◆•◆———

While we were walking to his house, I thought about the kind of work I could do at his house. My thin Somali dress had been very easy to wash. As soon as I soaked it in soapy water, the dust dissolved. After that all I had to do was rinse it and hang it up to dry on a tree. I thought I could wash twenty sarongs and dresses in one morning for the warden. The hardwood floor of the house would require waxing and rubbing for a long time to keep it shiny. I wondered how much he would pay us.

After about ten minutes, we reached his house. The outside was white like Ali Wollao's and had a small veranda. Inside, it had three rooms with minimal furnishings and decoration. There were one mattress and two chairs. No one was home when we arrived. The warden directed us to a room with a floor mat and two pillows where we were permitted to stay.

"We can't stay here," Meskerem confided to me once the warden had left the room.

"I would rather be at the refugee camp," I said, looking at my brothers.

"He is separating us on purpose, or else why would he want me and Asrat to leave. It is not safe for you at all," Yared agreed.

"What should we do then?" I asked desperately.

Meskerem said to Yared and Asrat, "When he takes you back to the city, pay attention to which way you are going, so when he drops you off, you know how to come back and get us. Until then, if he tries to bother us, I will know what to do. But you must come back for us in two days. If we manage to escape before you come, we will look for you at the camp or ask for you at Foad's shop."

"We have wandered in the desert for days, so this will be easy. Don't worry," Yared declared, sounding like my father.

"The Afar *dagu* is faster than an airplane, so be very careful not to tell anyone about our plan," Meskerem warned.

We now had to be careful about anything we did because a lot of people in the city had seen us driving through the streets in a police car. I suggested that we go back to Rhoda as soon as we escaped, and wait there until we heard from Abba. No one agreed with my idea, but Asrat and Yared left with the warden early that evening with a clear plan for them to come back and get us within two days.

Early the next morning, as Meskerem and I were wondering where to begin our work, since the warden had not given us any instructions, we saw two women let themselves in without knocking. They looked totally surprised to find us seated on the floor. They were both dressed in long Somali dresses and had their heads covered. One carried a metal jug and the other held two full bags in her arms. They headed to the kitchen without a word.

"*Aninay*," Meskerem shouted a greeting in Afar.

"*Negay*," one of them replied with a smile.

"*Amarigna tichilalachehu?* Do you speak Amharic?" Meskerem asked in Amharic.

"*Aown, enichilalen*," one of them replied.

Meskerem asked them who they were and what they were doing at the house so early in the morning.

"We are not related to the warden," one of them said, stopping at the kitchen door. She had a long neck and, when she smiled, I saw her gums were coloured black. The two of them slipped back into the kitchen and began preparing meals without further explanation.

A few minutes later, they came and gave us yoghurt and bread with some tea. We wondered why the warden had not told us about the women.

Finally, Meskerem got up and went into the kitchen. She asked them if they could show us what we should be doing.

"We thought we were hired to do the cleaning and the cooking," Meskerem said after they told us they were in fact the maids. Their names were Luba and Fatima.

They looked at each other and laughed.

"How much did he say he would pay you?" Luba, the one with the black gums, asked.

"We are not staying in Dikhil for long anyway," Meskerem continued.

"Where are you planning to go?" Luba asked with a smirk.

"To Djibouti. To meet my husband," Meskerem replied.

"You are married!" Luba sounded shocked.

I pulled Meskerem's arm and whispered to her not to tell them any of our plans. But she said she knew what she was doing. So she recounted some of the things that had happened to us. To my surprise, in exchange they were telling us the warden's secret plan.

"He is looking for a wife or wives to keep close to Dikhil as his other wife refuses to leave her hometown. He has been looking especially for Habesha women."

Meskerem won their sympathy when she said she was pregnant.

"I am not good at cooking, cleaning, or washing. The only thing I can do is go to school. I am in grade eight and I speak some English," I said flatly.

They both stared at me as if I had come from a different planet altogether. I was not sure if they had ever met a girl who never cooked, cleaned, or did any house chores. I must have sounded like a man to them, but I did not care. I was just too upset. After that they did not talk about marriage. They worked all day while Meskerem and I waited for something to happen.

For two days, we did not see or hear from the warden. The two women, Luba and Fatima, however, continued to cook, clean, and feed us. They said as long as we were under the warden's care, it was automatically their responsibility to look after us. They didn't permit us to go to the market with them or to leave the house. Meskerem and I wondered if Asrat and Yared were safe and if they would come back to get us.

On the third day, we noticed a few men arriving at the warden's house. It seemed there was going to be an important gathering. More men soon arrived, and once they were all settled, I peeked into the room. The scene reminded me of the first time Yared and I had taken our family to Rhoda's house. The men were sitting in the centre of the room smoking, drinking tea, and chewing qat.

When Luba and Fatima finished serving them food and tea, Luba came out to the veranda where Meskerem and I were sitting.

"The warden wants to speak with you," she said.

"He's inside!" Meskerem could not believe what she heard.

All kinds of thoughts raced through my head as I stumbled into the room full of men. They looked up and I looked down. I squeezed my sweaty palms, thinking that if they tried to separate Meskerem and me, I would run away.

When I finally looked up, I couldn't believe my eyes. Ali Wollao was sitting next to the warden. I was happy, frightened, and embarrassed all at the same time. It occurred to me that he must have known all that had happened to us from the day we left his house through the Afar *dagu*.

Considering how generous Ali Wollao had been, we should not have kept secrets from him. If we had been jailed for keeping secrets, that would have made better sense.

Luba acted as translator. Ali spoke gently and slowly, as he always did.

"He would like you to consider coming back to his house and wait for him to get you the refugee passes you need to enter Djibouti," Luba said.

Even Meskerem was speechless. But Ali continued, "I have learned that Terrefe is not in Dikhil. I don't know where he is, but he could be in Djibouti and I will have people look for him." It seemed as though we had always had some luck through all our bad times, and that luck had always rescued us.

Rhoda beamed with excitement at the sight of us. She had been missing us. She promised to share with us one of her beauty secrets and told us to be ready early in the morning.

After breakfast, Rhoda sat on the floor on the veranda with a metallic bowl. She called out to us to join her in the fresh air. In the bowl she was mixing a yellow mudlike substance with her hands, adding some kind of liquid and stirring it quickly, as if she were beating eggs. When she had poured in the last drop, she said, "Here, tie your hair with these." She handed me a purple bandana and Meskerem got one with a yellow flowery print.

Then Rhoda inspected our faces and fixed my hair properly. It was completely covered with the bandana. "You have a lot of hair," she commented and rubbed the yellow mud on our faces. It felt cool and tingly and smelled like turmeric. She said it would clean our faces and leave them spotless. She pasted the rest of the mixture onto her face while looking in a mirror, covering every spot, being careful around her eyes and nose, and applying it all the way down her neck. I couldn't wait to see what we looked like after we washed.

"You look like a yellow bird," Meskerem joked.

"How long do we keep it on?" I asked as I lay down on a mattress, making myself comfortable for a short nap.

"As long as you want, but you get the best result if you keep it on the whole day." She then went about her business, even to the market, looking like a yellow bird. In the evening, we washed our faces. My complexion had changed to a radiant yellow, more like the local women. My face had never felt so smooth and clean. I wondered if Yared and Asrat would notice the difference.

Meskerem also looked much healthier. For the first time since we started our journey, she decided to make up her eyes with *kohl* and wear lipstick, which she borrowed from Rhoda.

This was how Rhoda celebrated our return.

On the drive back to Ali Wollao's, Meskerem had asked to stop at Foad's spice shop to leave a message for Yared and Asrat, telling them where they could find us.

They came the very next day, happy to hear the good news of our rescue. They still had our original shelter at the camp and nothing much had changed. Suddenly everything was back to the way it was before we tried to escape Dikhil. Meskerem and I continued to stay with Rhoda, and Yared and Asrat came to stay if the house was not crowded, but otherwise they stayed at the camp.

We knew it would take another month to save enough money to get us to Djibouti. The escape plan was the only one anyone was willing to discuss; no one wanted to stay and wait for Abba. I was fine to stay here with Rhoda. In the meantime, I learned a few words of Afar from her.

There were three other official languages I could also learn: Somali, Arabic, and French. Even though Rhoda knew Somali and Arabic, she used them only when she went to the market.

So the little English I knew was useless in Dikhil. But when I told Rhoda that I knew some English, she was impressed—as though I had actually gotten a degree from a foreign university.

One morning I was having white bread with red sauce and goat meat with tea for breakfast on the veranda. I had had a good night's sleep and felt the most rested I had been in a long time. The brightness of the sun reminded me of our yard at home. It was a clear morning; the sun was warm and gentle and the dust had settled. I had never seen a morning like this in Dikhil.

Yared and Asrat were not coming to Rhoda's today. They would probably go to the city centre to visit Foad and have a Coke for breakfast while they planned our next escape. There was nowhere I could go by myself where I felt safe.

I dipped my bread into the red sauce, scooped up some meat, and took a big bite. The sauce was sweet. I was sure Rhoda had put tons of sugar in it. Rhoda loved sugar, even with her lamb sauce.

After breakfast, I took out my braids and combed my hair. I loved how Rhoda's rosemary oil made my hair shiny and soft, and how it restored the curly waves I had had in Ethiopia. I rubbed it all over my hands and legs too. I inhaled its fragrance and the strong aroma triggered a memory of my favourite mornings in Addis, when Yared, Asrat, and I would perch on the front veranda of our house, the yellow sun warm on our faces, and listen to the laughter of my baby sister Kalkidan inside the house. It was all coming back to me . . .

The sound of a car horn made me open my eyes at once and I jumped to my feet with excitement. "Abba!" I shouted. But what I saw outside was not my father's Land Rover but Ali Wollao's uncle's green Mercedes, shimmering in the Dikhil sun.

"*Aninay*," Habib greeted Meskerem and me on the steps of the veranda as he came up.

"*Negay*," Meskerem replied.

Rhoda was right about Habib coming back this way again to see his new wife, though I didn't expect him so soon. Still, my happiness didn't diminish upon seeing that it was not my father who had arrived.

To Djibouti

———————◗◆◖———————

"HABIB IS WILLING TO TAKE you to Djibouti city today," Rhoda announced as she joined Meskerem and me on the veranda. "He can take two people in his car." I stopped oiling my hair.

"Today?" Meskerem muttered not sure what she'd heard.

"Yes, this morning," Rhoda replied in a clear voice.

"You mean now?" I asked.

"As soon as he is ready, in about an hour."

"But we don't have our permits, besides Yared and Asrat are not here," Meskerem hesitated.

"You need not worry about those permits when you are with Habib," she said confidently and hurried back inside to attend to Habib and his guests.

I sat there somewhat confused about what to do: should I run and get Yared and Asrat or not? Only two people could go. It had been over two weeks since we last saw Abba and we had been worrying about him ever since. This was our chance to look for him in Djibouti.

"We should talk to Yared and Asrat about this," I said, looking at Meskerem. "You are right," she agreed.

"Let me go there and see what they say." I jumped to my feet, and put on my slippers.

Just then Rhoda came back to the veranda with more tea and Meskerem asked her what we should do about my brothers.

Rhoda assured us that Habib would be back again soon to visit his new wife and then she would make sure that Asrat and Yared got a ride with him. The prospect of leaving my brothers behind made my stomach uneasy. I felt unsure and fearful, as though the moment I separated from them something terrible would happen to me.

"I will convince Yared and Asrat to stay here. I will take care of them, I promise," Rhoda reassured me.

It was all happening too fast for me to think clearly. I had come to trust Rhoda. She had clothed, fed, and sheltered us from the unforgiving heat. In the Danakil Desert we had been betrayed by people we trusted, but there were others who upheld our trust and helped us survive. I would continue to trust Rhoda.

———◆·◆———

As I raced through the streets of Dikhil, past all the nice white houses with flowers, past the market area, past the police station and all the way to the outskirts where the shanty shelters of the refugee camp were concentrated, all I thought about was the chance for me to continue school when I made it to Djibouti city. I reached the camp totally out of breath and found Asrat sitting outside the shelter cutting his fingernails. He was surprised to see me drenched in sweat. "Beth, what are you doing here? Is everything okay?"

"Everything is fine." I stopped to catch my breath.

"What is happening?" Yared came out of the shelter. "Beth. Why are you here?"

"I came to tell you something."

I looked around and everything seemed exactly the same as the first time Yared and I stumbled into the camp—not a single thing had changed. The shelter still had no door. Animal smells and wood smoke filled the air. I could hear children crying. *If we stay here, nothing will ever change,* I thought.

"Ali Wollao's uncle, Habib, the man with the green Mercedes, is here again and he has agreed to take two people with him in his car back to Djibouti," I said.

"How much do we have to pay him?" Asrat wanted to know.

"I don't think we have to pay him. Rhoda said he was a very important person and does not take money from refugees."

"I just don't know if we should trust him," Yared frowned. "Remember what happened with the last person who promised to take us to Djibouti?"

"We have to take every chance we get," Asrat disagreed, "or else what difference does it make whether we are in this stinking camp or in jail? How about if you and Meskerem leave? That way we can check with Rhoda if anything happens to you. We have to trust somebody."

"Rhoda said you are welcome to stay at Ali Wollao's until Habib comes back . . . if Meskerem and I left now."

———— ◆◆◆ ————

The car started with a jerk and as it picked up speed, I looked back and saw Rhoda still planted where she was in front of Ali Wollao's house, her pretty dress waving in the wind. I knew that she was crying.

We sat in the back among a heap of qat leaves and a big box full of dates. I was surprised that the shiny Mercedes was not as clean as I expected. I carried a small plastic bag containing my miniskirt, Adidas, and the beige shirt I had worn in the Danakil.

Looking out the window, I could see camels and their sand trails billowing like smoke. The sand hills came and went and, from time to time, a big truck passed, whipping up a dust cloud behind.

How easy it had become to separate from my brothers, I thought to myself. Things seemed to have a way of unfolding in an unpredictable way. I concluded that it was better to be like the Afar: adaptable, fearless, and decisive.

"What's wrong?" Meskerem asked, noticing that I had been staring out the window a long time.

"Nothing," I whispered.

She rested her head back, closed her eyes, and took a deep breath.

"Are you worried?" I asked, looking at her.

"We will be fine," she whispered.

"Foad told us the checkpoint to Djibouti city is barricaded with a wire fence and the only way to enter is through a guarded gate," I explained to her.

I saw Habib throw a glance in our direction.

"Shhhh. Everything will be okay," Meskerem replied.

An hour later we approached the city of Djibouti. We lined up at the checkpoint to be searched. Foad was right. The officials in Djibouti had done everything they possibly could to protect their city from refugees. There was a single main building about the size of our house in Addis, and a few feet from it were about ten armed soldiers in uniform. In the full heat of the mid-morning sun, they were searching every car, every permit and identification. On each side of the road was a razor-wire fence twenty feet high and as far as the eye could see. It was obvious we could not enter Djibouti city any other way.

"We should have covered our heads," I said to Meskerem.

"We should have, but Rhoda was sure we did not need to."

Slowly our car approached the gate. I was perspiring and felt lightheaded. When I saw two officers marching toward us, I looked down and away.

What transpired between the guards and Habib happened so quickly that I couldn't grasp it right away. Suddenly we were on the other side of the wire fence with nothing ahead of us but a long stretch of highway. Was I dreaming? I turned my head to see if we had actually passed the soldiers and saw the dark shadow of their building behind us. I tried to recall what had happened. As we approached the soldiers, they stood in a line, feet together, rifles down, hands raised in a salute. Then our car pulled up and stopped before them. It couldn't be us they had greeted like diplomats, could it? Who was Habib? I looked at him from behind, at the back of his soft curly hair; he sat there talking to the driver as if nothing unusual had happened. It was hard to believe that we were finally where Abba wanted us to be.

The empty highway soon turned from brown dirt to black asphalt, and the desert horizon soon turned into a city scape. There were four- and five-storey buildings, which I had not seen in Dikhil. More men and women wore Western clothes. Because we had arrived before noon, all the shops and restaurants were open. The air smelled fresh but moist and carried the scent of the Red Sea. The trees looked thicker but not much greener than in Dikhil. People drove as if it were their last day on earth. There were no lines separating the lanes, so I did not know if we were driving on the right or the wrong side of the road. A truck or van travelling in the opposite direction would come into our lane and face us directly before swerving aside. My stomach would get knotted. If that were not enough to kill half the nation in a day, Europeans on motorcycles raced by, deafening us.

"Did Rhoda tell you where Habib would drop us off?" I asked Meskerem. Since neither Habib nor the driver spoke Amharic, they did not talk to us.

"She just said he will take us to Djibouti. I don't want us to be a burden on him. He can drop us off anywhere, it doesn't matter. If it is anything like Dire Dawa, we will find a mosque and we will be safe there," Meskerem said confidently.

Our driver made a sharp right turn into a street lined with beautiful villas. Between the houses, I caught glimpses of the rust-coloured water of the Red Sea; I took in a deep breath, and without knowing it I uttered "Djibouti" and tears filled my eyes. The car entered a road that went around a large circle the size of a soccer field. And then suddenly I felt that we were being chased.

The familiar rat, tat, tat from the sky above and, sure enough, there was a military helicopter hovering over us. But our car picked up speed and twisted and turned on the streets. I was now convinced that this was a trap and that Habib was handing us over to the Derg. Why else was a military helicopter following us? I was distracted by a blond Frenchwoman in white shorts, jogging by herself around the circle. The sound of the helicopter grew distant and our car slowed down. I noticed boats parked in the driveways of the beautiful houses. I looked at Meskerem and realized that she too was nervous.

We approached a blue iron gate. The driver stopped, jumped out, and ran to open it. At that same moment I saw the helicopter landing in the middle of a field not far from us, red dust swirling around it.

"We should run now," I said to Meskerem.

"What are you talking about? Please stop crying, they will get suspicious," Meskerem scolded me.

"Who is in the helicopter?" I demanded.

"It's a French military helicopter," Meskerem answered.

I felt as if a big rock was lifted off my chest. At the gate, a short man wearing a white hat opened the latch and swung it wide open. When our car rolled past him, I recognized him as the religious leader from Ali Wollao's house. Sheik Ibrahim. Habib had brought us to his home.

Habib's House

———————◆———————

If the only home you've known is a rock, then that is all you know. —AFAR PROVERB

HABIB'S HOUSE WAS BY far the biggest I had seen since leaving Ethiopia. It was encircled by a brick wall, which was surrounded on the outside by tall trees, making it seem as though the house were in the middle of an oasis. The air was scented with the fragrance of the sea. The veranda, as big as a tennis court, had a low, cement parapet and looked over the gravelled front yard. There was no grass and there were no flowers in sight.

The first room we entered was huge but bare, except for a large fridge—one of the most useful items in Djibouti—and a small table on the wall opposite the fridge. The walls were white and bare, but the floor was a smooth grey ceramic dotted in silver glitter. It was so clean and beautiful I hesitated to step on it with my dirty slippers. Even the clothes I wore felt heavy in the lightness of the room. Habib ushered us in quickly, and Meskerem and I had no choice but to follow him through the door into a dark narrow corridor that had closed doors on either side. Dim lights shone on a cloud of smoke and I smelled the room behind the door facing us before Habib even opened it. The scent was a mix of aromatic incense, cinnamon, and cigarette smoke. It was a beautiful bedroom. A king-size bed was in the centre, with white night tables on each side and a matching headboard with gold trim. The bedspread had a complex pattern of green, pink, blue, and white, and a telephone sat on one of the tables and a lamp on the other.

Then I saw a woman resting on her side on a mattress on the floor. Her large size reminded me of my grandmother. She was wearing a long Somali dress like Meskerem and I, except hers had a delicate pattern and the fabric was thick cotton, clearly much more expensive than ours. I had learned that Afar men and women dressed the same from city to city; the men wore *shirit* around the waist and women wore long flowing dresses called *dirac* over a full-length half-slip called *dree*. Another woman was sitting on the mattress, next to the sleeping woman, and just then two girls walked in behind us. We had all arrived together during a tea ceremony. There was some loose qat on the floor, but not as much as I had seen at Ali Wollao's house.

Habib squatted down near the big woman and whispered into her ear while Meskerem and I stood helplessly looking at the two girls who were staring back at us. The familiar aroma of the cinnamon tea blended with the incense, the perfume, and the scent of the sea instantly made me feel welcome.

Both girls had short hair. While the older had combed her silky hair back, the chubby one had hers natural with its soft caramel curls twisted around her ears. The older one couldn't have been more than nine, but the loud purple nail polish, the sleek wet look of her black hair, the heavy dark eyeliner, and the careful manner in which she arranged her dress when she sat gave the impression that she was a model.

When Habib finished talking to the big woman, he got up and headed for the bathroom next door.

"Selam. Why don't you sit down?" The woman's Amharic got

my attention right away.

"Selam." Meskerem smiled. "You speak Amharic."

"Yes," she said, and then she spoke in her language in a stern voice to the children who bounced off the mattress like kittens and perched on the floor.

"You must be tired after the long drive from Dikhil. Why don't you sit here?"

Meskerem sat next to the woman at her request and I managed to find a place near the children.

She told us her name was Isha and that she was Habib's first wife. They had five children. She then introduced the two girls as her own daughters. The older child was named Amina, and the younger one was Rokia. The other woman was the cleaning lady, also named Amina.

"Habib told me about your situation after he heard about it at Ali Wollao's house a few weeks ago," she said. "Have you located your husband?" She looked at Meskerem.

"No," Meskerem replied with a look of despair.

"Ali Wollao will take care of your two boys in Dikhil until Habib arranges to bring them here," she said.

Meskerem looked quite content in the company of Isha, a married woman with children who understood her situation. It didn't take long before Meskerem told Isha that we had left Kalkidan, my sister, behind.

"*Estafrullah!*" Isha cried out just short of screaming. "Habib did not say anything about a baby that was left behind."

Just then Habib emerged from the bathroom, his sandals still wet from the shower. Isha shouted something at him, and he squatted near her to hear the rest.

Isha sat up with great difficulty as her stomach was large. Her dress was as soft as silk and sparkled like gold. She had tied a similar fabric around her head, leaving only the soft black hair around her forehead visible. Both women were barefoot and their hands and feet were dyed with henna in intricate designs. We listened to Isha while sipping the cinnamon tea she had offered us. She had been born in Dewele, a small village in Ethiopia near the border with Djibouti, to an Ethiopian Afar woman and an Arab businessman. She spoke Amharic, Somali, and Afar. The only language she had not mastered was French. She understood everything we told her. She understood our way of life and our culture and the food we ate.

"*Injera* and *wot* are my favourite foods," she said with a smile. "In all of my experience, no matter how close I follow the recipe for *injera*, it never turns out the same way as it does when I make it in Ethiopia. Some days the mixture is so flat that we end up dumping it."

"Well, the mixture has to be left over a night or two, and with the temperature soaring so high here, I doubt if it rises in the same manner as it does in the mild climate of Addis Ababa," Meskerem said.

"That's just it. And you know, my friends in Saudi also tried to prepare it, but they completely gave up because their mixture always went bad. So what we do now is make *luh-luh*, the closest thing we can get to *injera*."

———◆◆———

"We are very thankful for what your husband has done for us. The soldiers didn't search us," Meskerem said to Isha.

"They never search Habib's car because of the license plate," Isha said. She then changed the conversation before we had a chance to ask what was special about Habib's license plate.

"When was the last time you saw your husband?"

"Over two weeks ago," Meskerem whispered.

"He probably is in Djibouti; he couldn't be anywhere else. I will have people look for him." Isha took down my father's full name.

I felt confident that the Afar news network, *Dagu*, would bring Isha my father's whereabouts in no time.

Isha continued, "I know you Addis Ababa women don't sleep on the floor. Until we get you an extra bed, you can use the couch in the living room."

Although we no longer carried dust on our feet as we did in the Danakil Desert, I was sure Isha knew we had been sleeping on floors during our journey. When Meskerem told her about our ordeal through the desert and in Dikhil, Isha raised her hands up high and shouted "*Stafrullah*. Forgive me, Lord. How great is Allah? How good of Rhoda to shelter you," she said with tearful eyes.

Isha kept crying when she heard about the robbers, "They are *waraba*. The hyena men who do not fear Allah."

My skin felt moist and cool in the air-conditioned room. Keda Amina went to prepare lunch. Isha said we could use the phone to contact anyone we wished.

Isha and Meskerem continued their conversation, now talking about Harar, the Ethiopian province where they were both born—Meskerem in the capital Dire Dawa, and Isha in Delewe: Suddenly the bedroom door was flung open and two boys and a girl barged in. They stood staring at Meskerem and me while Ounda Amina and Rokia giggled.

"These are the rest of my children," Isha said, introducing us.

Laoita was her eldest son, about sixteen, and Mohammed came next. The girl was called Medina. Laoita and Mohammed smiled as Isha went on to tell them about us in Afar, while Medina frowned and continued to stare.

Keda Amina brought in a large tray filled with enough rice to feed ten people. In a separate bowl, she served camel yoghurt. She also brought a jar full of ice cold water. She carefully placed the tray in the centre of the floor where we sat. As the steam rose into the air from the rice, I smelled onion, tomato, cinnamon, cardamom, and rosemary, and I could see big chunks of meat on roasted ribs.

"*Besmillah*," Isha blessed the food and ordered us to eat. All hands reached for the tray.

"Iyan Meskerem." Isha called Meskerem "Iyan," which meant "my sister and also looking in my direction." "Would you like a fork?" Meskerem and I declined.

It was nice to see Isha's children eating with us. They all had soft black hair. Amina had combed her hair flat to her skull and applied generous amounts of gel. Laoita most resembled his father and mother. His brown, even-toned complexion and his smile were like his mother's, but his gentleness resembled that of his father's. His face was rarely without a smile.

The only child who made me uncomfortable was Ounda Amina, who looked perfect compared to how I looked. My slippers were dirty, my donated Somali dress paled in comparison to her shimmering silver dress. My hair had suffered a great deal. It would be a very long time before I owned any gold jewelry like Amina. She was wearing a white bra, which I could see through her dress, and she didn't even need it.

After we finished our meal, Isha said, "Come. Let me show you the room where you will stay until I figure something out."

We followed her into the darkened hallway that Habib had led us through earlier and Isha stopped in front of a door and inserted the key.

"This is the living room," she announced.

I saw a burgundy couch and a rectangular glass coffee table in the middle of the room. Against the longer side stood a large, shiny, ebony wall unit displaying two polished elephant tusks. I had seen ivory rings, necklaces and bracelets before, but never had I seen a life-size elephant tusk.

"Ali Wollao slept on the couch and he liked the privacy of the room here," Isha said. "There is a small bed in the other room," Isha added, walking towards a door I hadn't noticed before. It was not locked and we were led into an even more crowded room, which contained the dining table with all the chairs turned over on it. Behind the table, in the corner, was a single bunk.

"Bethleen, you can sleep here," Isha said to me. I agreed right away, happy that the elephant tusks were in another room.

"Let me show you the rest of the house," Isha said, "so you know your way around."

We'd already been to Habib's bedroom, so Isha took us to the hallway and pointed to a closed door. "That room belongs to Fatima, Habib's other wife. She has a one-year-old boy," she announced.

I was amazed at how my culture differed so much from that of this family. I had a stepmother, but my father married her after divorcing my mother. I decided not to think too much about cultural differences because it was unsettling. What if they didn't celebrate *Enkutatash* (the Ethiopian New Year), *Gena* (Christmas), or any of the holidays that we did in Ethiopia?

Isha moved quickly from Fatima's door to the room with the large fridge. I stepped very gently on the beautiful floor. Isha explained that at times the room was full with travellers and visitors who slept there for a night or two. Behind the room was the kitchen, which was twice the size of Rhoda's, and next to it, facing the backyard, was the bathroom for everyone other than Isha and Habib. Outside, facing the kitchen and the bathroom was a big white house where an Arab diplomat and his family lived, and next to that, on the right, was a two-storey brown brick building owned by a French family.

After our showers, Meskerem and I sat on the couch in the living room enjoying the air-conditioning.

"Please make yourselves at home and let me know if you need anything," Isha told us. "But one thing I want to tell you is to please not leave the house on your own, because people have told me that the policemen on the streets are trained to spot illegal refugees and I don't want anything to happen to the two of you while you are under Habib's responsibility. Also, don't worry about what food to eat because Sheik Ibrahim and the other men do the groceries and anything else that is needed. Even I don't go out unless I really need to."

That night, as I looked up and saw hundreds of shimmering

stars and the Milky Way I thought of our home in Addis. I felt sad. Not too long ago, I had a country, lots of friends, a dog, a home, a mother, a father, two brothers and a sister. Was this new life real, or was it a dream? It had barely been half a day since I saw my brothers but I was starting to worry about them. I stared at the clear view of the sky, as intently as I had done many times in the desert, because every time I looked at it, it filled up the hole in my heart with its richness and powerful beauty, forever reminding me that this earth was still a glorious place.

For the next several days, Meskerem and I did mostly what we had been doing in Dikhil—wash our clothes, comb our hair, eat, take a shower—but the one big difference was that at night we stepped out onto the veranda to watch TV with guests or Habib's children and wives.

The TV programs in Djibouti started around seven in the evening and lasted for about four hours, beginning in Afar and then repeating in Somali, Arabic, and French for one hour each. People watched the shows in all the four languages, and turned the TV off at around eleven.

Together Again

WE HAD BEEN IN Djibouti more than two weeks. One day, Meskerem and I were in Isha's bedroom seated around the qat, when Isha announced, "Iyan Meskerem, Habib has found your husband and he is bringing him tonight."

"Where did he find him?" Meskerem's eyes bulged.

"He didn't say, but please know I am expecting him to stay here with you."

"Is Abba okay?" I asked, trying to contain my excitement.

"Yes, he is well," Isha said.

I now felt confident that Habib would bring Yared and Asrat from Dikhil, just as he had promised. We would get our permits; Abba would see to it and everything would work out just like Abba had planned it.

That night we waited and waited well past dinnertime, but Abba and Habib did not show up. I was falling asleep. It was past midnight when I heard men's voices behind our bedroom door. Soon there was a knock. Meskerem opened the door. It was Habib, and trailing behind him was my father, followed by Sheikh Ibrahim and two other people I had never seen before.

"Endemin nachehu?" (How are you doing?) Abba said with a wide smile.

"We worried so much, thank God you are okay." Meskerem rushed to give Abba a hug.

I couldn't take my eyes off my father. I was sure my face was shining like the desert moon from sheer happiness.

"You know how this place is, but I was not named survivor for nothing," Abba said with a twinkle in his eyes.

I fell into his arms, smelt the scent of his cigarette on his white shirt. If only I could be around my father all the time, life would be much better. His face was clean shaven and his black wavy curls had been smoothly combed back, just the way he combed his hair in Addis. He wore a clean white shirt with the sleeves rolled up and beige trousers I had never seen before, and he still wore sandals.

Habib spoke, but in such a low tone that only Isha was able to hear and translate. Of course, Habib was saying, Abba must stay with us and should get some rest.

"It was most generous of you to help my family and we are very grateful, but I promise you we will be well on our way once my sons join us," Abba told him.

Once everyone left the room, Abba told us why he was not able to get us out of Dikhil as he had promised. The day he left Dikhil, he hid in the back of a truck among the goats and sheep. "Never mind the animal's droppings and stink and one animal after another tripping and stamping on me, it took the driver three hours to get to Djibouti."

Abba continued, "I jumped off at the market and as soon as my feet touched the dusty ground, a policeman spotted me and ordered me to stop. He said he would shoot and kill me if I didn't stop and I understood him even though he was speaking in Somali. While he shoved me into the back of his van, I pleaded with him in Amharic, telling him I have children and not to put me in prison. But he ignored me and delivered me to a very crowded jail," Abba said.

It was upsetting, hearing his story and how the jail was filled with Ethiopian refugees. Why was being a refugee a crime? Why wouldn't the police let the refugees just be until their permits got sorted out? We were stateless, without our families and friends and everything else that came with losing a country overnight. The police came after us when they already knew our backs were against the wall.

My father continued with his story. He convinced the guards that he was sick, and they sent him to a hospital. At the break of dawn the next day, he escaped and found himself on the streets. He saw a well-dressed Ethiopian man and spoke to him in Amharic, asking him if he could help.

"Do you remember Melaku?" Abba asked. Meskerem and I drew blank and my father continued with his story. He stayed with the Ethiopian man for three days while looking for an old friend called Hailu he had heard was living in Djibouti.

Melaku didn't know Hailu, but took Abba to an Ethiopian restaurateur who knew every one in the city. Her name was Askalech Goshu. She fed them an Ethiopian meal and told him that Hailu often came to the restaurant. The next time he came she would tell him about Abba.

As Abba and Melaku left the restaurant, the police captured them at gunpoint and sent them to jail. Again Abba claimed sickness and was sent to the hospital where he was given pills and told to lie down.

"When they finally left me alone for the day, I fell asleep, but when I awoke, it was all quiet and I had my chance to escape. As I slipped out the door, I bumped into the big doctor, who stared me directly in the eye. I walked myself back to my bed and he followed me. It was then that he told me, with a patient in the next bed translating in Amharic, that my family was here in Djibouti and if I just stayed put until the evening, someone would take me to you."

And finally the doctor brought him to Habib's house.

"And so here I am."

I missed my brothers and my sister terribly. I was starting to understand what Abba meant when he asked us to trust him on decisions he made regarding the future, for he was sure it would make sense to us later. In Ethiopia, I had thought Asrat was obnoxious; we picked on each other and fought over almost everything. In Ethiopia, I had thought the tall grass of our lawn was too much work to maintain. In Ethiopia, I had complained that the food I ate was too spicy. Now, looking back, I could see that the fights with my brothers were actually play, the tall grass was a fortress, and the spicy food was my deep root in the rich soil of Ethiopia.

I was in a house full of people, but I felt at odds with them, not really connecting to anyone but Abba. Isha's sons were closer in age to me than her daughters, but they spoke not a word of Amharic and because of that I felt muted. Meskerem was lucky to have Isha. I sat silently on the mattress whenever they talked, about Dire Dawa, husbands, and children. But I couldn't complain. We had a roof over our heads, regular meals, a shower everyday, and people who cared about us. Things could be far worse. I gave thanks to God, but all I wanted now was to be with my brothers, so I could play, joke, fight with them.

A few days after Abba's arrival, one bright Djibouti morning as I lay on my bed in Isha's living room, listening to the chirping of the birds, I heard a loud bang on the front gate. The gate was usually opened early in the morning, but for some reason it was closed that day. I thought it was one of Habib and Isha's relatives. I stayed in bed but awake. Abba and Meskerem slept in the room where the tables and chairs were stored. More banging followed. I sat up and fixed my head wrap quickly. I had never heard such persistent banging; whoever it was was not giving up.

A long silence, then more banging. That's it, I thought; I will get Abba. I jumped off the couch and headed to Abba's room and as I stood with my hand ready to knock on the door, I listened quietly. Silence. Then a few minutes later, someone was knocking at the living room door.

Abba must have heard the knocking; he stormed out from the

storage room where he was sleeping, fixing his sarong, and marched
past me to the door, muttering, "For God's sake, are these people
dead or do they want their door smashed down? Who is it?"

Without waiting for a reply, he swung the door open. I stood
behind him, and Meskerem came and stood behind me.

Who could have delivered them but God himself? I couldn't
believe my eyes; there they were, my two brothers, standing at
the door. Someone must have let them in. I felt ashamed; I had left
Dikhil without them, and here I was staying in Djibouti in a fancy
house. They had found us instead of us finding them. My brothers
were nothing like my father when it came to enduring hardship. It
showed on their sunken faces; their cheekbones protruded and their
hair and clothes were covered in dust. If they had cut their Afros,
they might not have look so ragged.

I was the happiest I had been since we left Ethiopia. I hugged
them each and told them how I missed them.

"Let me take a good look at you," Abba smiled proudly.

Yared began sobbing. Abba gave him a big hug. "Everything is
okay now, my son. Didn't I tell you we were going to be just fine?"
Abba held him by the shoulders, and Yared wiped his tears. "We
are safe in Habib's house," Abba said with a gentle smile. "And it
won't be long before we leave Djibouti and start a brand new life.
Just keep staying strong as you have been, and everything will be
okay. How did you get here? Did Habib send someone for you?"

"We came on our own," Asrat said. "It didn't take us long to save
enough UN food. There were some new Ethiopian refugees who
came and stayed for just a few days and when they left, they gave us
their unfinished rations. So we sold the food and found a driver. It
was no problem getting to Djibouti, but once the driver dropped us
at the Megala, the police picked us up in seconds."

"I wonder what these policemen did before Ethiopian refugees
started to arrive in Djibouti!" Abba said angrily. "Sit on the couch
and tell us how you did it."

Asrat couldn't wait to continue. "They loaded us onto the back of a big military truck and drove around the city and picked up some other people from the streets. Some of the others said we were going to jail. Indeed, that was where we ended up, but the truck moved backward like the trucks in Addis Ababa backing into the butcher's shop. When they opened the door we were ready to get out, but they ordered us to make room and loaded more people from the jail, locked the door tight, and drove and drove. I thought they were taking us back to Ethiopia. But they stopped in the middle of nowhere and told us to get out and unlocked the door. Then we thought they had brought us to a maximum security prison, but once they made sure we were all out, they drove back just as fast and disappeared. We were in the middle of nowhere, no houses, nobody at all, just dusty hills all around and the intense sun on our backs. Some of the men started running in one direction while others ran in the other. One of the men, named Dawit, said not to worry. He had been left like that before and he had walked back to Djibouti. So we followed him.

"And so we came back to Djibouti. We kept a lookout for police and, following Dawit's instructions, we headed to the safest place in Djibouti, the mosque. At prayer times, we pretended to be praying, copying the men by bending our knees and putting our heads to the ground. Some of the men were looking at us suspiciously, but they let us be. We slept there for several nights.

"One day we were wandering around the market, doing nothing in particular, when we bumped into Dawit. He was unusually ecstatic when he saw us and shouted for all the market people to hear, 'You guys would never guess how lucky you are. Someone told me, your family is staying at a rich man's house.'"

"I am sorry," Abba said, looking at Yared and Asrat in turn. "You suffered so much. I'm sorry it took this long for us to be in Djibouti, but we have all made it, just like I knew we would. From now on, things will be much easier and we will get our permits in no time. I will work on it every day, you will see."

———— ◆•◆ ————

It did not rain much in Djibouti, and the year we were there, 1980, would be recorded as one of the hottest and driest in history. Everything was slow—the banks closed early; most business places were shut down before noon; people slept outside except for the handful of rich ones like Habib whose houses were blessed with air-conditioning—but Abba was hardly inside. He went everywhere his legs could take him to make his plan work.

The Birthday

HABIB'S BACKYARD WAS COVERED in gravel all the way to the fence. I chose to wash my clothes here at sunset to avoid the heat. I had found a spot near the steps where I set up the *safa* and the laundry detergent, and pulled the water towards me. I had a clear view of the backyards belonging to the French and Arab families living on the other side. The French family had furnished their yard with tables and chairs, and under one of the trees sat a ping-pong table. I had played a lot of ping-pong with Asrat and Yared in Addis. I noticed that there was a girl about my age in the French home who was often in the backyard with her parents, so I assumed that she was an only child, but she had lots of friends who came to play with her.

There was a long green plastic clothesline where I could hang my wash. I stayed in the backyard long after I had finished washing the clothes. I noticed in the French backyard a large collection of big colourful balloons, the size of which I had never seen before, hanging from the trees, on the walls, and even on the fence separating us; light bulbs in green, yellow, red, and white shone on the faces of the people whose numbers were increasing by the minute.

I had not seen so many people in one place partying ever since I left Ethiopia. On one table there was a cake with candles, and on another all kinds of pastries, and there was an area just for drinks. It was the daughter's birthday party.

I went in and got my brothers to come out and watch. The three of us sat in the dark as though watching a movie. Suddenly, I saw a shadowy figure step out our kitchen door and come marching toward us. As the shadow got nearer, I recognized it was my father, who rarely came to the backyard.

"What are you all doing here in the dark?" He looked surprised. "I was looking for you everywhere. What is going on?"

"We are watching the party," I said pointing across the fence.

Abba observed the party quietly for a moment and then looked in our direction.

"I need all three of you to come out to the front because I have something to share with you," he said.

The birthday celebration going on in the French backyard was so wonderful that I didn't want to leave, but my father looked serious.

"I hope it is good news," Asrat said as we all followed Abba to the front.

When we reached the veranda, the TV was on and the Somali show had already started. Meskerem was seated by herself on a mattress across from the TV; Habib and a few of his close associates were sitting nearby, and the children were sitting with Isha on the mats.

"Come, sit here," Abba offered us seats on the mattress and the mats.

"We have two things to tell you," Abba began once we were settled. "The first thing is that Habib just told me that our refugee papers are ready." There was a wide smile on his face.

"That is really good news," I said.

"It is what we have been waiting for," Meskerem agreed.

I really had expected Meskerem and Abba to be much more excited about this, even to the point of kissing the ground, but aside from their smiles, they were emotionless.

"Does this mean we can go out without having to worry about the police?" Yared was curious.

"I hope so. But we are still refugees, so it is best not to trust the police so much and be as careful as you have been so far," Abba warned.

"I can't wait to get out of Djibouti," Yared sighed.

"Can you sign us up for school now?" I looked at my father.

"Not in Djibouti."

"But we will have the papers soon?" I asked, hopefully.

"Yes. The first thing we have to do is go to the government office to have our pictures taken and then we will be given our papers. The papers will help keep the police off our backs, but as you now know nothing is guaranteed here. One thing that we can do is go to the embassies of different nations and apply to be citizens of those nations. All we need is for one country to say yes to us. This is what I plan to do once we have our papers. This is the best plan for us."

"That is what all the other refugees want to do," Meskerem said.

"What I need from all of you is to stay out of trouble while I go to the embassies and fill out application forms and anything else that has to be done."

Ounda Amina and Medina headed our way, each with a plate full of mango slices and cookies for us. As I was enjoying the treats I saw Abba and Meskerem whispering to each other. Abba was very serious and Meskerem looked worried. "What should we do?" I heard Meskerem say to my father. He looked at the TV for a moment.

"I have one other thing to tell you," he then turned to us and said. "Actually, Meskerem and I had planned to tell you this a few months ago, but we wanted to wait until we were all together again."

They had our full attention.

"Meskerem is pregnant," Abba announced.

I was motionless; I stopped chewing and my eyes raced to Meskerem's stomach. She was wearing a large Somali dress and I could not make out her condition. Now everything was making sense to me, beginning in the desert when she refused to take the malaria pills, when she kept on telling the jail guard who was trying to assault her in the Dikhil jail that she was pregnant, all the vomiting and listlessness and how she became close to Isha so quickly.

"We already told Isha," Meskerem added.

For once I didn't mind that Abba and Meskerem had kept this news from us for a while and had told something so important to someone else first.

"Isha has been saving extra camel milk, vegetables, beans, and goat meat for me," Meskerem said. "The baby will be here in about three months and that is when I am praying we will have Kalkidan also," she added full of hope. Her eyes met my father's. My brothers and I also turned to Abba, hoping to hear some kind of miracle he had managed to make happen about our sister whom we had left behind. Abba looked at Meskerem while my brothers and I kept staring at him. His face was without a wrinkle and his eyes were shining. Happiness shone on his face.

"We will find a way. There has to be a way, Terrefe," Meskerem said to him.

"I promise, it won't be long. Are you thirsty? I will go see if there is any cold water left in the fridge." Abba got up and Meskerem was quick to follow him.

Asrat and Yared began playing cards with Laoita.

————— ◆•◆ —————

Early the next morning Abba was anxiously waiting to take us to the immigration office in Habib's blue Toyota. I took my time combing my hair and making it shiny with Isha's hair oil. It had a rose fragrance. I then tied my hair back in a ponytail. I decided to wear a red shirt and a long beige skirt that I had found. Red was now my favourite colour.

We were all together in a car after a long time. It felt good to see Abba driving again. He had his side of the window rolled all the way down, his left arm on the door while he balanced the wheel with his right.

"I will drive around the city and show you some of the places I go to when I am not at the house with you," Abba volunteered with a wide smile on his face. I could see his face in the rear-view mirror and it reminded me of the drive from Addis to Dire Dawa, except this time Kalkidan was not with us. Outside, the heat had soared beyond words; but Abba was too happy to close the window and turn the air conditioning on.

We drove around Habib's affluent neighbourhood, slowly passing the rows of villas with expensive cars and boats outside. We were delighted to hear the Amharic song *"Tizeta"* playing in one of the houses. How refreshing it was to hear it so unexpectedly, but Abba pressed on the gas and the sound of the music faded into the hot morning air. Soon after we made a right turn into a frightening snarl of traffic. The corner was jammed with about twenty small white commercial buses packed with people.

"This is the last stop for these buses," Asrat said loudly. "I take one of these buses when I go to work at the church."

"But it is so crowded," I said.

"If you stand, it is not so bad, but if you are lucky enough to get a seat, well, everyone else sits on your lap."

"Once we cross to the other side and head to the city centre, the traffic is not so bad," Abba said. He zigzagged through the crowds of people who were getting off one bus and onto another with their qat and parcels and bags. By now, the dust on the streets covered us inside the car, but we kept the windows open anyway.

The Orthodox Christian church where Asrat had found a job as a gardener was to our left. My father slowed down the car, turned and faced the church, bowed, and made the sign of the cross three times.

"Can you see through the gate?" Asrat asked, his voice full of excitement. "All of those flowers were not there when I started." He pointed to a bed filled with rose bush, herbs, and a small olive tree.

"The garden was just half the size it is now."

"You really have transformed the church garden. Even the herbs are doing great," Abba said.

There were all kinds of people at the city centre—men in suits, women in skirts, and children in shorts mingled with others dressed in traditional clothing. People drove along the narrow, paved street in cars, vans, and trucks, and bicycles threaded their way through. Goats and sheep lounged on the hoods and roofs of parked cars. We passed the mosque where Yared and Asrat had spent many nights after their escape from Dikhil. We heard the Muslim call to prayer from the top of the minaret: *"Allahu akubar, ashaud laila ilalah."*

"I don't think there are as many tall buildings in Addis Ababa as there are here," I said to my brothers as we approached a bridge.

"This part of town is actually called Tall Buildings. Look over there," Yared pointed to a huge white house.

There was no missing the home of the prime minister of Djibouti, Hassan Gulaid. The huge white house ran parallel to the bridge. Like the bridge, it had rows of fancy lights that resembled Olympic torches. I could imagine how beautiful the lights would look at night, reflected in the water. Behind the torches stood lush palm trees. It reminded me of the Menilik Palace that we loved to look at from the roof of the Kokeb restaurant, except that there was no water surrounding the palace in Ethiopia. My father slowed down so we all could have a good look. It was beautiful. I noticed there were several European-looking couples strolling hand in hand along the bridge.

"My friends and I come here and we sit on the edge and eat our sandwiches sometimes," Yared explained.

We then headed to Kartede, a section of the city centre, which was popular with Ethiopians, refugees, and merchants alike, for its famous tea houses that specialized in flavoured teas and fresh tea biscuits called *paste*. Many times Yared and Asrat had brought the biscuits home. They were round like balls and deep-fried. Isha liked Kartede because camel milk was cheaper here. In comparison to the other sections of the city centre, like Palace Rambo and Tall Buildings, Kartede was crowded and the streets were littered with broken beer bottles, flattened soft drink cans, empty cigarette boxes, and camel dung. The houses were small and in disrepair.

We finally arrived at a plain white building where we were to settle our refugee status. Even this early in the morning there were many people lined up in the office, Somalis, Afar, and Ethiopians. Abba told us there was no need to ask for a translator as someone was bound to speak Amharic here. People we spoke to described their frustrations with having to return either because the last time the office had closed before it was their turn or they had run out of film they used for taking photographs.

For once we were lucky—within the hour our names were called and we were taken into the picture room, an area sectioned off with an old cotton fabric. Here there was a stool and a camera. Once our pictures were taken, we were given our papers and our names were written down in an official book.

Now that we were listed as official refugees, we were some-what free to move about the city, but we were still stateless, and this is what Abba did not like. As well, there were some uncertainties. Abba was not convinced our refugee documents would protect us from the Derg's informants in Djibouti. Nor could we contact anyone in Ethiopia. Once again, he warned us that the police in Djibouti could do what they wished with us, whether we had documents or not; it was best for us to be as careful as we had been before getting our papers.

Abba talked about his plan all the way back to Habib's house—which embassies he would go to, and how we would all have a brand new life, a fresh start once we were accepted. Most refugees talked about going to Saudi Arabia and America, but Abba said he was not putting in an application for Saudi Arabia because none of us was familiar with Arabic; instead, he was applying to America, Australia, Sweden, and France since we had some knowledge of English and, in his case, French.

"Can we pick any country we want?" Yared inquired.

"We can, if they have embassies here," Abba replied. "I will go to the embassies and inquire about their immigration rules. But people I've met in the city have already told me some of the things I need to know. We will be out of Djibouti in less than six months."

I wondered if Asrat had sent the letter we had written to our mother. In some strange way, I now realized, it was better that Abba did not tell us about our escape until we had actually left Addis, because I would have told her about it for sure. But this way, when the Derg interrogated her, she would have nothing to tell. I hoped our letter would reach her soon and she would not worry. Slowly, we were leaving Ethiopia behind.

Hiyaw's Birth

———◆◆———

WE MADE PROGRESS. IT took over three months, but Abba finally secured an interview at the American Embassy. He had applied to a few other nations as well, including Canada, but the Americans were the first to respond.

"Didn't I promise you things will get better?" Abba said confidently, the day he announced the good news.

Luckily, only my parents were required to be at the interview and I was sure Abba would know how to respond in that situation. He had been to Israel, after all, and in my eyes that outside contact had given him the advantage of being able to communicate better with the American officials.

"The interview is in a week. Then we will know when we can leave Africa," he said.

Just like that, it became a sure thing that we were actually going to set foot on another continent, far away from the Derg. No more watching our backs, no more fear of deportation, and no more waiting for something terrible to happen. We were going to have a normal life again, with schools and our own home in a brand new country. The months of languishing in Djibouti had helped me realize that the only way for a better life was if we abandoned the old life altogether, so I had accepted leaving Ethiopia behind.

There was also progress being made in Habib's house. Abba had convinced Isha and Habib to send Laoita to school in France. Laoita had been accepted to a school there and had purchased his plane ticket. He would be leaving soon. Abba was very happy about that, and at every opportunity he reassured Isha that this was the best decision she had ever made.

"It is a good thing for the entire country and also for the Afar people to have more educated people," he told her. "My brother, Paulos, will greet him at the airport and make sure he is well accommodated in every way," he assured her.

<hr>

Our immigration interview at the American embassy was scheduled for early in the morning. That day, Abba got dressed in a pressed white shirt and grey trousers and put on black leather shoes. He was clean shaven and had had his hair cut professionally. Meskerem wore one of Isha's long Somali dresses because there were no other clothes that would fit her. Following my parents' departure, my brothers and I stayed put at the house, waiting for them to come back and tell us how the interview went. They had not returned by lunch time, so Yared, Asrat, and I sat together for lunch with a tray full of rice and goat meat in front of us.

Finally, our parents returned.

"Sorry if we had you worried," Abba said as soon as they arrived. "After the interview we stopped by Madam Askalech to tell her about it, and she insisted we stay for lunch."

"I am so tired. We walked from the city centre all the way to the restaurant and my feet are swollen," Meskerem sighed and sat on the bed.

"Did everything go okay at the embassy?" Yared asked.

"I believe it did," Abba said confidently. "They asked what my job was in Ethiopia and if I had any relatives in America." Abba took off his shoes.

"They also asked us why we wanted to go to America," Meskerem added. "Of course, we have no country, that's why."

"Well, that is true, but what I said was that there was a good opportunity for me to find a job in my field and that all three of you would have the opportunity to go to school," Abba said, looking at me. "They also asked me why I left Ethiopia. Overall it was a good interview."

They had been interviewed by a Black woman. I had heard of Americans who were once Africans but had become Americans in my grade five geography class. Our teacher had just returned from a visit to America and was telling the class about it.

"Most Americans who are Black speak English, and they don't eat *injera*," he had told us.

Abba said, "If we pass the interview, we will have to do a complete medical examination, and once that is cleared we'll just need to get our passports and will be on our way to America within a few weeks."

Meskerem, who was lying on the bed, suddenly said, "I think my water just broke," and sat straight up, her face flushed.

I looked at her, shocked and not quite sure what she was talking about. But my father quickly asked if he should take her to the hospital.

"I don't think it will come now, but I feel the pain," Meskerem said.

"Beth, go get Isha," Abba said.

I barged into Isha's bedroom, hoping the baby would not come while I was away.

"Isha, the baby is coming. Abba would like you to come and help," I said, almost crying.

"Now?" Isha muttered something in one of her languages. She pushed the tea tray out of the way and placed her hands on the cement floor to lift herself up, quickly fixing her dress. "Please, find me my slippers."

She was already out the door in bare feet before I had located her sandals, but I caught up with her. She slipped them on and walked right into the room where Abba and Meskerem waited, with a smile as wide as the half moon.

"My sister, Meskerem, this is the day. You looked so tired last night, I knew you were ready to have your baby," she said and sat on the bed next to Meskerem, who was now uncomfortably positioned on the edge.

It suddenly dawned on me that tomorrow was my birthday and it would surely have been forgotten, just like the New Year and other holidays we had failed to remember in Djibouti, but for the excitement of a new baby on the way.

"Where is the pain?" Isha began firing all kinds of questions.

"It is unbearable, too much, too much." Meskerem scrambled to hold the crib that was beside her for support. "It feels like the baby is coming now, this is not like my first one."

Isha hurried out the door to fetch Sheik Ibrahim.

I wondered how pregnant women could possibly survive without air conditioning. Having to go through labour must be like the inferno of hell considering how much Meskerem was sweating inside the cool room. In the refugee camp I had not seen a doctor or a nurse. Giving birth in those conditions, with flies and other insects and dust, and the sun pounding on the thin aluminium roof, was unthinkable. What if we had still been there?

Isha returned with Sheik Ibrahim. He did his own assessment of the situation and declared, "I think it is a boy and if I am right you must name him after me, and then I shall give him a camel."

"I will. I will," Meskerem agreed, willing to do anything to be free from her pain.

Then Sheik Ibrahim dashed out to get a car ready for Abba.

In no time, the news had travelled through Habib's house and our room was overflowing with people: Laoita, Mohammed, Ounda Amina, and all the guests. All were disappointed when they found out that Meskerem would not be delivering the baby in the house.

After a long while, we had dinner and even managed to sleep a little because the heat was so exhausting.

As the sun went down, we played table tennis. The news of the baby did not arrive until we had all fallen asleep in front of the TV on the veranda and most of the night was gone. Abba came home by himself and went to where each one of us lay asleep, gently waking us to tell us in a soft whisper, "It is a boy."

Aside from jaundice, which required the baby to be in an incubator for two days, he was in excellent health. It was a miracle. And I could not wait to see him. His name was Hiyaw.

From time to time Abba invited other Ethiopian exiles to Habib's home so they too could have a meal and a shower. But the person who accompanied my father one hot Djibouti afternoon did not look anything like a feeble and distressed refugee. I had just finished gulping down the last half of a glass of cold water when I saw them approach the entrance. I quickly ran to our room undetected, knowing they would soon follow.

The guest wore denim pants, a white long-sleeve cotton shirt, a brown cowboy hat and matching cowboy boots. I had never seen such an outfit except on TV. I hurried inside our room where I found Meskerem nursing Hiyaw. When I told her about the guest in the cowboy hat, she quickly placed the baby in the crib.

"Look who I met in Kartede!" Abba beamed with excitement as he walked in.

"Hello everyone," the guest followed with a tip of his hat.

"Don't you remember Mr Hailu?" Abba looked at me.

"She was small when I last saw her, and look at how beautiful she has become. She won't remember me." He smiled at me.

I did remember Mr Hailu; he looked different, though, in his unusual outfit. He was taller than my brothers, slim, and walked with his head high. He had a warm smile and his teeth were milky white.

Meskerem shook his hand warmly and greeted him with three kisses on each side of his face in keeping with Ethiopian tradition. He would have lifted me up high if I were still small; instead, he gave me a warm hug and repeated kisses all over my face and forehead without giving me a chance to kiss him back. Then off he rushed to the crib and in seconds my four-month-old brother, Hiyaw, was up in the air flying like an airplane in the arms of Mr Hailu.

"It's a miracle!" he declared, staring at the baby. "What a great name, Hiyaw."

"Beth picked the name," Meskerem said.

"He is also named after one of Habib's relatives, Sheik Ibrahim; it's just Ibrahim for him," Abba added. "In the Afar tradition, it is important to name a boy after a person you want your child to be like. They keep a long list of all their favourite people handy and the person your child is named after is so overjoyed at being picked that he gives the child an important and significant gift. Sheik Ibrahim gave Hiyaw a camel and carried him on his shoulder to ensure that he turns out just like him."

Mr Hailu looked at me, surprised that I had come up with the name Hiyaw, which means "The immortal."

My favourite picture of Mr Hailu in our family album showed me in his arms, held close to his chest, and my two brothers standing on each side of him. He was so tall that my brothers came just above his knees. I must have been around three years old.

Mr Hailu was the best man at my parents' wedding, and my mother liked him very much. He was a well-known businessman in Ethiopia, trading in coffee and oil, which required him to travel extensively, including to the United States. He had just returned from Texas which, he told us, was just as hot as Djibouti; wearing the hat truly helped.

"My other children have gone swimming in the sea," Abba said.

"I am sure I would not recognize them," Mr Hailu said.

Abba and Meskerem sat on their bed and a small stool had been brought from the kitchen for Mr Hailu. With white teacups in hand, they conversed late into the afternoon.

"When I last saw Kelem she told me she was fasting and praying that you were alive and unharmed," he reported.

"How is she?" Abba lowered his voice as he inquired about his only sister still living in Ethiopia.

"Well, she really did not look all that well. She has lost weight and she looked frail. So I asked her if there was anything I could do and told her she could trust me. But she cried, saying her world had shattered, she had not been able to eat or sleep well since you vanished. I told her not to listen to the rumours; some people were saying—mind you some of them are our own relatives—that you had been captured by the Derg on your way to Sudan, and others said you had gone to Europe."

"So she knows nothing then. Please let her know we are doing fine when you go back, but be very careful," Abba pleaded.

"That will be the very first thing that I will do and don't worry about me." Then he continued, "A relative who worked at Emanuel Hospital told me that Getenesh was seen there." He glanced over to where I was seated.

Emanuel Hospital? But that was the biggest hospital in Ethiopia for treating people who had gone mad. My own mother at Emanuel Hospital! Didn't she get the letter Asrat had posted to her?

"I have not seen your mother, but if I see her I will tell her you are okay," Mr Hailu said to me.

I was troubled beyond words.

"Do you know what happened to our house?" I asked.

"Well, I did read in the newspaper that the Derg had repossessed your house and they auctioned it, and it was bought by a local businessman."

"Did they find our dog Metew?"

"People saw your dog at the house for a couple of days, but it disappeared after that."

Tears filled my eyes, and when everyone was quiet for a moment I slowly walked out of the room. I wanted to vomit. I stormed to the back of the house where I usually did the laundry. There was nobody there and I sat on the steps with my chin on one knee and cried ceaselessly. I knew very well by now that crying would not bring back the past; perhaps if I had said goodbye to my mother with a simple hug and kiss, I would not have been so miserable every time her name came up. Some days I could not forgive Abba for having been so cruel as not to give us a chance to bid farewell to the people and things we loved. If I had rubbed Metew on her tummy and spent a whole day playing her favourite games, perhaps the pain would not have been as deep. I resolved to be tough. This was what I said from the bottom of my shattered heart: once I got out of Djibouti and once I got to the end of the universe where my father was dragging us, I would not have a dog. I would never discuss my mother with anyone, and I would forget Ethiopia.

Much later, no one having bothered to come look for me, I finally got up and dragged myself back inside. Nobody was in our room. I rushed to the veranda where I heard my family. I was glad Mr Hailu had not left without my saying goodbye to him. It must have been around six in the evening. "Quick everyone, the sun is going down. Let's take some pictures," Mr Hailu said and gathered everyone around as he got his camera ready.

After Mr Hailu left, Abba told us he had gotten from him the address of my aunt Abby in New York. In no time he was drafting a letter to her. He could tell her everything that had happened to us without fear because she did not live in Ethiopia. Mr Hailu had insisted on leaving some money for us, and for once Abba wanted us to tell him how we would spend the money. We agreed that each of us would get some pocket money and we would go to Madam Askalech's restaurant for a family dinner and pay for it.

Within a couple of weeks, we learned that we had passed the interview at the American embassy. My father read the letter giving the details of the required medical tests—where we had to go and what was needed.

For the first time in my life, I was with Abba everyday. I could be certain that he would come home every night. Although he would be exhausted and worried, he was home to help me practice my English and to tell us jokes and describe all the places he had seen in our country.

"There isn't a place in Ethiopia that my feet have not touched," he said once.

"Was it during your travels that you got the scars on your legs?" Yared asked.

"These?" He said with surprise. He pulled up his pant legs to show the scars. "Oh, my goodness, I got these before any of you was born." He added proudly, "I must show you something else." I waited curiously, almost sure we would hear a story about the hole I had seen under his rib cage.

But instead he took off his socks so that we could see the shattered toenails on both feet. Some looked as though they had wilted back inside his toes. I had seen them before, but I did not expect a story about them. Regardless, Abba was happy to tell us that before any of us was born, he was a star soccer player for his college. "I was like Pele, the Brazilian player. There wasn't a school we had not crushed. I loved the game, but with my job sending me everywhere, I could not play professionally."

"Did it hurt?" I asked.

"Not that I remember," he said. "Now let's practise some more English words."

One afternoon, after siesta, Abba came home and asked us to gather for a very important family meeting. He began as if he were Emperor Haile Selassie himself addressing the United Nations! "As you all know, our application has been accepted by the American embassy and they have told us we will depart in three short weeks."

I recognized the look on my father's face. It was not long ago, sitting between the sand walls of the Danakil Desert that he announced we were escaping from Ethiopia. The look on his face was now similar, and I knew he had made a major decision without us. He was trying to find a way of delivering it to us after the fact.

"As you know we had put applications to other nations as well. I am happy to tell you that we also passed the interview at the Canadian embassy. Isn't this great news? Didn't I promise you that everything was going to be okay?" Abba could not contain his excitement. I was very happy that a lot of things were finally working out in our favour. I was hopeful.

"But what does that mean now?" Yared asked, confused.

"I want us to go where you will get a superior education and, of course, somewhere very far away from the conflict in Ethiopia. We don't want to make a mistake by going to just any country. We need to have choices. We have suffered too much to go anywhere out of desperation and regret it later." Abba spoke with some emotion. "I've decided that we shall go to Canada."

"But you told us we will be leaving for America. Isn't that far enough?" Asrat asked. My brothers and I did not really know where Canada was.

Abba had had second thoughts about emigrating to America. I wondered if the heat was confusing him.

"When do we leave for Canada then?" Asrat wanted to know.

"Well, we won't be going to Canada for another three months," Meskerem put in.

She had known about Abba's decision all along and I wondered how he had convinced her.

Yared could not bear the thought of waiting another three months and got up and walked out of the room. The last time Yared was unhappy with my father's decision was in the desert when Abba told us about our escape. Yared had tried to leave us there and walk back to Ethiopia on his own, but my father had talked to him and nudged him along all across the desert. Abba was quiet, but Meskerem tried to reason with Asrat and me.

"The schools are really good in Canada and the people are very nice," she said, so full of confidence that one would think that she had just returned from a visit there.

"Are we really turning down the American offer?" I asked.

"It is better this way. It is not just my life, it is all of yours. It means more to me that you go where it is better for you than I take you just where I want to go," my father answered.

"Why did he bother applying to the United States and make us go through all the awful medical tests when he was so certain that was not where he wanted to go?" Asrat was furious long after the meeting was over. Now we had to do another set of medical examinations for the Canadian embassy.

Later I found Yared sitting on the cardboard mattress outside on the veranda. He was crying. As soon as he saw me sitting next to him, he wiped his tears.

"I can't take it any more, this heat, everything. Things are not the way they were back home, and they'll never be the same again. Why do we have to wait another three months? All we have been doing is waiting for this, waiting for that, and now that we have a chance to go somewhere, we are turning that down just so we can wait again. It doesn't make any sense to me. He thinks we have no feelings, why can't we just go somewhere and just live?" Tears rolled down his face.

I begged my brother not to cry even though I knew what he said was true.

Abba brought in as many English magazines and books as possible to distract us and keep us busy preparing for life in a country where we must speak English. I could read anything in English, but I was weak in word meanings and spellings. We spent so much time practising that Laoita, who was multilingual, wanted to learn English as well. Even with the few words we knew, we could appear to be English-speakers.

Laoita came up with the excellent idea to memorize the English that was in the music we listened to. That way we could practice English with music.

I memorized Bob Marley's songs one at a time.

I was amazed that Laoita already knew most of the words to the songs, but like me he did not always understand the meanings. We played Boney M's "By the Rivers of Babylon" a lot too. Part of the song made my heart ache for something whenever it played.

We became obsessed with music; some days all we did was listen and dance. Yared, Laoita, and Asrat went to watch Bob Marley's concert in a theatre. They told me what they saw. "Bob Marley dances just like Laoita and his hair is long, just like the people we saw in Abaya. Remember those families who lived across the bridge with their two children and who spoke English?"

I liked being around Laoita. He was always doing something that caught my attention. One morning, I found him practising skateboarding. In a few days he was excellent at it and skated inside the empty rooms and hallways of the house. If I was not doing my wash, napping, watching TV, or looking after my baby brother, my favourite past time was watching Laoita dance, skate, swim, talk, or do anything else. He was pure life. His presence filled the empty days of Djibouti with excitement.

Laoita had been accepted as a student in a small town in France. He was to go for a year. Habib, with the advice of my uncle Paulos in France, purchased all the necessities: a winter jacket, a pair of jeans, a suit, gloves, shirts, and a suitcase. If my father had not insisted, Laoita would have left for France with just the clothes he was wearing.

At times, life was funny, as Meskerem said. I could not believe that Laoita, who never even thought of leaving his beloved Djibouti before, was now packing to leave the continent of Africa before we did. His flight was scheduled to depart at five in the morning. No one slept the night before. We all wanted to go to the airport to say goodbye. After we watched all the news and the TV station had signed off, relatives and friends gathered to bid him farewell. He enjoyed the farewell gathering and played some of the Bob Marley cassettes. But there was a new disco cassette that he had been listening to for several days and it became my favourite instantly. It made me feel happy and alive whenever I heard it. Laoita called it the disco song because it repeated the word *disco* all the time and it became the best song for practising our English.

Just before we left for the airport, Laoita came out of the bedroom wearing a pair of jeans, a white shirt with thin black stripes, and a pair of black leather shoes, and holding a brown, heavy jacket. This was the first time I had seen Laoita dressed from head to toe. He was already sweating.

He looked sad, but his sense of humour saved him from crying openly. "Look," he said to Meskerem. "These pants are too tight for me." He turned around to show the back. The pants were tight and in a strange way, they outlined his muscles and he looked good in them. But in his favourite sarong and bare feet, his movements had always been graceful and free and he did not look so stiff.

As the final hours approached, I was in tears. I was not his mother, or his sister, or even a relative. It was not the place for me to cry, that was for his mother and sisters. They were not crying since they knew he would be back during the school break. I knew Yared and Asrat would tease me if they saw me crying. But I would miss Laoita terribly. I felt miserable. What if I never saw him again? Perhaps it was for the better that we were not leaving for America, because he might be back before we left for Canada.

Laoita's Air France plane rose into the sky just as the sun was rising. The gentle desert wind blew on my skin as the tears I could not control rolled down my cheeks. Silently I wiped them off, absorbed in my misery and unaware of my surroundings. We were called back to the car when the plane was out of sight. I had followed it with my tear-filled eyes as long as I could. In the car, I saw that Yared's and Asrat's eyes were also red. What would we do now? Who would fill our empty desert afternoons? The swim at the Red Sea would not be fun without Laoita. For the rest of that day, I felt alone; I was the only one who was still crying after dinner.

A Promise Kept

———◆—◆◆—◆———

THE WEEKS FOLLOWING LAOITA'S departure were slow
and depressing, just like the heat, except for one morning when
Meskerem and I met Munira, Isha's younger sister, who had come
to visit. Isha invited us for tea in her room to introduce us. Munira
was seated next to Isha on the purple and gold velvet-covered mattress. They were both light skinned with round faces. Munira's
purple nail polish with its perfect shiny finish competed with Ounda
Amina's. The fragrance she wore reminded me of my mother's
perfume. She wore a spotless, long white dress, and her red henna-
coloured hair fell to her shoulders. In Ethiopia, Munira would have
been given a name like Birtukan (orange) to suit her light skin.

"Iyan Meskerem, Betleen, come meet my sister Munira," Isha
announced in excitement as Meskerem and I walked in.

"Isha told me you are from Ethiopia," Munira said in perfect
Amharic, getting up to greet us. Her gold bangles clicked together
when she extended her arms to hug and kiss us. We kissed lightly
three times on each cheek.

"My husband was Ethiopian, but he was killed six months ago in
the Red Terror. Allah was watching out for you. He is the one who

got you through all the bad things you have endured," she said with tears in her eyes. "Isha is all I have now, and I come to visit her at least twice a year."

Munira had no children of her own, and every time she came from Dire Dawa, she showered Isha's children with presents—shirts for the boys and dresses for the girls, not to mention leather goods, coffee, and tea.

After Meskerem and I had sat down with hot cups of tea between our palms, Munira continued, "So, you want to leave Djibouti? Well, I agree with you. There isn't much to do here and your children need to be in school. Isha told me you are from Dire Dawa," she looked at Meskerem. "Would you like me to contact your family when I go back to Dire Dawa?"

"I am sure we would like that very much, but let me talk to my husband first," Meskerem replied cautiously.

———— ✦ ————

That evening, as soon as Abba walked into our room, Meskerem demanded his attention.

"You would not believe who we met today!" she began.

"Tell me."

"Munira, Isha's sister."

"How come you are so happy about that? Do we know her?"

"No, we don't, but she lives in Dire Dawa and she is willing to take a message. Don't worry, I have not told her anything. I just said I would talk to you."

Abba paused for a moment as he took off his socks and placed his bare feet on the cold cement floor. The calming effect was visible on his face as he closed his eyes to enjoy it for a moment. After much discussion, Abba accepted Munira's offer.

"You must be extremely careful whom you talk to. Only the people whose names we give you should know this," Abba explained to Munira the next day after inviting her to our room. He quickly took a pen from his shirt pocket. He found a notebook under the piles of newspapers and foreign magazines he had been reading and began to write.

"First, contact Miriam. She is Meskerem's sister with whom we have left our daughter. I am drafting a letter for you to take with you, but please don't say anything to anyone just in case the plan does not work," Abba cautioned again.

When Munira left, Abba and Meskerem whispered about what to put in the letter. Munira had agreed to pick up Kalkidan and bring her back. They would refer to my sister as "what they left behind" knowing that Miriam would understand.

"I miss Kalkidan terribly," Meskerem said in a shaky voice.

"We all do. But remember, we are not going anywhere without her." Abba paused for a moment and then said, "Okay, now read it back to me." He handed the letter to Meskerem, and she read out loud:

Dear Mrs Miriam,

Please accept our apologies for it was not out of lack of respect that we did not tell you of our plans. You must understand why we did what we had to do. As you know I can't talk about the details of the past few months, but all I can tell you is that we have been trying to find ways of contacting you, but it had not been easy. I am happy to tell you that Meskerem and the children are doing well, and I am grateful to God for keeping us safe. You can now be relieved of your worries, which I am sure were more than I can ever imagine. The bearer of this letter will tell you more details if you desire to know. She will ask you to give her the one thing we have left behind and please accept her request, as we trust her so completely with what we have burdened her to do for us.

We are so grateful to you for taking care of what we left with you. I pray that one day God will grant me the opportunity to show my gratitude for all the trouble we have caused you.

"No one will suspect anything," Abba said, confident about his new secret plan, and this was as much as my brothers and I were permitted to know about the scheme to get Kalkidan back.

A photographer was on hand a few days before Munira's departure for Dire Dawa. He was hired by my father to take family pictures that Munira could show to Meskerem's family as proof that she had met us and we were alive. I was curious why the photographer was keen on taking a special picture with just Munira and my new baby brother, Hiyaw, sitting on Munira's lap. It looked like she was his mother and I wondered what good it would do for Meskerem's family to see the two of them like that.

Following Munira's departure, we waited anxiously for her to call. I was not sure what I was anxious about, but my father and Meskerem obviously were expecting some big news from her. They were in Isha's room practically every few hours asking if Munira had called.

The days were hotter than usual, even in late evening. The afternoon heat was unbearable and the air conditioning in our room did not cool the room enough. My brothers and I went to the beach every day. I loved watching and feeling the warm water come up to my knees and I would stretch out my arms like an eagle and let myself fall back onto the crest of the waves. I swam until my arms ached and my legs felt disjointed. When I finished my swim, I collapsed on the sand and rested.

———◆◆◆———

The Red Sea was different. Its beaches were littered with beautiful seashells and colourful rocks that sparkled like gold. The air was filled with moisture and laden with rich scent. The moisture accumulated on my skin and my body glistened in the sun. When I licked my arm, it tasted of salt. My feet toyed with the yellow sand which felt soft and warm. Small boats were floating in the water.

Behind me, stretching as far as my eyes could see, was a garden, in which was the heavily fenced French Army base. The French military personnel were always fully armed. I could see the soldiers walking about inside the fence, but I didn't let my fear of them keep me away from the beach.

Three days after Munira left, she called.

"Let me speak to her first," Abba said.

Isha handed over the phone.

"Munira, how are you?" Abba said, and paused to listen. "Good." He paused, then: "What kind of problem?"

"What is she saying? Terrefe?" Meskerem demanded, sounding worried.

"She is saying Mrs Miriam will not give up Kalkidan," Abba said.

"Why not? Did she show her the letter?"

"Look, I can't talk to her if you are like this. We have to find a solution so we must stay calm." Abba resumed the phone conversation.

He listened for a long time. Finally he said, "Could you try that and call us tomorrow? We will wait for your call." The bulging veins on his forehead betrayed his concern.

"What happened? Why did you hang up? What is she going to do? Please tell me." Meskerem was frantic.

"Your sister is saying that she does not know anything about a baby."

"Maybe she does not trust her," Meskerem said, crying now.

"Well, crying is not going to help," Abba glared at Meskerem. "I am telling you she will go back again first thing tomorrow and see if Miriam will reconsider. She may have become attached to her and is afraid to let her go."

Meskerem couldn't stop crying. We could not even call Miriam directly for fear that a Derg agent might trace the call. For the first time I thought about how Meskerem's family must have felt, having to care for a new baby abandoned by its family. Did they know that her favourite formula was Fa Fa? Would they know how to make her stop crying? Did they know her favourite games? Did Kalkidan sense that we were not returning?

Isha cleared the room of everyone except Abba and Meskerem, and closed the door behind us. I could hear her talking to Abba and Meskerem as I headed to our room. *Maybe I will sleep*, I thought to myself, *and when I wake up things will be sorted out*. In the desert, I had learned that sleeping stopped all the bad thoughts in my head. As I lay my head on my mattress, I thought of Kalkidan. Her name meant *promise* in Amharic. When she was three months old, Meskerem had allowed me to take her out on the veranda to warm her body in the morning sun. I rubbed her hands and feet with oil and I felt happy when she smiled for me. My brothers took turns playing with her, making her laugh.

"Beth, wake up, wake up!" I heard a voice, and when I opened my eyes, I saw Asrat, kneeling near my face.

"What's going on?" I asked.

"Get up! Look what came." He shoved a piece of paper in my hand. "You have to be quick."

I sat up, adjusting my eyes, and studied what had landed in my hands. An open white envelope with a red and blue border; the picture on the stamp was an ibex. My heart pounded. I read the name on the envelope over and over again. Getenesh Debebe: my mother. Under the name was a post office box number.

"It came today. You can't read it here. Maybe go to the back of the house or the washroom. As soon as you are done, give it back to me. I have not shown it to Yared yet. He is still at the beach."

I folded the envelope and tucked it under the elastic band of my skirt. I headed for the kitchen and out through the back door where I was sure I would find no one else. I sat on the steps, and nervously began reading my mother's letter:

My dearest Yared, Asrat, and Bethlehem,

I am crying as I write this letter to you and praising the Lord for keeping you safe for me. It was really hard getting out of bed for many days after I found out that you had gone. I kept going back to the house hoping to one day find you there. I could not believe that all my three children could go missing all at once. Thank God that I am now able to write this to you, go to church and pray for you. I admire you, my children, for your strength, courage, and bravery, for surviving such a dreadful journey and for writing to me, as I am aware of the obstacles you had to withstand just to do that. My eyes are swollen red from crying, but this time I am crying because I am happy. I had to wear my sunglasses all the time so no one could see my swollen eyes and suspect something. Please don't worry about me. I just want you to know that I love you very much and miss you very much. There are so many reminders of you around me that I always have you in my heart.

I heard a noise coming from the kitchen and I was sure it was a goat as usual looking for food. I peeked through the back door to make sure no one was there looking for me. I took in a deep breath, wiped my tears and continued reading:

I was having lunch with old friends when I first learned where you had gone. One of the people who joined me was Hailu, and it had been such along time since I last saw him and I looked forward to hearing about his recent travels. He pretended to be gossiping like everyone else about your disappearances so that no one would suspect that he had actually met you. "I saw Terrefe's two sons in the city centre in Djibouti while I was driving. Boy, someone needs to tell them to cut their Afro," he said, looking at me. When I looked into his eyes, I knew he had met you and he stayed behind after everyone else was gone, then he slipped a picture of the three of you into my hands. After that I went straight home, closed my bedroom door, lit a candle and fell on my knees.

Please be careful and don't make too many friends. Even if you are angry with your father, you must respect him. I will pray for you and the people who are helping you every day. Please write me as often as you possibly can so I don't worry as much. I love you very much. May God keep you safe now and always.

Until we meet again, your loving mother, Getenesh.

I folded the letter neatly and placed it back into the envelope and felt happy when I stepped out onto the front porch. There I saw Isha, my father, Meskerem, and even Habib engaged in a serious conversation. I did not feel like joining them so I turned back unnoticed, collected some dirty clothes from our room and headed to the backyard.

Much later, after I finished my washing, I returned to the veranda. The TV had been turned on. Isha and Habib were in a group with new Afar visitors, and Meskerem and Abba were talking with Yared and Laoita, who had returned from France already. They all looked grim.

"What happened? Why do you all look so worried?" I asked.

"Someone wanted me dead," Yared said, fighting back tears.

"What? Why?" I asked.

"I was swimming with Laoita and before I knew it I had gone too far out and for some reason I couldn't swim back and the waves kept taking me further and further from the shore. All of a sudden, a big wave turned me upside down and no matter what I did I could not see under the water. I struggled hard to get to the top but the waves were too strong. I thought I was going to die, when I felt a hand grabbing me and pulling me up to the top. It was Laoita who saved me . . . " Yared blurted out his story practically in one breath.

"No one wants you to die," I said in a soft voice, thinking how lucky we were that Laoita saved my brother. "It must have been too windy," I added.

"There was a Somali kid with us at the beach. While I was drowning, he told Laoita not to save me. He said, 'Let him die, he is a habesh (a highlander).'"

"You know it is war time," Abba interrupted my thoughts. "Ethiopia is fighting with Somalia and there is a drought along the border of Ethiopia."

"But why would the Somali kid want Yared dead? It is not Yared's fault that there is war and a drought," I said.

"Those are very good questions," my father said, his face turning thoughtful. "You see, all that other boy knows about Ethiopia is whatever he hears from his family and friends, and when he sees Ethiopian refugees in the conditions we are in, all he is thinking is that we are good for nothing."

"God bless Laoita," Meskerem said.

I had always liked Laoita, whose name in Afar means the beautiful morning sun, like the warm, bright, and comforting Addis Ababa morning sun that I loved so much. Now he was my hero.

The very next morning, when the sun was shining brightly through our window, there came a call from Dire Dawa. It was Munira. My father and Meskerem ran to Isha's room where the phone was. As usual I trailed behind them hoping they wouldn't notice me in their excitement. This time Meskerem got to the phone before Abba. After the usual greetings, Meskerem listened quietly. Then she screamed out, "That is so terrible! That is so terrible!" She began crying. I felt my stomach churning. I had not still completely recovered from the shock of hearing of Yared's ordeal at the beach yesterday, but seeing Meskerem cry so desperately was wrenching.

"What is going on?" Abba finally got a chance to ask.

"She is saying that my sister has sent Kalkidan to Harar province. Oh my God, where is my baby?"

"Give me the phone." Abba reached over and took the phone.

"Please, you promised me, Terrefe. You promised me. Make her bring my baby," Meskerem pleaded and collapsed onto Isha's bed, holding her head between her hands.

It was then that my father noticed me seated on the mattress on the floor. I was asked to leave the room right away and I left without protesting, but feeling totally devastated. As I was walking down the hall to our room, I could hear my father, but I couldn't make out the words.

For several days following that phone call, Meskerem kept crying. She was only distracted when she had to nurse Hiyaw. Hiyaw was not a fussy boy. He laughed for me much easier than Kalkidan did. All I had to do was tickle him on the neck and he would squeak and giggle right away. I didn't have to jump around or try different tricks. He also went to sleep faster and without fuss.

Abba went about his business of researching on how to settle in a western country such as Canada while Asrat kept busy keeping St. Gabriel's garden green. He said it was the only green grass in the whole area and he was extremely proud of himself. The scare at the beach didn't keep Yared away from it. He was often out with Laoita and his new Ethiopian friends.

Meskerem was not eating much. There were dark circles around her eyes and the absent look on her face reminded me of how she looked while we were waiting in Dikhil. She was in her twenties, but there were already a few strands of grey hair on her head. Abba tried to comfort her often. One day he announced that we were all going to Madam Askalech's restaurant for lunch because the Madam wanted to celebrate the birth of my brother.

"I really don't feel like *injera* now," Meskerem protested.

"How can you say no to *injera*?" Abba convinced her with just that one question.

I was happy to go to Madam Askalech's restaurant. It was the first time we took the baby to the beach, and he was excited to see the crashing waves. A tray full of *injera* and *wot* was served in celebration, their spicy aromas filling the air around us. Since Asrat couldn't come with us because he had to go to work and Yared was out with his friends, it was just Abba, Meskerem and I feasting on the food, while Hiyaw sat quietly.

Then Madam Askalech did something unexpected. She gave me a big *gursha*—a big wrap of *injera*, filled with all the different *wots* on the tray, the size of a tennis ball.

"Here, here, open your mouth before it falls apart," she instructed.

I opened my mouth as wide as I could and she pushed the *gursha* into my mouth and my cheeks bloated up. The *gursha* was ten times bigger than what I normally put in my mouth. Before I even had a chance to finish it, I heard the Madam instructing me to open my mouth for a second round.

In our tradition, it was common to feed one another this way; it was mostly adults who engaged in this. It was a sign that everyone was happy and that they had respect for one another. My grandmother made the biggest *gurshas* I had ever known. One *gursha* was lunch on its own and I dared not pick out onions, collard greens, or any of the foods I disliked. That would show complete disrespect.

The Madam wouldn't hear my protests and gave me three more *gurshas*. My parents were happy to see her celebrate with us this way. She looked satisfied knowing that she had rejoiced in the birth of my brother. For me it was as if I had just eaten six lunches all at once.

That evening I told my brothers, "I don't think I will ever be needing food again," and that was how I went to sleep.

A knock on the door woke me up from one of the deepest sleeps I ever had in Djibouti. By the time I realized what was going on, Abba and Meskerem had opened our door. Someone was there and then I heard Meskerem crying, "My baby, you brought my baby. I know this is my child, my Kalkidan, my Promise."

Just like that Kalkidan was brought to us. Meskerem and all of us had held on to Abba's promise to have her reunited with us, and at times it had seemed impossible that it would happen, but it did. It was a miracle. Abba jumped high, holding his child in his arms like a soccer trophy he had just won. Tears streamed down his face. "Look at you! You have gotten so big!" he whispered and kissed her while Meskerem waited for her turn. Soon she was in Meskerem's arms and Meskerem hugged her tight, crying, "My baby, my baby, I am so happy. *Igziabher ymesgen*, may God be glorified."

When I held my sister in my arms, I couldn't believe how light she was. She was wearing a white tank top with a floral skirt and no shoes. Her skin was an even brown, and I could see she had rashes on both cheeks. Her eyes were twinkly but watery at the same time. For the first few days, she cried a lot because she didn't recognize us. But soon she was comfortable with us, calling our father "Abba" and her mother "Mama." She was almost two and had learned to walk; she especially liked walking on her toes. For some reason, she kept calling me and my brothers "Tato." So to make her feel good, we started calling each other Tato too, and we called her by the nickname we had given her back home—Billie.

To the West

—————◆—————

I wanted the world to know that my country Ethiopia has
always won with determination and heroism.
—ABEBE BIKILA, OLYMPIC MARATHON CHAMPION

I COULD NOT BELIEVE our journey or "vacation" had lasted
from June 29, 1980 to November 24, 1981. It was our last day in
Djibouti. Only when we were aboard the Air France flight would I
be convinced that Abba's plan to get us off the continent and away
from the Derg had finally worked.

"The immigration officer told me that we are going to Canada at
the best time of the year; soon it will be Gena, or Christmas, which
is the biggest celebration in the country. Almost all the houses, the
streets, shops, and trees will be decorated with lights and orna-
ments. The Canadian prime minster, Pierre Trudeau, is a very good
leader, not like the Derg at all. I am a hundred percent sure you will
like Canada," Abba said, sounding as though this new country was
our Christmas present.

On the day of our departure, Habib and his entire extended
family—at least all who were in Djibouti at the time—came to the
airport to wish us farewell. Tears were rolling down Laoita's face. It

was one of the saddest days of my life. The end of my Ethiopia as I knew it and the beginning of something that was going to be so new, it was beyond comprehension.

It was six in the morning and I was sweating profusely. The white cotton sweater and the worn-out pair of jeans I wore (both donated by Madam Askalech) were making me feel hot. It was our last hour in Djibouti. Sweat, more sweat, and tears.

The last time we were at the airport was to welcome Laoita from France. Laoita never returned to France after his first semester of school. He said he felt very cold there and most things he touched seemed to electrocute him. He may have missed his country too much just as I was missing Ethiopia, but at least he had a choice of returning to his Djibouti. Of course, Abba had flatly objected to Laoita's decision not to return to school. "Education is everything. Our children have to be educated. Why do you think I left Ethiopia with my children?" Abba said to Isha, shaking his head in disappointment. But Laoita was adamant.

We stood under a group of trees while Laoita took some pictures. Click. Click. *I must remember everything*, I said to myself. I would miss Laoita's music and his dancing.

I had learned that an inferno like the Danakil could still have some inhabitants who were kind and generous, like the Afar woman with child who saved our lives from the armed bandits who fired at us, or the man tending to his goat who gave us the last drop of water we needed to survive, or the family who sheltered us for four nights at their camp. The desert had actually been kind to us—it had allowed us to survive in order for us to learn the most important lessons in life so that we could share what we learned with others. In turn, we had been respectful of those we met. We were destined to pass through the land of fire to find a new life on the other side.

My mother had told us not to forget Ethiopia. She had known from Asrat's dream that we would travel to a remote land and, surprisingly, she had known we would survive. I understood now that on life's journey, one could have such a powerful experience as to make one forget who one was in the first place. In Addis, it had seemed so easy to remain who I was—eating *injera* and *wot*, speaking Amharic, and going to church. But for fifteen months I had eaten rice daily (other than the few days we were served *injera* at Madam Askalech's restaurant), not attended church even for a day, was without school and my best friends. But I had survived and learned.

The airport was crowded. French soldiers were lined up in front of us and the group of Djiboutian men who had just landed distracted them. The Djiboutians were abandoning their Western clothes and putting on their sarongs in the open space of the airport just as Laoita had done upon his return from France. I stood motionless, thinking about a journey so long it would take two days on a fast plane, a journey into a Canadian November. All that I knew was that we had to leave this family and that someone on the other side of the ocean, outside the continent of Africa, had our names in their hands and would be waiting at the airport for a family of seven to arrive from Djibouti. This was the day I was hoping would come quickly, and now I wanted it to be over and without so much pain.

Everyone was crying, so I cried openly. All of us stood in a group and took more pictures. We took pictures of Habib and Isha alone, of their children with us, and Munira took pictures of us with Hiyaw and Kalkidan. We could not stop taking pictures. I would treasure them. They would be a reminder of the times we had shared with Isha and Habib's family and of my family's journey.

"Don't forget me," Laoita said, hugging Yared and crying.

"I can't forget you. You saved my life at sea. Thank you," Yared said, crying.

I waited for my turn to say goodbye to Laoita thinking he would never know how much he had made the empty hot days in Djibouti full of life for me with his music. When it was my turn, I kissed him on the cheeks and we hugged. "Maselama, Betleen," he whispered.

"Goodbye and thank you," I said in Afar.

What could we give them in appreciation for all that they had done for us? At Rhoda's and Habib's houses we were treated equally and with great respect during our stay in Djibouti. In the Afar tradition, a guest is welcomed first with water to wash off the dust from the long journey, then with food. Only after that would they ask where the guest had come from and if the guest knew where he was heading. If the guest was lost, they would walk with him and show him the way until he could do the journey on his own. Goodbye, Laoita. Goodbye, Djibouti. Goodbye, Tetye. Goodbye my beloved Ethiopia, I said under my breath.

Laoita seemed to have finished the film in the camera. He opened it to take out the film and give it to Abba. Abba promised to develop the pictures in Canada and mail back a set of the prints to him. But then, there was a look of dismay on Laoita's face. He stood frozen, holding the open camera in his hands.

"What is wrong?" Abba inquired.

We all looked at Laoita.

"The camera is empty. There is no film."

I could not believe it. What would remind me of everything now? I would have to remember it in my head and, if I could find the music we had listened to, that would also help me remember. I felt sad that they might forget us.

◆

The greatest lesson I learned from all the despair was that there was a much better way for human beings to live on this planet. The kindness we received from strangers had made all the troubles, wars, homelessness, statelessness, and hunger more bearable. By sharing their spare water and food, the nomads had helped us survive and reach this place. More generosity and kindness is what was needed to stop the war between Somalia and Ethiopia, between Eritrea and Ethiopia. If only our people saw each other as brothers and sisters, sharing the same land for the prosperity and future of the children.

The Derg would not wipe out my fellow citizens. There was too much kindness in our people despite its attempt to take that away from us. I had witnessed how one small act of kindness, like giving a glass of water to a stranger, could have an effect, its miracle multiplying, touching the lives of so many and shaping history for generations to come, just as it had done for my family.

Afterword

———————— ◆ ————————

THE DERG REMAINED IN power in Ethiopia from 1974 until 1991, when it was overthrown by the Ethiopian People's Revolutionary Democratic Front (EPRDF), led by the Tigrayan People's Liberation Front (TPLF). The TPLF has now been in power for a quarter of a century.

After many years of conflict between Eritrea and Ethiopia, Eritreans voted to separate from Ethiopia and formed a new country in April 1993.

Although Ethiopia appears to have enjoyed economic growth over the years, tensions have been simmering among the various ethnic groups over the question of fair representation in government; draught, famine, disease, and high unemployment have only worsened the situation. In the past few months, as of this writing, there have been waves of protests across the nation, demanding fair elections and a change of government. Conflicts between protestors and government forces have broken out, and hundreds of protestors are reported to have been killed.

In 1981, arriving in Canada as a refugee, my family settled in Lethbridge, Alberta, where I went to high school. My father could not find employment as an agricultural expert, therefore he worked first as a meat packer and then as a taxi driver to support our family. Meskerem attended a college there, but a few years later, she and my father decided to move to Toronto with Hiyaw and Kalkidan to open an Ethiopian restaurant. After finishing high school in Lethbridge, I attended the University of Toronto and now work for a local municipality. I got married and have two children.

Yared attended a college in Calgary, where he continued to live for a few years. He tried to move back to Ethiopia a few times but abandoned the idea eventually. He now lives in Toronto and has one son.

Upon completing high school, Asrat moved to Toronto, where he studied business and later began his career in the hospitality industry. He is also a photographer. He is married and has three children.

Abba and Meskerem were successful and happy running Blue Nile, an Ethiopian restaurant. But a few years later they closed it and got a divorce. Soon after, my father's health worsened. He moved into an apartment in downtown Toronto, where he lived for a few years. He passed away in 2003. Meskerem moved to the United States, remarried, and is managing her own Ethiopian restaurant there.

Hiyaw and Kalkidan also moved to the United States. Hiyaw lives in Washington with his family; he has one son. He is a professional chef and distributes packaged Ethiopian vegetarian food in North America. My sister Kalkidan lives in California with her husband and three children where she has become a fashion designer.

Yared, Asrat, and I sponsored our mother, Tetye, for an immigrant status in Canada, and the four of us were reunited in 1990 in Toronto. She lived with each of us in turn, catching up on lost times and just being a mother to us. She spent a lot of time with her six grandchildren and enjoyed going out for coffee the way we did when we were in Addis Ababa. She attended the Ethiopian church in Toronto regularly. She passed away in March 2015.

Since 1981, I have visited Ethiopia twice, once in 1993 and again in 2008. I am grateful to be able to enjoy my Ethiopian culture within Ethiopia and outside. But over the years, the pull of the future has been stronger for me than the pull of my past. Like my ancestors, I will always pray for lasting peace in Ethiopia, wherever I am in the world. Its flag, the green, yellow, and red symbol of freedom, is forever engraved in my heart.

Beth Gebreyohannes
September 2016

Tetye and Terrefe

Tetye with the three children

Tetye

The family in Djibouti

Terrefe, Yared, Asrat, Bethlehem

Ali Wollao (Djibouti)

Meskerem with Hiyaw

Beth with brothers

Acknowledgements

———————◆————————

I AM FORTUNATE IN having had many wonderful people in this second and new life of mine, who have supported me during the writing of this book. I deeply regret that neither my father nor my mother are here to see it, now that it's finished. They shared many memories with me, which I have been able to weave into this book. Their unconditional love and their unceasing prayers for my well being have shaped the person I have become. Without their care, emotional support, and guidance this book would not have been completed.

My deepest thanks to my brothers Asrat and Yared Gebreyohannes for sharing their memories of our Ethiopian childhood; their compassionate views about life and our fervent debates about our desert journey helped me to find clarity and meaning. My thanks also to my brother Hiyaw Gebreyohannes for always willing to help; to my stepmother, Meskerem Gebreyohannes, for sharing her memories of the desert and for her encouragement; and to my sister Kalkidan Gebreyohannes for her love and encouraging words, which gave me the confidence to keep at the task.

Professor Paulos Milkias of Concordia University read the first draft and gave me valuable comments. Professor Michael Gervers of the University of Toronto, Kate Merriman, Beth McAuley, and Adriana

Montesano provided honest editorial feedback. From Ann Ireland at Ryerson University I received my initial guidance in writing. And my immense gratitude to the members of my writing group, Ann Chrichton Harris, Kathy Vatcher, Jane Little, and Susan Wall, for their genuine curiosity and many suggestions.

Rebecca Teshome passionately shared her rememberances of Dire Dawa. My dear friends, Rahel Amare, Zeynaba Hassan, Genet Abraha, Hiwot Besha, Meseret Getachew, Elizabeth Bezabh, Hiwot Tafesse, and Beletu Yadeta shared their memories of Ethiopia during our regular get-togethers.

I am very lucky to have had Mohammed Ibrahim read the manuscript and check my knowledge of Afar culture. My further thanks to him for giving me the chance to thank the Afar community for supporting and protecting my family during our long journey.

My thanks also to my friend Seble Afework for her faith in my ability to finish this work, for encouraging me to visit Ethiopia with her, and for her compassionate heart; also to Etye Eyerusalem Afework for openheartedly inviting me to stay at her home in Ethiopia and for answering all my questions during my visit.

My uncle Gashe Paulos Asrat was the person I went to for everything—for wise counsel, for checking and validating the contents of the draft, and for kindness. I will never forget the financial support he gave my family when we were homeless. My aunt Abaynesh Asrat was a source of information and connections. My aunt Kelemwork Asrat watched over us when we were children.

My manuscript could not have found a better home than Mawenzi House Publishers. My thanks to MG Vassanji for his faith and encouragement and his compassionate handling of this very personal story to the very end. And to Nurjehan Aziz who saw through the publication.

Finally my family: My husband, Sam Wozan, thank you for your patience and understanding. I am grateful to you my children, Nathaniel Wozan and Samra Wozan, for listening to the story over and over again all your lives without complaining. You believed in me and many times you have kept me company as I sat writing for hours.

BETHLEHEM TERREFE GEBREYOHANNES was born in Addis Ababa, a direct descendent of Emperor Menelik II and Haile Selassie. After her family's escape and arrival in Canada in 1981, they settled first in Lethbridge, Alberta, where she finished high school. She is a graduate of the University of Toronto and lives in Toronto with her family.